WITHDRAWN

A COMPLETE GUIDE
TO
EGYPT
AND THE
ARCHAEOLOGICAL
SITES

A COMPLETE GUIDE TO

EGYPT

AND THE ARCHAEOLOGICAL SITES

A. Hoyt Hobbs
and
Joy Adzigian

WILLIAM MORROW AND COMPANY, INC.
New York   *1981*

Library of Congress Cataloging in Publication Data

Hobbs, A. Hoyt.
  A complete guide to Egypt and the archaeological sites.

  Includes index.
  1. Egypt—Description and travel—Guide-books.
2. Egypt—Antiquities. I. Adzigian, Joy.
II. Title.
DT45.H6   916.2'0454   81-3982
ISBN 0-688-00647-7   AACR2

Printed in the United States of America

First Edition

1 2 3 4 5 6 7 8 9 10

BOOK DESIGN BY MICHAEL MAUCERI

*With deep affection
we dedicate this book to the people of Egypt.*

Acknowledgments

Thanks, in the first place, to Bess Adzigian whose love and generosity made this book possible and to Eunice Riedel, the most considerate and professional of editors, who made this book actual. Thanks to Bob Brier who showed us a new world and taught us more than we could learn. Thanks to Barbara Benton for suggestions of genius, to Ira Meistrich for artistic excellence, and to both for exercising the patience of Job. Thanks to Sherry, George, and Milton for constant support and concern and to Elaine Brier who played her role.

Contents

Introduction

This is a somewhat unusual guidebook, both in subject matter and arrangement. It covers more historical material than most, and interspersed are highly detailed discussions of sights—all of which leaves less room for extended treatment of hotels and restaurants. Frankly, Egypt does not have any of those wonderful, little-known hotels which could profitably fill a guide to, say, France. Nor is there much point in devoting long sections to the restaurants of Egypt when a prominent city might offer only five restaurants—three not worth discussing at all and the other two mediocre. So although hotels and restaurants are covered adequately in this book, we lean heavily on history.

The first time we saw Egypt, it was evident that this was a special place. We loved France for its elegance, cathedrals, and food; Italy had its people, pasta, and the Renaissance; Spain had passion and the Alhambra; Portugal had immense churches and tiny fishing villages; Greece had vitality and the Acropolis; Turkey was magical Istanbul; and Morocco showed us a different time and world. We were near the end of a year's journey around the Mediterranean when we landed in Egypt. We were overwhelmed. Old! The Colosseum and the Acropolis would both count as modern in Egypt. Egypt was almost as exotic as Morocco had been; its pyramids and tombs were as old when the Greeks built the Parthenon as the Parthenon is to us now—and had been less ravaged by time. Egypt seemed a traveler's dream that was real.

But as we looked with awe at pyramids, temples, and tombs, questions nagged about a carving here, a hole for some purpose there, a statue out of keeping with the rest. And no one, not even professional guides, knew many answers. The more we were impressed, the more frustrated we were to know the purpose of the temples we were seeing and the characters of the pharaohs who erected them. What was the nature of this ancient civilization that allowed it to begin so early and to accomplish so much?

Home we came, enchanted by Egypt, and before our second visit we spent a year studying intensively. This time, Egypt was like a book in a language we could read: so much now made sense. Scenes on temple walls told stories; overlooked elements now stood so clearly it was hard to imagine how we could have missed them. Each ancient edifice was now more alive, evocative of having once been used by real people.

Our experience proved to us that Egypt presents tourists with a special difficulty. The average person can appreciate a splendid cathedral without explanation: we have all seen churches before. But the great age of Egyptian monuments, which contributes so much to their drama, also makes them more foreign, more distant in conception. On its own, Egypt can be more than adequately impressive. But without explanation—general background and specific details—Egypt is perplexing and its wonders are obscured. We planned this book to supply those explanations, and its arrangement reflects this.

The important phases of Egypt's ancient history, which spans 2500 years, are fascinating but take time to ingest. How much will you remember about Thothmoses III by the time you reach his tomb? Luckily, your tour of Egypt can be arranged in historical order. Information about Thothmoses III is important in Luxor, but not in Cairo or the places in between. Almost every visitor lands in Cairo, then goes south to Luxor—perhaps stopping off in the middle of Egypt on the way—and travels on to Aswan and Abu Simbel next. This route follows the chronology of the surviving monuments exactly. Before each chapter on a city and its sights, therefore, we've placed a preliminary chapter describing the historical events and people germane to those sights. In this way, all the important information is covered, but in manageable, relevant pieces. So do not wonder that the history section "Background for Cairo" stops at the end of the Old Kingdom; later history continues in the prelude to the next stop on your route, Middle Egypt. If it happens that your trip in Egypt skips some of the normal stops, skim through the history of skipped areas so as not to feel gaps.

The one exception to this arrangement is Alexandria. Because it is so near Cairo, and north, where there is little else to see, you will commonly visit Alexandria as an excursion from Cairo before heading south. Historically, however, Alexandria comes at the end, where you will find it in this book. It hardly matters, in practice, whether you visit Alexandria early or late; its history is self-contained.

Guides to Egypt are all subject to two insoluble problems. First, prices change these days in Egypt, as in much of the world, more quickly than publishers can produce books. Prices in this book are the latest available at time of printing, but should be used only as guides—correct relatively, but perhaps incorrect in absolute terms by the time you land.

The second problem is that no good systems exist for writing Arabic or ancient Egyptian words in English. Neither language is spelled in our alphabet so that we can only transliterate—match sound by our letters. *Muhammad* can be spelled five ways in English, and one author's favorite spelling is despised by the next. To match any Arabic word in this book with one you see elsewhere, sound both out, and if the sounds are alike, they are the same word.

The situation is even more complex with ancient Egyptian

words. Hieroglyphs usually do not include the vowels, giving great leeway for variant transliterations. Some conventions have gained a degree of currency, but occasionally through poor choices. The conventional spelling *Amenhotep*, a pharaoh's name, obscures the fact that he was named for the god conventionally written *Amun*—a historically important point. In this book that pharaoh's name will be spelled *Amunhotep*, and the same point gives us *Amunemhat*, another pharaoh, though these spellings flaunt convention.

Frankly, the business of transliterating hieroglyphs is a mess. One pharaoh's name has been spelled Sesostris, Senusert, and Usertsen. The first spelling is the way a traditionalist would do it, deriving from the Greeks—never mind what Greek spellings have to do with ancient Egyptian. The second and third spellings derive from the ancient Egyptian, but they differ about whether the hieroglyph placed first in the pharaoh's name is first only for honorific reasons—because it was also the name of a god—or first because the pharaoh's mother spoke it in that order. No matter what spelling we choose, somewhere else you will undoubtedly encounter a different spelling, so different that you may not realize it is the same word or person. Except to hope for intelligent standardization in the future, all you can do in the meantime is to ignore at least the vowels when comparing two spellings. Such problems will not spoil your trip.

1.
Practical Matters

In this chapter we provide specific information for planning and outfitting a trip to Egypt, along with what you can expect by way of food and shopping. Chapter 2 explains the principles of visiting Egypt on your own, in contrast to package tours. It offers help both in making your own reservations and in selecting tours. Chapter 3 provides general background information on the land and the people of modern Egypt.

The addresses of the **Egyptian Government Tourist Office** are 630 Fifth Avenue, New York, NY 10022 and 3001 Pacific Avenue, San Francisco, CA 94115. You can reach **Egyptair**'s U.S. reservation service at telephone 212-581-5600.

PLANS: Egypt demands early decisions and arrangements because hotel space is limited. If you make your own arrangements, you must decide exactly when you will go, decide your itinerary (at least the number of days you will spend in each city), and then place hotel reservations. For a winter trip, Egypt's high season, you should make hotel reservations six to twelve months in advance. Even then, reservations do not come easily. (See Chapter 2 for ways to improve the odds.) Companies that offer group tours, faced with such a scarcity of hotel rooms, simply book blocks of rooms a year in advance. In most cases, this means that the size of a group is fixed. To avoid disappointment if you wish to join a specific tour group, enroll at least three months before the scheduled date of departure.

Arrangements are easier for trips in seasons other than winter—the time when 70% of the European and American visitors arrive. A trip in spring or fall would not require such advance planning and reservations. Summer is even less pressured, but only air-conditioned hotels should be considered, except in cooler Alexandria.

HOTELS: When choosing a hotel or assessing those offered by a tour, be aware that official Egyptian ratings are more generous than those in Europe. *Deluxe* does not signify a palace and *First Class* will prove to be second rate. In general, Egyptian ratings are about one class higher than those Westerners would expect; if possible, it is usually wise to stay in hotels rated no lower than *Second Class*. Deluxe and first-class hotels will be acceptable for most tourists, with rooms smaller and not quite as comfortable or clean as their European counterparts—particularly at the lower rating—but at much more reasonable prices.

In Egypt, a comfortable hotel is of genuine importance. Because most require that you take lunch or dinner there, you will be booking not just a room but also a main meal. Since you will spend days prowling through tombs and hiking across dusty landscapes, a soothing bath or shower and a clean room become raised to the level of eagerly awaited pleasures.

CLIMATE AND SEASONS: Egypt has only two seasons: winter and the rest of the year. Egypt is among the driest countries in the world, and ranks with the hottest, but is less dry and less hot from November to March.

Seven inches of rain fall on Alexandria and two inches on Cairo annually, with almost all of it during December and

January. Only then should you consider taking an umbrella—
it might be used once or twice. South of Cairo, no matter
what the season, rain would be an event discussed for
months afterward.

Except for the winter months, Egypt boils. Peak temperatures in Aswan, the southernmost city, normally reach 110° to
120° F in June and July. Luxor will be a few degrees lower;
Middle Egypt almost ten degrees still lower. Because of the
absence of all humidity, the heat is less discomforting than
might be expected, but also more dangerous. Perspiration
evaporates as it reaches the skin, so that you can dehydrate to
dangerous levels without familiar physical signs. Shops close
during the middle of the day in summer, and you would do
well to restrict activities to early and late in the day. During
this time of year Alexandria, to the north, enjoys cooling
Mediterranean breezes which draw the citizens of Cairo to its
90° temperatures. Rooms are all but impossible to find in
Alexandria then but are plentiful in Cairo—which steams
from the moisture of those same sea breezes at close to 100°.

From the summer peak, temperatures slope approximately
three degrees lower each month until they reach the 90s in
Aswan late in the fall and early in the spring, with Cairo and
Alexandria about 15° cooler. By the middle of winter, Egyptian temperatures correspond to our northeast spring—80° or
lower in Aswan, and middle 60s in Cairo and Alexandria.

Nights are unexpectedly cool, often 25° cooler than daylight temperatures. Winter evenings may be chilly anywhere
in Eygpt, but the air in Middle Egypt—which is neither as
close to the equator as southern Egypt nor as close to the
moderating influence of the sea as Cairo—commonly descends to the 40s and can reach freezing. Sweaters, even
coats, are needed for winter nights, and you may welcome a
jacket on many summer evenings.

Fall is the ideal Egyptian season—warm, but not over-
powering. Spring comes next and would rival the fall except
for a vicious wind that can blow at 90 miles an hour for days
on end for as much as a two-week period. Europeans call the
wind *sirocco* or *mistral*, and the Arabs call it *khamsin*, but
whatever its name it is unpleasant, both physically and

psychologically. Usually the two weeks of wind come in the middle of April, but this can vary by a month. Winter in Egypt is a pleasant contrast to our colder version, though it calls for warmer clothes than do other Egyptian seasons. Summer, given caution and a leisurely pace, can be managed well enough, but the heat matches our expectations for the land of Ra, the Egyptian sun god.

HOLIDAYS: With one possible controversial exception, Islamic holy periods need not affect the timing of your visit. The possible exception is Ramadan, a month of fasting that usually falls in August. This is a time of atonement when nothing is allowed to pass through the lips of a Muslim while the sun casts any light. After sundown, the devout make up for their temperance with large meals, then take to the streets for shopping and promenades until midnight. Travel agents generally advise travelers to avoid Egypt during these holy days because shop and restaurant hours change. (Citizens may be cross, some agents claim, from the discomfort of their abstinence, and some Muslims may be angered by the sight of a visitor eating, drinking, or smoking while they cannot.) Such cautions are excessive. Egyptians are as used to visitors of different religions as they are to non-Muslim Egyptians. Nor do all Muslim Egyptians follow the religious rules of Ramadan to the letter, any more than would be true for people of other religious groups from other parts of the world.

Ramadan and other Islamic holy days throughout the year include festivities that overflow from crowded mosques onto the streets, providing memorable sights for visitors. Unfortunately, it is not simple to plan a trip to coincide with a particular festival because the Muslim calendar is based on a lunar year, shorter by ten or eleven days than our solar calendar, so dates move each year—by our reckoning. For the dates of Islamic holidays that might fall near the time of your proposed trip write to the Egyptian Government Tourist Office.

Museums are usually closed on important secular holidays, which do follow our calendar. National Day celebrates the revolution that ousted King Farouk on July 23, 1952. Liberation Day, on June 18, memorializes the final departure of British troops from Egypt. On Friday, the Islamic sabbath, most museums close from 11 to 1 or 11:30 to 1:30 so employees can attend services. In the summer, museums commonly do not reopen on Friday afternoons.

Despite the temperance rules of the Koran, Egyptians have taken over the celebration of our New Year's Eve, with late parties and toasts in hotels and cabarets. Egypt is an unusual and enjoyable place to ring in the new year.

ITINERARIES: Some travelers on flights around the world jump off their plane when it lands to refuel in Cairo and hop into a taxi which speeds them to the Pyramids for a photo, followed by a race back to catch their waiting plane. But most people have a longer stay in mind. The ideal minimum would be a 22-day trip—detailed below and followed by adjustments for shorter or longer visits.

22 days: The plane trip from or to the United States eats up 14 to 16 hours, which effectively eliminates the first and last day, leaving 20 days. Because of the loss of seven hours in time zone changes, those who take the evening flight from the U.S. will land in Cairo on the evening of the next day and have only 19 full days in Egypt.

7 days for Cairo: 1. Giza for the Pyramids, Sphinx, and the Valley Temple of Khaefra; afternoon free. 2. Museum of Antiquities, Khan Kalili bazaar. 3. Memphis and Sakkara excursion. 4. Islamic, Christian, and Jewish sights in Cairo. 5. Alexandria excursion. 6. Faiyum excursion. 7. Free time.

2 days for Middle Egypt: 1. Travel, visiting Beni Hassan on the way to Minya. 2. Tell el Amarna and Tuna el Gebel.

6 days for Luxor: 1. Travel to Luxor, stopping at Abydos and Denderah en route. 2. Valley of the Kings; Luxor Temple in the evening. 3. Valley of the Nobles and Valley of the Queens; Karnak Temple in the evening for the Sound and Light show. 4. Karnak Temple and Luxor Museum. 5. Ramesseum, Dier el Bahri, and Medinet Habu. 6. Free time.

2 days for Aswan: 1. Travel, with stops at the temples of Esna, Edfu, and Kom Ombu. 2. Aswan sights; free time.

1 day for Abu Simbel: 1. Fly there from Aswan; visit; fly to Cairo.

2 days for Cairo: 1. Free time. 2. Depart for home.

This itinerary adequately covers the sights in Egypt with time for rest and leisure. The ordering of days in a given city is flexible.

A pleasant modification would be to incorporate a cruise on the Nile in a hotel boat. Several of these boats run regularly from Aswan to Luxor, or vice versa. (Details about such trips can be found in Chapter 2.) Though cruising uses five days to cover sights that you can see in one day on wheels, the experience of life on the Nile is memorable and relaxing. The four days lost can be made up by omitting the two days for Aswan, or by omitting the two days for Middle Egypt plus foregoing the free day in Cairo (or the Faiyum excursion) and the one in Luxor. If it comes to giving up the time in Middle Egypt, that would mean missing the ruined city and tombs of Akhenaten's era and the paintings at Beni Hassan from the Middle Kingdom. Most visitors to these sights find them moving, but those who take the time to go usually are students of the ancient civilization.

More than 22 days: Add the Nile cruise between Luxor and Aswan. Spend more time in Luxor, for everyone complains that the stay there is always too short. You might also add three days of sun and superb scuba diving at the Red Sea resort of Hurghadah. Take three more days to do the other "Off the Beaten Track" excursions described in Chapter 14.

Less than 22 days: Sacrifices of one sort or another are in order. With greater industry and less time for leisure, you can cover Cairo in five days. Alexandria and the Faiyum may be omitted, and, if you are still pressed for time, Middle Egypt may prove to be a two-day luxury that time does not permit. You can avoid the two days for Aswan by flying to Abu

Simbel directly from Luxor. By diligent—and leisureless—work, Luxor can be compacted into four days. The minimum, below which sacrifices become too painful to consider, would be:

3 days for Cairo: 1. Giza and the Museum of Antiquities. 2. Memphis and Sakkara excursion. 3. Islamic sights in Cairo, plus Khan Kalili bazaar.

4 days for Luxor: 1. Travel to Luxor, Karnak Temple. 2. Valley of the Kings, Dier el Bahri, Ramesseum. 3. Excursion to Abydos and Denderah; Luxor Temple in the evening. 4. Medinet Habu and the Valley of the Nobles; Luxor Museum in the evening.

1 day for Abu Simbel: 1. Fly there; visit; fly to Cairo.

1 day for departure from Cairo.

Such a trip would be full and tiring; any added days will help.

FORMALITIES: A visa is required for Egypt. An application will be sent on request from the nearest Egyptian Consulate: 1110 Second Avenue, New York, NY 10022; 2310 Decatur Place, NW, Washington, DC 20008; 3001 Pacific Avenue, San Francisco, CA 94415. Return the application with a valid passport, one passport-sized photo, a self-addressed return envelope, and a money order for $3.00 (for U.S. citizens; $4.50 for others) to cover processing charges and the costs of registered mail postage. Personal checks will not be accepted. Allow three weeks for the two-way transaction.

In Egypt, visitors have one week in which to register their arrival. The management of the first hotel at which you stay will take care of this process when you hand in your passport overnight.

For stays of over six weeks, the processes of securing a visa and registering must be reinitiated in Egypt.

PACKING: In summer, protection against heat is paramount. Avoid clothing that exposes skin; protect whatever may be exposed with effective sun blocks. Take a tip from those who live in Egypt and cover up with loosely fitting garments. Wear a hat. For cooler evenings and air-conditioned dining rooms, do not forget a sweater or light jacket.

Near and during the winter season, you must deal with the problem of swings in temperature. Layering, taking off articles that can be put back on later, works well to carry you from cooler mornings through hotter middays to cool evenings without unnecessary trips back to your hotel.

Because so much time will be spent hiking around the desert, casual, comfortable, and durable clothes are the order of the day. In the evening, in hotel dining rooms, guests tend to change to slightly better—and less sandy—clothes: you may want one or two less casual outfits. Sunglasses are needed, whatever the season, for the bright, transparent Egyptian sky. Comfortable shoes with gripping rubber soles prevent both blisters and slips.

A flashlight, the brightest one that can be carried comfortably, is indispensable for dark tombs and temple corners. Consider taking one roll of bathroom tissue—without the cardboard center, so it can be flattened—for out-of-the-way calls of nature and occasional rustic restaurants or rest houses. Salt tablets help your body deal with the summer heat. Individually wrapped, premoistened towelettes are cooling as well as cleansing. Remember to bring a shoulder bag or knapsack to tote all of the day's paraphernalia.

A kit with some sort of adhesive bandages, first-aid cream, safety pins, aspirins, needle and thread, scissors, and any other miscellaneous items you normally like to travel with is valuable as insurance, even if never used. The kind of penknives with all sorts of blades and a corkscrew also often comes in handy. For the inevitable pile of souvenirs and gifts you pick up along the way, an extra parachute nylon suitcase that folds into a small packet can be a tremendous help; or you can purchase inexpensive camelskin bags and suitcases in Egypt.

CUSTOMS REGULATIONS: Bring what you wish for personal use. Egypt has extensive and expensive duties on imports, but cigarettes, liquor, and other items that you take with you in reasonable amounts for your own use are exempted. Expensive personal equipment such as cameras and jewelry should be listed on the form supplied by the flight attendant before landing so that, if ever checked, you can show that you still have these things and did not sell them in Egypt.

Leaving Egypt, no regulations affect the normal tourist, other than those for undocumented antiquities. But remember to save LE 3 in Egyptian currency for the Departure Tax.

MEDICAL: Rules change, but at most times an up-to-date smallpox vaccination is the only required shot for Egypt. Since various diseases do break out in Eygpt from time to time, however, it is foolish to risk the chance of infection. Check with local health authorities, who are regularly advised by the World Health Organization regarding potential health problems—although occasionally there may be an interval between outbreaks and international reports. Malaria, typhus, and cholera are possible infections. Though these illnesses are unlikely, protection can easily be secured by appropriate inoculations before you leave home. To avoid the unlikely possibility of need for reinoculation, ask your doctor for a letter to take with you indicating the types, dosage, and dates of any shots taken prior to your departure.

"Mummy tummy" is the most common traveler's ailment. Our systems are taken by surprise by the effects of microbes on foods in Egypt that are different from those our bodies are used to. The results frequently are diarrhea, sometimes accompanied by a low fever and cramps for an unpleasant day or two. Cooking kills enough of these microbes to make hot dishes safe for Western stomachs, but anything raw—unless peeled from its skin—may bring on the problem, as may tap water. Some people avoid salads and drink only bottled water. Some of them come down with mummy tummy anyway, and some people who wash down their salads with tap water never suffer a moment's discomfort. Ask your doctor to prescribe a symptomatic aid.

MONEY: The basic unit of Egyptian money is the pound,

abbreviated LE (from the French *livre Egyptienne)*. American tourists receive a special favorable rate of exchange, which has been stable for several years, of LE 1 for $1.45, give or take a few cents.

The Egyptian pound is divided into 100 piasters (pt.), which in turn are subdivided into 10 milliemes (rarely encountered). Bank notes come in denominations of LE 1, LE 5, LE 10, and LE 20, with smaller sized notes for 5 pt., 10 pt., 25 pt., and 50 pt. These smaller notes are graded in size to show their value. Nickel-colored coins, graded in size, represent 1, 2, 5, 10, 25, and 50 pt.; brass coins bear denominations of 5, 10, and 20 pt.

Rough calculations are simple; add 50% to the denominated value. One pound is roughly $1.50; LE 5 is $7.50; 10 pt. is 15¢; 50 pt. is 75¢, etc.

Credit cards have not generally caught on in Egypt, except in the better hotels and shops catering to tourists; expect to pay cash.

PHOTOGRAPHY: Strong sun and the clean air (outside of Cairo) in Egypt make dramatic pictures easy—especially in late afternoon when shadows increase and everything turns orange in the setting sun. Let your friends think it was all your skill. You will, however, want to deal with two situations at extremes from one another—temples in the very bright outdoor sun and paintings deep in dark tombs. For best results, bring a flash and two kinds of film for these two situations.

Professional photographers advise tourists to take a polarizing filter to remove outdoor glare; it enriches colors too. A skylight filter is a good idea on all lenses: it prevents dust and grit, present everywhere, from ruining the lens. For slide pictures outdoors, professionals would use Kodachrome KM or its equivalent, and for flash pictures, Ektachrome EL or its equivalent. For print pictures, use Kodacolor 100 ASA for sun and 400 ASA for flash, or their equivalents. Bring more film than you expect to use—Egypt causes most people to take more pictures than they had planned, and film bought in Egypt will cost much more. Spare batteries are also a good idea.

The sand-dust in the Egyptian air will eventually ruin any camera. Keep equipment covered as much as possible while in Egypt, and give it a thorough cleaning when you arrive back home.

TIMES, HOURS, WEIGHTS, ELECTRIC CURRENT: Egypt is seven hours earlier than Eastern Standard Time.

Business hours vary by type of business in Egypt. Regular banks close at 1 p.m. and all day Friday. All better hotels have facilities for exchanging currency or traveler's cheques, however; these remain open into the evening and accomplish such transactions more speedily than a bank because they do them all the time. Museums sometimes close on Friday afternoons or for lunch—check under the description of a specific museum in this book before visiting it at such times. Shops usually will close from 1 p.m. until around 4 p.m. but remain open until 8 p.m. or 9 p.m. Government offices close at 2 p.m. and are closed all day Friday and on every conceivable holiday. Remember that Friday is the sabbath in Egypt and Sunday is just a day of the week.

Egypt is on the metric system of weights and measures. One kilogram equals 2.2 pounds; a kilometer is six-tenths of a mile; a liter holds a few drops more than a quart.

Electric current generally is 220 volts AC, 50 cycles. A few hotels have adapters for American appliances, but a converter will be necessary if you expect to use, say, a hair dryer throughout your stay. Also bring an inexpensive adaptor for round-prong Continental sockets.

You may discover candles in your room. Current outages are frequent enough in Egypt to explain these precautions, though the darkness seldom lasts for long. Tutankhamun's curse has nothing to do with this problem, needless to say. Generating equipment that is too old for accelerating demand loads is responsible.

TELEPHONES AND MAIL: International calls all go through the Cairo system, which never was the best and is now hopelessly insufficient. Waits of half an hour or more to clear a line for a local call only hint at the difficulties of placing a call overseas. If you must call anyone, whether local or outside of Egypt, allow abundant time and have an operator in the hotel do the constant dialing for you. The wait for a long-distance line averages six hours, but you can reserve a line for a given time. Telex, which is accessible at all major hotels, is the easiest way for those at home to reach you, so it is wise to leave a schedule of your hotels and their telex or cable addresses with a friend or relative.

You can write home, but if you return after three weeks away you may well beat the air-mail letters you sent on your first day.

In Egypt you will be getting away from it all, like it or not.

BAKSHEESH: The first word of Arabic most tourists learn is the one they hear most often: *baksheesh*. Literally it means "gift," and so it may be meant by the utterer as he extends his hand. In actuality there are two forms of *baksheesh*. As a tip in return for a service, it is honorable and proper; as a gift, usually demanded in an arrogant voice, *baksheesh* is a Middle Eastern disease. Most Egyptians are themselves quite dismayed by the sight of adults crying for money—an unearned largess. Even more, Egyptians are concerned when children attempt this trick, for the success of it teaches all the wrong lessons to a character in process of formation. Tourists would do a great service if they consistently refused to give *baksheesh*, in the gift sense. Too often money is given to a child for his or her cuteness, or to an adult just to avoid being pestered, without a thought for this action's effect on the next group of visitors or on the person who receives the gift.

Baksheesh should not be confused with begging, which is viewed in this culture as honorable when done by a person who has suffered debilitation. Egyptians are generous to those who ask for alms, encouraged by the religious promise of future rewards. No Egyptian would ask another for *baksheesh*. He knows he would receive a tongue-lashing in return.

On the other hand, life is hard for many healthy Egyptians who often look for ways to earn extra money. People offer to carry bags, get tickets, guide visitors; in short, to perform any service they think that a visitor might want. If someone performs a service, a tip is certainly in order. For such purposes, a pocketful of coins, 20 and 50 pt. pieces, is a convenience. Egyptians also do favors without any expectation of reward. Offer a gratuity with grace, not fanfare, then accept a polite refusal if it comes or pay with your thanks. Be aware too that sometimes a person who assists by guiding you to a store may refuse his tip because he plans to obtain his reward from the shop owner, who will adjust his prices upward to cover that fee.

The economy of Egypt functions at a different level from that of Western nations, a situation that visitors cannot individually change. Tourists can only throw parts of the economy out of gear by heaping on individuals what seems to them a small sum, but which is out of proportion in the economic context of Egypt. Many Egyptians work hard for LE 2 per day. Keep that in mind when someone performs a half-hour's service.

BARGAINING: Except for businesses owned by the government, such as major transportation companies, and except for a few large department stores and the shops in large hotels, business in Egypt is conducted by bargaining—a negotiated trade of money for goods. The price that a shopkeeper mentions will be a first offer. To accept it would please him greatly for the windfall profit yet disappoint him for the lost chance of a contest.

Bargaining is engrained in this culture, tied to moral and sporting values as well as to economic principles. It is a contest in which one side endeavors to get more, the other side to give less, than the value of the product. The contest can be played gently with covert maneuvers or may be conducted theatrically with mock wailing and breast-beating. Any appreciable purchase involves a ceremony of polite conversation and most likely mint tea or Turkish coffee brought by an errand boy who discreetly watches the proceedings with wide eyes.

There are rules. To depreciate the quality of the product under negotiation is bad manners, though any flaw, any factor at all that lessens its desirability for the buyer, should be mentioned while simultaneously acknowledging the high quality of the product. Lies, if they are cleverly told, are silently applauded by the other side. Above all, each party feigns disinterest in consummating the deal—to the point, on the buyer's side, of preparing to leave and sometimes actually walking out the door with the seller in pursuit.

The first moves usually signal the eventual conclusion. If the seller's initial price is not far above the actual value, he will fight hard against every lowering. A ridiculously low response on the buyer's part may end negotiations without a sale. If, on the other hand, the seller's first price is ridiculously high, the buyer's first offer should be laughingly low. The seller will come down in successive large steps, provided that the buyer will go up in successive small steps. For a high initial price, a deal struck 50% lower represents victory for the buyer, while for a low initial price, a 25% saving would also count as a buyer's win. Prices generally are low enough in Egypt that we visitors can lose these contests and still come away with pleasingly inexpensive purchases.

With all the dissembling involved in the bargaining process, two scruples are never violated. Once a deal is made, it cannot be changed. We watched while a seller learned that his agent had accepted prices resulting in a loss of over LE 1000. The seller acted as if a relative had just died, but he never considered using the excuse of a mistake to renegotiate the prices. Also, talking about money may include untruths of many sorts, but when money changes hands both sides will be honest to the last piaster. The seller will urge that the buyer count his change. Good manners decree that the buyer refuse, and in this culture, he need not worry.

FOOD AND DRINK: Until World War I, Turkey dominated the Mediterranean from Greece around through Egypt and instituted the cuisine we call Middle Eastern. Stuffed grape leaves, skewered lamb, and spicy ground lamb are staples on the tables of twenty countries which otherwise have not much in common today. Though Egypt cooks a few dishes of its own, most of its cuisine would be considered Middle

Eastern because of the use of mint, cumin, and dill as dominant spices.

The most convenient way to discuss Egypt's food is by way of the kind of place one might be dining—from hotel to restaurant to sidewalk fast-food stand.

Hotels generally stick to vaguely Continental food, avoiding any dish that a foreigner might dislike. The cooking, therefore, tends to be bland, although it will satisfy your hunger. Breakfasts, included in the room price, are the lighter Continental sort—roll, jam, juice, and coffee or tea, though eggs may be ordered for a supplement. A few hotels in Cairo do have separate dining rooms for Egyptian food; those are discussed in the Cairo chapter.

Food is more interesting in restaurants. Appetizers include dips of ground sesame seeds, redolent of garlic, called *tahina* and of *babaganoug* with mashed eggplant. Grape leaves stuffed with seasoned rice, marinated in lemon juice and olive oil, are called *wara einab* in Egypt. But tomatoes, green peppers, and squash can also be filled with the same rice mixture, in which case the term will be *mashi*. *Turshi*, a pickle of almost any kind of vegetable, makes nibbling fun. For a treat, look for *batarikh*—pressed caviar. Cheeses include *gibna beyda*, goat cheese similar to feta, and *gibna rumi*, cow's milk cheese similar to cheddar. Creamy, thick, fresh yogurt, called *leban zabadi*, will spoil you for the American version and is beneficial for the intestines. Breads are good. The most common sort is flat and unleavened like pita bread and comes in two varieties: refined white, *aiysh shami*, or whole wheat, *aiysh baladi*. *Taamiyya*, sometimes called *falafel*, is a serving of fried patties made from spiced fava beans and tastes much better than its description might sound. You can eat it either as an appetizer or as a main course.

Main courses include lamb *(kharoof)* prepared in many ways—from familiar *kebabs* to less familiar *kuftas* (spiced ground lamb cooked on skewers) to stews. Chicken *(farak)* can be a tasty surprise because the birds raised in Egypt are not fed on the flavorless prepared feeds that fatten chickens today in much of the world. Pigeon *(hammama)*, especially when stuffed with rice and spices and grilled *(rosto)* over charcoal (as at Casino des Pigeons in Cairo), will change anyone's attitude about these delectable birds. Seafoods are served in great variety—grilled crayfish *(gambarey)* are, perhaps, the most outstanding. Look for *moulukeyeh*, a stewed green, resembling spinach in appearance, that may be served as a sauce, a thick soup, or a side dish. Strong in flavor and not to everyone's taste, it is an Egyptian specialty. *Khalta* is a rich pilau of rice, raisins, nuts, and bits of meat that is a much more interesting accompaniment to an entree than French fries.

For dessert, delicious, fresh fruits, which change with the season, are always available. Fresh dates will make you forget the sticky preserved ones we normally encounter. Otherwise, the dessert choices are very sweet. Of course there is *baklavah* and *kanafa*, a similar dessert made with shredded wheat instead of layers of pastry. *Mahallabiya* is Egyptian creamed rice pudding topped with pistachios. Egyptian ice cream, *dondurma*, resembles sweet sherbet. The Egyptian specialty is *Um Ali*, a hot bread pudding topped with milk and pine nuts.

The rule for beverages is that whatever Egypt did not produce will cost double its normal price. But Egyptian wines and beers are good and impossible to beat at their prices. Omar Khayyam is an eminently palatable dry red wine; Grenaclis Village is a dry white; Rubis d'Egypt is a dryish rosé. Other wines are sweeter. The national beer, Stella, may be the lightest beer made anywhere and is certainly among the cheapest, at about 60¢ for a double-sized bottle. Beer lovers should try Marzen, if available, a bock beer produced only during the spring. Try dark Aswali beer in Aswan. For liquor, Egypt produces bad brandy, suitable only in mixed drinks, and reasonable anisette ouzo, called Zibab. Tea *(chai)* is strong in Egypt because it is brewed, not steeped, as is the coffee *(gawa)*. Only in large hotels catering to foreigners will "American coffee" be more than just instant coffee. Egyptian soft drinks do quench thirsts, even if they do not quite match expected flavors: Pepsi bottled there does not taste like Pepsi bottled here; Spathis hints of Sprite; Si-Cola will do if no other colas are available.

Fast food, a stand-up snack or lunch, is available in countless tiny shops along Cairo streets. The Cairenes' favorite is *fool*, a bland serving of fava beans in sauce; *kushera*, an equally bland serving of noodles and lentils, is a close second. For our taste, a more savory snack is fried vegetable burgers in pita-style bread with *tahina* sauce, variously called *taamiyya* or *falafel*. Look for what appears to be a side of meat turning on a vertical spit to find *shwarma* (called *giro* in the U.S.)—a large meatloaf of lamb and spices which is roasted, sliced into slivers, then packed into pita-style bread along with lettuce and salad. *Fiteer* is a delicious Cairo specialty, a kind of hot pie which can be filled with eggs, meat, vegetables as you may choose, including raisins for a dessert. Sandwich shops exist, but serve small versions with skimpy fillings. Do not worry. There are also Kentucky Fried Chicken franchises in Cairo, and pizza is available too.

SHOPPING: Handcrafts generally present good values in countries where machines have not yet taken over. Quality can vary greatly because not every hand is tasteful, but prices will be pleasing.

Egypt produces inexpensive leatherwork, tooled by hand, available in suitcases, boxes, handbags, hassocks, stuffed animals, and camel saddles in many souvenir shops. Egyptian alabaster is widely available in the form of pharaoh's busts as well as vases, plates, and ashtrays. Technically, this substance is calcite, softer than true alabaster although similar in appearance. "Factories" in Luxor turn out most of what sells in Cairo at higher, though still reasonable, prices. For the best reed baskets, wait until Aswan for the Nubian crafts.

Cairo is the perfume center for the Middle East. Scents are not the most subtle, but they will be mixed on the spot according to your taste in countless shops of the Khan Kalili bazaar in Cairo. You will not soon forget the experience of trying different mixtures while sipping tea or coffee and then seeing the astonishing quantity produced for a few dollars. Kohl for the eyes and henna for the hair are also available in such shops.

Hammered brass trays for tables can be found in Khan

Kalili by following the tapping sounds to rows of hammerers. Prices are fair and dependent on the weight of the brass. In this area there are also brass and copper pots, pitchers, and candlesticks.

Tapestries woven by children in the village of Harraniya are world famous. These naïve woven pictures cost over $150 for the smallest works and should be judged by the standards of art not of carpets. Your hotel concierge can direct you to a shop that carries them in Cairo or you can visit the village on your way to Sakkara.

Although long-staple Egyptian cotton may be the world's best, much of the best is exported. Fabrics in Egyptian stores as often as not prove to be just regular cotton, but this does not affect the popularity of kaftans for souvenirs. They look so Middle Eastern, are comfortable and becoming, yet sell at prices lower than friends at home will ever guess. One can be made to measure in a day for about LE 2, plus the cost of the fabric, totaling about LE 5–8. Tailors abound (all are men or boys), but those in Luxor ask slightly less for their work, and in Luxor's smaller, less harried shopping district, buying is easier than in bustling Cairo. Kaftan refers to the woman's garb, a simple A-line shape. More popular with tourists are the closer fitting *gallabiyahs*, worn by men in Egypt but by both sexes elsewhere. *Gallabiyahs* come in two styles: *effendi* amounts to a tailored, shoe-length man's shirt; *saudi* is similar but even closer fitting. You will have choices in collar, front, and embroidery.

People are surprised at the quantity of ancient Egyptian objects offered for sale at prices substantially less than a king's ransom. Indeed, people should wonder. The only ancient objects that legally can be sold are those which experts from the Museum of Antiquities have approved for sale, and approvals ceased in 1976. By today, the last legal object surely has been sold. You may be told otherwise and sometimes offered official documents to confirm the story—but many more "official" papers exist than legal objects. Probabilities argue strongly that any purchase will be illegal, hence subject to confiscation at an Egyptian airport. Legality aside, fakes outnumber genuine articles by hundreds to one.

Museum curators have been fooled often, for the fakery business is old and experienced in Egypt. Of the two sources that sell "ancient objects," licensed stores and unlicensed dealers, the odds approach certainty that the latter will offer only fakes, while the odds are still better than two to one that a licensed dealer will push good, but modern, fakes at you.

The story of ancient Greek and of Coptic artifacts for sale in Egypt covers all the same plots.

TIPS ON VISITING MOSQUES: In the art of Islam, mosques must be given first place. They were raised for the glory of God, of Allah, and thus show the soul of Islam. Originally they were simple in plan, literally "places of prostration," the meaning of the word *mosque*. A large courtyard formed the hub for three meditation corridors and for a fourth that faced holy Mecca and ended in an ornate wall called the *mahrib*. The faithful gathered in the courtyard and bowed toward the *mahrib* in prayer. The Ibn Tulun Mosque is one of the finest examples in the world of the original simple plan. Later mosques grew more complex. More than just gathering places for the faithful, mosques were the only schools and needed areas for teaching and other services. The congregation area became smaller, the surrounding area larger and more complex. The *mahrib* toward which the congregation faced was made wonderful by an intricately carved dome that looked like glittering stalactites. Tall minarets, from which the calls to prayer could go out over the city, were added. Inside, all around, words flowed from the sacred Koran in beautiful script. The artistic culmination of the more developed form is the mosque of Sultan Hassan.

The Koran, like the Old Testament, includes prohibitions against images. Because these strictures were more rigidly enforced during some periods than others, however, you still see animals and sometimes even human figures portrayed, especially in early Islamic art. In general, though, Islamic artists were denied whole realms of expression and concentrated all the more on what was left to them. Abstract designs, therefore, have seldom been more extensive or beautiful than in Islamic decorations, and simple writing became veritable art. Kuftic writing (named for the town where it developed) is the simpler and more angular style, compared to a more florid type with fluid curves; but both attain high levels of abstract design.

Islamic people used to remove their shoes (and stockings) and wash their feet upon entering a mosque. Visitors once had to remove their shoes too. Many mosques now have cloth slippers to cover shoes. You find them right inside the entrance. When mosques do not have shoecovers, you are expected to remove your shoes, but not stockings.

Egyptians are pleased when visitors admire their mosques. Feel perfectly free to enter. The one exception is during times when services are held—no one wants tourists walking through their place of worship during sacred rites. This means that for mosques that offer services the Sabbath (Friday) is a bad time to visit. On other days services usually are held from noon to 4, intermittently. Needless to say, a quiet attitude will be appreciated.

2.

By Tour Or
On Your Own

More than 80% of the Americans who visit Egypt use package tours to avoid the worry of dealing directly with such a foreign-seeming country. The proportion of British who come "packaged" is far lower; more of them prefer the freedom to tailor their own schedules. Both Americans and British enjoy their visits, apparently, to equal degrees. There are advantages to both sides. Here we set out procedures for visiting Egypt on either basis.

PACKAGE TOURS

The fundamental advantage of buying a travel package is that someone else works out the arrangements. In Egypt's case this is no small asset. Not only does it save work, but by using expertise and clout a company can secure transportation and hotel space that most individuals could not. Also, by dealing in larger lots, packagers sometimes get discounts substantial enough to make a profit and still offer a trip for less than an individual would have to pay. However, the issue of price savings is complex. If a package involves a trip different from what you would arrange on your own, how can you compare the two? One solution is to look further, to find a package even closer to your ideal or one that permits modifications that would allow you to tailor the trip to your plans. Many packages of various types are available—some provide more freedom from the prearranged itinerary, others less.

Before considering the types of packages and examining some actual packages, we should mention possible negative aspects of packages. In the tour business are some very substantial companies whose solid reputations are based on well-earned accomplishments, and other, less substantial, organizations. Consider the name and the size of the company offering any package tour before you buy. From time to time there are incidents of trips cancelled at the last minute and of trips that turn out to be very different from the impression created by a brochure description. Fortunately such stories are rare. But, please, read the fine print in any brochure—which is like a contract and just as important to understand before signing.

A major problem with travel in an escorted tour is a psychological pressure that drains grown people of their wills. It begins innocuously as people in a group ask their leader what he advises that they bring on a given outing. The leader has been there before, the tourist has not; so the question is reasonable. As days pass, as all problems that arise fall on the shoulders of the leader—who solves most or all of them—a situation develops in which the group depends more and more on its leader. Eventually members of the group look to the leader for advice not just about what to wear in a given situation, but what to eat and what to do. Grown people revert to children unable to make normal decisions; the leader looms larger before them than any parent. These pressures are subtle, thus powerful. Unless you want a trip resembling a grade-school outing, maintain your independence from the beginning. Do things—anything—from time to time away from the group. The other problems that arise in groups of people who travel together are those to be expected in most social situations: what to do about the chatterer who insists on sitting with you; how to avoid arguing with the insistent person whose politics are distasteful to you. Fortunately, Egypt is so fascinating it distracts almost everyone, so such small social problems seem less extreme. If you maintain your independence at the beginning—the trip is long and there is adequate time to get to know your fellow travelers—you can usually avoid awkward situations later on.

Not all packages herd people into groups; there are varieties. A package trip means only that some, not necessarily all, of the elements of a trip are assembled and sold together at a single price. It may involve no more than an arranged flight and a series of nights in designated hotels. You may even have choices of how many nights you want to stay in any city and which hotels you prefer in different cities. These are sometimes called *freelance tour packages*. Other names for packages mean something different. A *package tour* does include sightseeing and touring together. An *escorted tour package* includes a leader who accompanies the group throughout its travels. A *hosted tour package* only guarantees that a representative will meet you at your hotel to deal with questions and help with arrangements.

Some packages are sold directly, usually through advertisements in newspapers and magazines. Often a university or a large museum will offer escorted package tours. Many other packages are sold through travel agents. If the travel agent you use has a large business, he should know of five to fifteen different sorts of packages for Egypt. Gather information on as many as you can. Compare services and decide which services you want. Note the class of the hotels to compare the prices. If a tour includes some travel by boat, it will be more expensive because boat accommodations cost more. Check to see how many meals are included. Above all, remember that whatever is not specifically mentioned will not be included.

As a rule, the cost per day is less the longer the stay—the

airfare of about $700 (or more, depending on season) is averaged over more days. Airfares rise in the summer, but land arrangements decline to make prices average out. Roughly, a one-week trip (8 days) costs in the neighborhood of $1400 per person, which includes airfare and first-class, or better, hotels. This price, as are those following, is based on two in a room; single rooms are more expensive. Ten days will cost about $1700 to $2000; two weeks (15 days) costs about $2300; three weeks should cost less than $3000. With a three- or four-day Nile cruise included, 15 days costs $2500 or so. We have seen budget trips to Cairo offered for under $830 with all normal expenses included, but with hotels at the three-star, second-class level.

We supply the following list for illustrative purposes. It far from exhausts all the packages available, though it hints at the variety. No suggestion is intended that the listed offerings are in some way better than those not included. We have omitted prices—which are subject to change. Write directly, or see a travel agent for current costs.

American Express (65 Broadway, New York, NY 10006) offers half a dozen tours. These vary in duration from ten days to three weeks and cover a price range from moderate to expensive, depending on accommodation and services.

Arthur Frommer International (380 Madison Avenue, New York, NY 10017) charters planes to reduce prices. At present all that is available is an 8-day visit to Cairo, but other packages may be offered in the future.

The Cortell Group (3 East 54th Street, New York, NY 10022) offers a 10-day tour without, and a 15-day tour with, Nile cruise.

Cunard (P.O. Box 999, Farmingdale, NY 11737) lets you fly to Egypt for as long a stay as you like, then brings you back on the *Queen Elizabeth II* through the Mediterranean, to England, and across the Atlantic.

Esplanade Tours (38 Newbury Street, Boston, MA 02116) are the U.S. agents for the British Swan Ltd. They offer a 19-day cruise down the length of the Nile from Aswan to Cairo, or vice versa, escorted by an expert in Egyptology. The trip involves flying to London, but from there on every expense, other than drinks and laundry, but including tea, is covered.

Four Winds (175 Fifth Avenue, New York, NY 10010) offers fully escorted tours of 10 days and 15 days. The 15-day tour is on board a cruise ship.

Lindblad Travel (133 East 55th Street, New York, NY 10022) offers various escorted tours, all of which include a Nile cruise. Shorter visits of 16 days include 6 nights on a boat; the 19- or 20-day trips involve a cruise from Cairo to Aswan, or vice versa.

Maupintour (900 Massachusetts Street, Lawrence, KA 66044) offers escorted trips of varying duration, with and without cruises, some including stops at the British Museum in London.

Persepolis Tours (667 Madison Avenue, New York, NY 10021) offers tours of 8 or 15 days. The longer trip can include a three-day cruise.

Sunny Land Tours (166 Main Street, Hackensack, NJ 07601) has a variety of 10- to 15-day tours, all involving cruises of from three to seven days. They also offer a budget 14-day escorted tour for students.

TWA Getaway Tours (605 Third Avenue, New York, NY 10158) TWA flies directly to Egypt and offers escorted packages of 8, 10, and 15 days. One version of their 10-day trip includes four nights on board a hotel-boat.

Each of these companies, and others as well, provide a variety of tours that visit other countries along with Egypt, in addition to their strictly Egypt tours, but we are purists.

EGYPT ON YOUR OWN

Unquestionably, making arrangements for yourself involves work, but it also carries satisfactions. The trip will be yours, tailored to your interests and a true adventure.

The awareness that Egypt is a very foreign culture does tend to worry travelers. Indeed, Egypt is different in a thousand ways from any European country, but not in frightening ways. Unfamiliar procedures and styles of operation all work themselves out. The saving grace of Egypt, among all other Middle Eastern countries, is that Egypt has been in the travel business since the time of the ancient Greeks. Long-range planning may be difficult from an ocean away, but when the preparations are settled and you actually arrive in the country, willing assistance will be offered on every side. He who asks will receive—whatever he wants.

Egypt may be dealt with in three stages: reserving hotels, booking a flight, and managing following arrival on Egyptian soil. Reservations, to repeat a point that cannot be made too strongly, must be secured months in advance of a visit. You can write to hotels or have a travel agent cable to ask for bookings. This approach might succeed. But letters and cables may be unanswered; or the response may be that the hotel is full, even if it isn't. This is just Egypt's way, at times. If possible, it is better to be direct: make bookings through agents in the U.S. Most hotels in Egypt can be reserved this way. For this reason we have listed the company that owns a hotel after its description, unless the hotel is privately owned.

Egyptian Hotels Company through: Misr Travel, 630 Fifth Avenue, New York, NY 10022; Telephone: 212-582-9210.

Hilton International Hotels, 401 Seventh Avenue, New York, NY 10001; Telephone: 212-594-4500.

Meridien Hotels, 888 Seventh Avenue, New York, NY 10019; Telephone: 212-265-4494.

Oberoi Hotels, 666 Fifth Avenue, New York, NY 10019; Telephone: 212-841-1111.

Sheraton International Hotels, 1700 Broadway, New York, NY 10019; Telephone: 800-325-3535 (toll-free).

When you secure a reservation, it is better to pay in advance. Then, when you confront the hotel clerk in Egypt, your indignation, if it is needed, can be honest. If the clerk continues to insist he has never heard of you, *baksheesh* as a reward for his trouble in rechecking his list may assist him in finding the reservation. In the case of privately owned hotels, writing is the only way. Again, prepayment is advised.

Because Nile cruises are so popular and the available boats are so few, arranging reservations is a chancy matter for private individuals. Tour companies gobble up almost every cabin. The long cruises—from Cairo to Aswan, or vice versa—constitute an entire tour and are booked as such through a company offering them. Shorter cruises ply between Aswan and Luxor (some go as far north as Abydos and Denderah). These trips last between four and nine nights with stops en route and can be pursued by people who are not on organized tours. The odds are at best only fair and efforts should begin long in advance of a trip. Try travel agents, but ask the agent to try a direct approach. Hilton Hotels Corporation and Sheraton Hotels each operates several of these cruise ships.

Air transportation inside Egypt is also heavily booked. If you settle on your schedule early, you or your travel agent can make plane reservations by contacting Egyptair. Fares inside Egypt are reasonable—about $40 per person from Cairo to Luxor, for example.

Train transport is reasonably good in Egypt and cheap enough that first class is well worth the privacy. Of course getting there takes longer (12 hours from Cairo to Luxor, compared to an hour by plane), but arrangements can be made after landing in Egypt; make them on arrival through the concierge at your hotel.

For any questions or problems, contact the Egyptian Government Tourist Offices who will try to help.

At present, few airlines fly to Egypt. TWA is the only U.S. carrier with direct flights, but Pakistan International Airlines also flies direct and most airlines that fly the Atlantic connect with Egyptair in Europe to complete the trip. Since plane fares have been deregulated, they fluctuate chaotically, but principles and approximations can be stated. The shorter your stay and the later you reserve and pay for your ticket, the more it will cost. The least expensive fares are Advanced Purchase Excursions (APEX), which must be paid for some weeks or months in advance—the timing depends on the airline and season. Next in price are excursion fares, which involve minimum stays—usually of two weeks—and the purchase of a minimum hotel package.

In order of rising prices, next comes 21- to 120-day

extended stay fares; 14- to 21-day excursion fares; and regular fares. The advantage of regular fare, and often for a small supplement, of 14- to 21-day excursion fares, is that they allow one or more stopovers along the way. If such is not your desire, go for the APEX fare which presently costs about $685 off season, round trip. But shop—fares differ with different airlines.

Airfares vary by season and are wholly out of phase with desirability. High season runs from June through August; low season runs from September through May; the rest of the year is mid-priced shoulder season. The popular seasons in Europe, which are altogether different from those in Egypt, determine the seasonal scale. Do not tell the airlines; just take advantage of a terrific situation. Hotel seasons in Egypt are the reverse. Summer is low season and lower prices—except for the summer resort of Alexandria.

Having gotten to Egypt and secured reservations, the rest is easy. You can easily do anything that groups do. Your hotel will have lists of excursions offered by various local tour companies from which you can select what you want. But to follow the groups is to be in a group and lose the advantages of your independent situation. If, for example, you wish to see the Sound and Light show at the Giza pyramids and book through a tour operator, you are tied to someone else's schedule and will pay about $25 per person for the arrangements and admission. Alternatively, you can walk outside your hotel on the evening of the show, hire a taxi for about $5 (however many people there are in your party), and buy a ticket at the box office at Giza for LE 2—less than $3 per person.

If you buy an excursion to Memphis and Sakkara through a tour company, it will cost approximately $100 for one person, $120 for two, $150 for three—unless you go packed with a group of strangers at $36 for each person in your party. For this price, you will get lunch and a guide whose information can be generally uninteresting. Alternatively, you can hire a car and driver for about $25 to take your entire party to the same places. You view the monuments you wish to see at your own pace. On the way back you can, if you wish, stop off at the crafts villages of Harraniya and Kerdassa, then drop by Andrea's Chicken Restaurant for a late lunch. Or if you want to do something truly memorable, stop at the Giza pyramids the day before you plan to go to Memphis and Sakkara. Ask any of the eager dragomen where you can hire horses. They will bring someone who will agree to provide as many Arabian horses as you wish, along with guides—which will be waiting for you in Giza the next day. For less than $20 per mount and $20 per guide, you can ride through the desert to Memphis and Sakkara, passing tiny villages along the way.

To make the most of an independent trip to Egypt, you need only know that almost anything is available at a reasonable price, if you ask. Know that private transportation anywhere can be had for $20 or so for the day just by asking at the hotel desk or walking outside to the waiting taxis. With your own transportation, you can go where you wish and stop along the way when anything strikes your fancy.

Traveling in this manner puts you in direct contact with all levels of Egyptians. You do not have a group around you and a leader to smooth over all difficulties. Such contact can involve irritations in addition to wonderful opportunities. You will be in situations in which you will have to bargain for things. Most people soon catch the spirit of bargaining contests and enjoy them. You will be pestered by people asking for *baksheesh* and others who will try to thrust unwanted services or items to be purchased at you. Only in a few, tourist-filled places—such as Giza, the west bank in Luxor, and Tell el Amarna—is this pestering so insistent that it can become a serious annoyance. In these places you can hire a guide who, in addition to guiding you, will fend off intrusions. Or you can struggle through your first few encounters and learn how to communicate with a firmness that will ease your way through successive occasions. But through all these situations, you will meet many Egyptians and learn about an extraordinary culture and its people. Some people you meet may suggest restaurants and other places to go. They will invite you to tea or to dinner at their homes. You are almost certain to be invited to at least one unforgettable village wedding somewhere along the way. You will hear about camel auctions and village celebrations, and experience the life of Egypt that in a tour you might miss altogether.

3.

Land and People

The unique landscape of Egypt has always been intriguing. It was an enigma to the ancient Egyptians and remained a mystery until Victorian times. Egypt is the world's largest oasis—astonishing fertility surrounded by millions of miles of sterile sand constituting the largest desert in the world. This desert stretches in a band across North Africa, pausing for the ten-mile width of the Red Sea, then continues on to the rivers of Iran. The top of this band, the Mediterranean coastline, retains enough water to support proper soil and large populations. Otherwise, humans live only in widely scattered oases that dot the desert. For five million square miles only one country has length as well as breadth for population—Egypt.

The mighty river Nile is the life-sustaining force that runs the length of Egypt. Its water allows green crops to replace the gray-brown sands of the desert. Ancient as well as modern travelers have asked, What is a river doing in the middle of such vast, arid wasteland? For this desert is not the average desert; it is the standard by which others are judged—no other is drier and few are as hot. Water should be as alien in this portion of the world as it would be on Mercury. Yet here a half-mile wide river flows, surrounded by verdure. And of all the great rivers in the world, only the Nile runs north. Even stranger, before the construction of the High Dam, the Nile turned red, then green, before mounting its banks every summer to inundate the surrounding land.

Expedition followed expedition to find the cause of these phenomena, the source of the Nile. Eventually the source was found in Lake Victoria—so filled by the constant rains of tropical Africa that it could nurture a 1500-mile river and push it through a final thousand miles of desert. As to why this river flows north, scientists learned the answer recently through the new theory of plate tectonics. We now know that continents move, almost imperceptibly, on roads of molten rock. For eons the northern half of the African continent has been inching toward southern Europe, while the continental shelves met under the Mediterranean Sea two million years ago. In this mammoth meeting impelled by inexorable forces, something had to give. What gave was North Africa, whose crust passed under Europe, tilting North Africa downward. The Nile flows north because north is downhill.

The summer color changes in the Nile and its regular flooding were caused by torrential rains—not rains that fell on Egypt or anywhere else along the course of the Nile, but spring monsoons in Ethiopia. The mile-high Ethiopian plateau, southeast of Egypt, caught clouds filled with the evaporation of humid central Africa. Every spring, 20 feet of deluge fell on Ethiopia, eroding the soil and sweeping away vegetation in sudden rivers that emptied into the Nile near Khartoum. Except for the boil and rage of the water, little happened for three hundred miles after this infusion, for the Nile flowed on a granite bed in the Sudan, funneling the floods through to Egypt. Egypt lies on softer sandstone and limestone carved by erosion into mile-wide plains. After Aswan—the last granite obstacle—plains beckoned the Nile to release its surplus and the green vegetation and red soil of Ethiopia.

This summer inundation of Egypt more than replaced the rain that other countries depended on. From the earliest times, Egyptians learned how to save as much of their flood as possible by building basins and canals. As water slowly seeped back to the lowered Nile, the mix of suspended soil and vegetation settled behind on the plains, forming a rich topsoil. Egypt's fertility was legendary, dependable, and inexhaustible. But there was not enough farmland for the population explosion that took place in this century. In 1967 the High Dam at Aswan ended the floods. Today the farming process is more prosaic—canals, dykes, and fertilizers—but the configuration of the land remains the same.

The quieted Nile flows half-a-mile wide down the center of Egypt; rich crops stretch flat and green on either side. Desert shale prefaces abrupt hills (though actually it is the Nile valley that has dug itself 300 feet below the surrounding land), behind which are the deserts. To the west the Sahara continues almost to the Atlantic Ocean in Morocco. To the east lies the Eastern Desert, a series of small mountains where the land buckled to make the Red Sea. All the life of Egypt concentrates in the river valley. Villages of gray adobe rise 10 or 20 feet above the farms on their own crumbled predecessors. Quiet people go about their measured routines, almost as features of the terrain.

The Egypt that maps present has little to do with the real Egypt or with anything but political history and the convenience of map-makers. Maps show Egypt as a virtual square, 674 miles long by 770 miles wide. Libya forms the western border; the Sudan lies south; the Red Sea separates the African part of Egypt from the Sinai in Asia; and the Mediterranean Sea seals the top of Egypt. No one lives in any of this area except in the center 3% where the Nile flows. Living Egypt takes the shape of the Nile, a 600-mile-long flower stem whose flower is formed just above Cairo by 70 miles of river delta that opens 150 miles wide when it ends in the Mediterranean. More than half of the population lives in Cairo and the Delta. The rest live south in the valley or in the Faiyum, just below and west of Cairo, near Egypt's only large natural lake.

The Faiyum's loamy black soil anchors grove after grove of date palms. The Delta grows the long staple cotton for which

Egypt is famous, along with rice and grapes, and provides pastures for sheep and beef cattle. The south produces grains, rice, dates, olives, vegetables, and fruits. Egypt is a farm, populated by farmers.

Egyptians have varied ancestries, but on the whole they are different from every other people. Although they are not Arabs, they speak Arabic and call their country the Arab Republic of Egypt. True Arabs are Semites. Anthropologists class Egyptians as Hamites, putting them in a collection with the blue-eyed North African Berbers to whom Egyptians bear little physical or cultural resemblance. No one, it seems, knows exactly how to classify the Egyptians. Many Egyptians work hard in total silence, then meet their friends in cafes for ceaseless chatter. In general they are desperately poor, but smile at the slightest excuse. They are a handsome people whose skin shade ranges from olive to deepest black. Their facial features are strong; their brown eyes are soft.

Religion and culture, however, do align Egyptians with Semitic Arabs. More than 80% of the population is Muslim, which establishes a tone of morals and broad culture in Egypt, as it does throughout the Middle East. Egyptians combine benevolence and fatalism in a complex mixture that derives from the two fundamental currents of Islam.

According to Islamic belief, the living shall die on the day of judgment at the sound of the first trumpet note by the angel Azrael. The dead will reawaken at his second note, then set out for paradise on a bridge no wider than a hair. Those whose devotion has been exact and whose charity has been ample will pass safely across the bridge, while the rest will fall into a hellish abyss. Charity, which encompasses hospitality as well as donations to the less fortunate, is thus a high moral principle for Muslims. Religious devotion ranks still higher, and the requirements are simple and clear. Three fundamental duties are asked of every believer: pray five times every day, endeavor at least one pilgrimage to Mecca, and profess the credo daily that there is no god but Allah and that Muhammad is his prophet. But paradise has levels, and angels keep records of every action, so Muslims attempt to earn better places in the next world by extra fidelities. They try to avoid "unclean" foods, such as pork; resist intoxicating beverages; and fast during daylight for the month of Ramadan to atone for any sins. Many of these practices are fading now, especially—among the upper class—the abstention from alcohol.

Such religious duties and the moral principle of benevolence are not, of course, very different from what other religions preach. Muslims do excel, in degree, both in the percentage of serious practitioners and in the energy expended for their religion, compared to the performance today in Judeo-Christian cultures. Muslims act on the belief that Allah controls everything. Every human plan, they believe, represents a mere wish which Allah effects or not according to a grander plan. Muslims strive, but at the same time feel that efforts and intentions have no effect. The least consequential arrangement—say to meet a friend on the next day—ends with the phrase *Inshallah*, "If God wills." Yet their attitude of predestiny does not interfere with keeping appointments or with working hard.

Egyptians living in Cairo, like the French of Paris, are quite different in attitudes and dress from those who live in other parts of the country. Cairenes are more worldly, pragmatic, and enterprising. Their dress deviates more than elsewhere in Egypt from the norm of flowing robes and floppy headcloths. In Cairo, people frequently wear European fashions and carry briefcases; others wear ragtag eclectic collections; and there is a middle ground of those who aim for European fashion but who can afford only one suit jacket, which they've worn every day for 20 years.

South of Cairo one finds more fundamental Egyptians. Especially pure are the *fellahin* who live opposite Luxor, where veiled women are a common sight, otherwise unusual in today's Egypt. Children dress in brightly patterned pajamas, adults in somber plainness. Throughout the south homes are single-story mud houses with flat thatched roofs, just as they have been for five thousand years. Women in black—for almost every family has suffered some bereavement—bear the day's produce on their heads; men plant with hand tools. Water for irrigation is lifted by water wheels driven round and round by water buffalo or even more primatively, by *shadouf*—mud-weighted counterpoises. Practically naked men and boys wade near their nets in the canals. On the Nile beautiful lateen-rigged boats fly like sparrows; close inspection shows them to be mosaics of salvaged wood and sails. The south tends to be poor, superstitious, and proud.

Egyptians have never experienced democracy. Pharaohs gave way to Roman emperors replaced by sultans, pashas, kings, and finally, revolution in 1952 which resulted in the leadership of strong-man Nasser. Today Egypt would be called a benevolent dictatorship under President Sadat's rule. Regular elections are held, but only the parties authorized by those in power may contend, and the president can fill ten of the 350 legislative seats by appointment. One party, the Arab Socialist Union (ASU) wins every election, both locally and nationally, by huge majorities. Real politics in Egypt consists of individual struggles to rise in the ASU and of efforts to keep the ASU planted firmly in popular favor. The thrust of President Sadat's policies has been to hold basic foodstuffs at artificially low prices and to personally shine on the international stage for Egypt's pride. He has dealt with Egypt's serious economic problems in a socialist manner. Every college graduate is guaranteed a job in government, if he or she desires, which makes bureaucracy endemic. Education is free and compulsory between the ages of six and twelve, though the system is strained by the rapid growth of population. New industries are government financed and owned, at least in part.

Through all its history Egypt survived as an agricultural country, but it can no longer. Its population, the fastest growing in the world, can use all and more than Egypt grows, leaving nothing to trade for imports. Today Egypt searches desperately for new industries that can earn international credits. Imports have been drastically restricted until the time that Egypt can pay its way. The High Dam at Aswan accomplished no miracles; Egypt's new eastern oil fields are only large enough to gain some time.

Those who visit Egypt help—tourism is one real asset for Egypt's trade balance. Feel proud when you visit for the help you bring to a deserving country. Indulge yourself correspondingly, and wish Egypt well.

4.

Background for Cairo

Cairo is many things—belly dancers, camel drivers, men in gallabiyahs, women in veils (occasionally), as well as American soft drinks, train stations, fast-food chains, and skyscrapers—but most of all, Cairo is history. The life of modern Cairo is striking, impossible to ignore. History is never so evident. Yet however splendid these historical monuments may be, the past requires a portion of understanding. Understanding enlivens piles of stone, helps them shine with the richness of context and purpose.

Cairo's history is immense. Her sights span five millennia and cover three cultures as different as an Islamic civilization is from a Christian culture, with ancient Egypt still more different. Cairo presents her history with delightful mosques, churches, pyramids, and museum treasures. The sights are not overwhelming; they create a thirst for more—and for more understanding.

Our job in the following pages is to supply the background to Cairo's sights, from the beginning of ancient history and the establishment of the very first capital of ancient Egypt at

Memphis (near Cairo) to the early Christian Copts to the Islamic art that survives in the Islamic capital of Egypt—Cairo.

ANCIENT EGYPT

On the outskirts of Cairo stand the oldest buildings in the world. The Giza pyramids were completed over 4000 years ago. Near ancient Memphis, 20 miles away, are tombs and paintings that are older still. The great Museum of Antiquities in the heart of modern Cairo exhibits the art of those ancient people who raised the buildings and painted the tombs. Cairo is the place to meet our oldest civilization and to think about its beginnings.

Who were the people of the Pyramids? Why did they raise 50-story monuments at a time when the rest of the world still huddled in tents? How, without machines or wheels, were such mammoth structures possible? What secret enabled Egypt to produce wonders of architecture and art an eon ago?

THE FIRST PHARAOH: No great civilization existed in Egypt before 3100 B.C. No great civilization existed anywhere. It was a time when mankind still lived in mud dwellings and scratched subsistence from the dirt. In this primitive age Egypt was perhaps a small step ahead of most other countries simply by having towns, some temples, and the rudiments of writing. But so, too, was Sumeria on the Mesopotamian plains. In fact, Sumeria could boast of larger towns and temples and older writing. In the race to create the first great civilization Egypt was in second place.

In 3100 B.C. Egypt crowned her first pharaoh—2100 years before the Exodus, 1500 years before Stonehenge, 1300 years before the flowering of China. Suddenly Egypt was a nation, the first one in the world. Egypt sped toward greatness, leaving Sumeria behind.

Narmer, the first pharaoh, molded the character of ancient Egypt. Religion, morality, attitudes toward life and toward death all interwove in ancient Egypt—interwove around the pharaoh. It was Narmer who created the institution of a living, ruling god. Every subsequent pharaoh copied him. His achievements are the key to ancient Egypt.

Unusual prehistoric and geographic conditions helped Narmer. Egypt was among the earliest lands where humans settled. Theories contend that our species evolved not far away in east central Africa (where Tanzania, Kenya, Ethiopia, and Uganda come together) and followed the Nile, a natural road, northward. Evidence of humans living in Egypt more than 500,000 years ago—stone axes and ostrich eggshells (the first pots)—is found far from the Nile in what is now desert. In prehistoric times rain in this region created streams with trees and flowers, providing sustenance for early men. When the ice melted after the last ice age, the climate changed. The rains stopped. The Nile was left as the most peculiar of geographical phenomena—a desert river. Thanks to its waters men could live, but they became more and more concentrated at the river as the land around turned to sand. Concentrated population was one ingredient of nationhood.

Primitive Egyptians, forced by the drying of the land, gathered along the Nile and found natural occupations as farmers. Egypt could grow three crops every year. Population increased, towns grew, innovations—the bow, pottery, domestication of animals—were happily adopted in Egypt as they passed around the world. The first Egyptians accomplished a number of "firsts." Apparently they first domesticated the donkey (as a beast of burden; it was not ridden until later times) and the cat (from a wild desert ancestor). Some experiments failed—for centuries Egyptians tried to domesticate antelopes. In other ways Egypt marched in step with various advanced civilizations, though more comfortably because of its assured supply of food. But geography also encouraged the separation of northern and southern cultures and precipitated war.

Just north of modern Cairo the Nile seems to sense the Mediterranean, 70 miles away, and breaks apart in fanning branches searching for the sea. The shape reminded ancient Greeks of the triangle of their letter *d*; they called this part of Egypt *Delta*, their name for the letter. Later, the word came to mean any estuary. In Egypt, this low and marshy expanse contrasts dramatically with the 600-mile ribbon of fertile valley, five to ten miles wide, embedded in desert, that constitutes the rest of the land. In the south, a farming civilization developed, raising grains and vegetables, and building houses of bricks made from dried river mud. Their challenge was to spread water from the river over as much land as possible through complex irrigation systems. In the northern Delta, in contrast, nature took care of the water, spreading it freely over hundreds of square miles where grazing herds of cattle, flocks of sheep, goats, and pigs flourished. The Delta had ports opening onto the Mediterranean to receive ships, and it lay at the end of overland trade routes that brought goods from throughout the Middle East. The south was jealous of her richer neighbor to the north. Pig flesh, eaten in the north, was a religious anathema offensive to the south. In turn, the Delta had designs on the fertile southern farms and considered the southern farmers barbaric. Competition and war were inevitable.

The war was interminable. Towns built adobe enclosure walls up to 20 feet high and almost as thick. Defense had the upper hand by far, for there was little that spears, arrows, clubs, and knives could do against such massive fortresses. The war lasted for generations, leaving a permanent scar on the psyche of Egypt.

Narmer was born approximately 5000 years ago during this war and lived near Abydos in southern Egypt. Somehow he gained leadership in the south and thus possession of the leader's hat—a tall, white crown shaped like a cone but with a ball-like tip. (You will see this southern crown often in carvings of pharaohs.) He called for volunteers from all the southern towns and collected an army of farmers, perhaps 4000 strong. At first light on a morning in early spring, they set out for adventure. Narmer rode in a boat while his army ran on hardened feet beside the river.

Some genius, no one knows who, found a way to conquer fortresses. Men constructed reed shelters to cover a dozen of their fellows. Safe from the arrows of the defenders, the crew dug at the fortress walls with farmer mattocks. Mattocks that could break the hard ground for planting could in time go through dried mud walls, however thick. One after another, the Delta fortresses fell, until Narmer held all the power in Egypt.

The military victory brought Narmer power, prestige, and a new problem. A defeated people stood before him, but what would prevent renewed hostilities after Narmer's army returned home? Extermination of an enemy was neither a moral nor a practical possibility until more modern times. Narmer needed a way to make peace between two hostile peoples. He needed a union, a nation. But nationhood, which is so common today that it seems an obvious idea, did not exist anywhere in Narmer's world. True, long before Narmer towns reflected a certain kind of community or government. Towns then sometimes even extended their powers by conquering neighboring areas. But the idea of a government that supervenes, one that does not replace local rule but is superior, one that governs other governments, had yet to occur to anyone.

What had to be created was political authority, a reason that would legitimize governing and replace force. Narmer's achievement was the invention of national government. Its form, peculiar compared to governments of our time, suited ancient Egypt well. Narmer allowed both the people of the Delta and those of the south to preserve their separate religions and different ways of life. He recognized that no device would transform foes into friends or two peoples into a single community. To make a nation, he merged their gods and customs into himself. Power that had come initially from spears and arrows soon became moral power. Narmer himself became the unity of Egypt and the only means of peace.

On his brow he placed a vulture head, the icon of a great southern goddess. Beside it he wore a cobra head, the icon of a great Delta goddess. Every ceremony was performed twice, once with Narmer in the cone hat of the southern leader, then in the hat of the northern leader—an odd, flat, red hat with a spike behind and a curl in front. (Later, a clever milliner would combine the two hats into one, producing the crown most often seen on pharaohs' heads.) Narmer called himself Lord of the Two Lands, giving ancient Egypt its name. The falcon god Horus was worshiped—in different ways—both in the Delta and in the south, so Narmer claimed Horus as his special patron. Thus, two different peoples could look to Narmer for leadership, regardless of their feelings about each other. He allied himself with both by raising their gods above a nation—his person was the nation.

He married the most important woman in the Delta, using the marriage to further justify his claim to rule. From that time forth, the throne of Egypt belonged to a woman. Although in theory only a man could rule Egypt—there are but a few exceptions—he could attain office only by marrying the most royal eligible woman. With his strategy of favoring neither area, Narmer could not live either in the Delta or in the south. He built a new city to be the capital of his new nation at the place where the Delta began, where the two lands join. For 1500 years after, Memphis was the great capital of the first and mightiest nation in the world. Narmer held a ceremony to celebrate his new city, new nation, and new position. He began a tradition by changing his name on that day of coronation. He became Menes: "I who establish."

Thus Egypt began as two lands united only in the person of her pharaoh. For this reason, the pharaoh was revered. He was viewed through the ages as the provider of unity and order, as Narmer incarnate, always wearing Narmer's famous crowns with cobra and vulture heads on the front. The fundamental artistic motif of ancient Egypt became unification, two in one. Pairs of matching scenes were carved on many temple walls. The favorite Egyptian composition was of lotus plants, the emblem of the south, entwined with leafy headed papyrus, the emblem of the Delta, on the sides of a throne. Horus became the god most often pictured because he stood for the pharaoh (who was referred to as "the Horus So-and-So"). Above almost any portrait of a pharaoh one can see the spread wings of a vulture, the old southern goddess who protected the king.

Of Narmer's death we are only told that he was carried off by a hippopotamus and perished. His new nation Egypt was just beginning to wield its power.

THE FIRST TOMBS: The long perspective of history gives order and seeming inevitability to what must have looked very different to those living through the times. After Narmer, Egypt moved toward increased power, greater wealth, and improvements in living, but not always in smooth succession. Politics and religion became wholly inseparable in the years after Narmer combined them. The office of the pharaoh grew enormous in its potential, but Egypt lacked direction. If a clear goal were revealed, a pharaoh could direct all the energies of his country toward a single challenge. Such a goal developed gradually. As pharaohs grew stronger and more sacred, new theories of death and resurrection inspired Egypt.

From earliest times Egyptians believed in the exact reverse of Western ideas about death. They thought you *could* take it with you. Predynastic graves, filled with prized possessions and practical things like meat, bread, wine, beer, clothing, cosmetics, and tools, teach us a great deal about early life.

The hereafter was believed to be an actual place, though of uncertain location. It might have been above or perhaps below the earth, although it was always referred to as the West, where the sun sets. There the dead receive a second life, better than in this world but not altogether different, so the deceased's body had to be preserved. Work would be necessary, clothing worn, and time set aside for play. Naturally the more important a person was, the more goods he planned to take along and the larger his tomb would be.

Before Narmer, the largest burials were pretty drab affairs—simple pits in the sand away from the houses of the living. Because moisture is necessary for most forms of decay, in a climate as arid as Egypt's bodies dried too quickly to rot. Placing bodies in tombs was to impede this natural process and lead to the need for mummification. One of Egypt's assets was a life so long that it permitted her to learn from her past: the principle of mummification was discovered in this primitive drying process.

The construction of substantial tombs began with the advent of pharaohs. A pharaoh's burial was important because its splendor was in everyone's interest. The pharaoh wanted to take as much with him to the next world as he could. His successor, as heir, had a stake in the respect shown to his father. Ordinary citizens could expect religious favors from any contribution to their lord, who was a god after death as in life. They worked happily on his tomb.

Tomb dimensions grew and grew in the competition for devotion. Within two centuries after Narmer, a pharaoh's tomb had reached the size of a football field. Chambers were dug underground for storing possessions and food. The corpse lay in the center in a chamber decorated like a palace room (sometimes complete with latrine). Over this subterranean complex, rubble was piled and faced with adobe bricks to protect both the valuable objects and the honored body. The shape above ground was a low rectangle with a gently curved top. Early excavators christened these tombs *mastabas* because they looked like giant versions of the benches you may see outside of houses in rural Egypt today: *mastaba* is Arabic for "bench."

What worked for the pharaoh would work for other citizens on a scale appropriate to their rank. Tombs sprouted beside the pharaoh's for his wives, children, and officials. During these early times when Memphis was Egypt's greatest city, the cemetery of the capital was two miles north in the desert at a place called Sakkara. Here, in the reign of the pharaoh Zoser, an innovation pointed the way to the famous pyramids.

DYNASTIES: A framework is needed for following the development of pyramids, one that will simplify the discussion of long periods of time. Among Egyptologists it is traditional to use units called *dynasties*. In fact this tradition goes back to the very first Egyptologist of all, the Egyptian priest Manetho, who lived in the 3rd century B.C. Manetho wrote the first history of Egypt so that the Ptolemies, who ruled Egypt after its conquest by Alexander the Great, might learn about the country they governed. His problem, like ours, was that over 300 pharaohs had reigned during the course of Egypt's history. He divided them into more manageable lots, into the generations of a single family. In theory all the pharaohs of Dynasty XII, for example, would be descendants of each other; Dynasty XIII would start with new blood. Manetho's ordering device helps, but over the span of 2500 years there were 31 dynasties. To further simplify, we can treat the "ups," the times of power and national unity, each as a single era and the "downs," times of weakness and disorder, as intervals.

There were three great ups: the Old Kingdom, the Middle Kingdom, and the New Kingdom. Separating each Kingdom is an Intermediate Period, or down. In addition, there was a period before the Old Kingdom—from Narmer through the Second Dynasty—called the Early Dynastic Period, and before that, Predynastic Times. After the New Kingdom ended, there was a long slide downhill, called the Late Period. What we have then is:

Period	Dynasty	Dates
Predynastic		about 4000–3100 B.C.
Early Dynastic Period	I–II	3100–2686 B.C.
Old Kingdom	III–VI	2686–2181 B.C.
First Intermediate Period	VII–X	2181–2040 B.C.
Middle Kingdom	XI–XII	2140–1786 B.C.
Second Intermediate Period	XIII–XVII	1786–1570 B.C.
New Kingdom	XVIII–XX	1570–1086 B.C.
Late Period	XXI–XXXI	1085–332 B.C.

The Late Period ends—at a time that would be early for most countries—with Egypt's subjugation by Alexander, the Ptolemies, and the Romans.

PYRAMIDS—THE OLD KINGDOM: In the years after Narmer, the political power of Egypt matured and consolidated. The borders of Egypt spread outward as armed expeditions pushed farther and farther afield. They traveled south into the Sudan (called Gold Country or Nubia by the Egyptians), west into Libya, east into the Sinai. They returned with perfumes, rare woods, semiprecious stones, and precious metals. Wonderful art flowered, thanks to the infinite patience of Egyptian artists and their adoration of the pharaoh.

Social complexity developed along with wealth and power. Writing evolved from pictures into the language called hieroglyphs. Egypt had grown powerful, rich, and civilized— ready for something new. It was time to show off. In Dynasty III Egypt visibly demonstrated her greatness in the form of the first pyramid. It was not, however, a pyramid of the familiar shape.

A pharaoh named Zoser (sometimes written *Djoser*—the sound, not the spelling, is what counts) dominated Dynasty III. His fortune lay, as much as anything, in a brilliant vizier named Imhotep. What a genius Imhotep must have been! Since the pharaoh did not dirty his hands with practical matters, Imhotep managed the whole country. He was renowned for his knowledge, especially of medicine, down to the time of the Greeks who came to his tomb as pilgrims to worship a demigod. Naturally, when Zoser thought about a tomb, he called on his genius vizier. We do not know what prior experience Imhotep had had with architecture. At the least, he learned fast.

Every pharaoh's first project was to arrange for his own tomb. His architect could work on that commission from the beginning of a reign until its end. Indeed, there was obvious bad luck to finishing a tomb before the pharaoh died. For Zoser, Imhotep would have 19 years. He had time to experiment.

Imhotep wanted something very special for his master's final rest at Sakkara. He thought first of a traditional mastaba, but one with a unique feature. Instead of adobe bricks, Imhotep decided to use brick-shaped stones. The idea, after all, was to build a long-lasting structure so it could be enjoyed by the dead for as long as possible. What could be more lasting than stone? So Imhotep improved on the durability of a tomb, but at the cost of slowing its construction: it takes time to hew stone. He also wanted to honor his master with an impressive building, larger if possible than any existing tomb.

The limiting factor in the size of a mastaba was the difficulty of roofing so large an expanse. That realization gave Imhotep his solution. He could make the largest mastaba ever if he omitted the roof. So he created a structure fully one mile in circumference, a wall in stone of characteristic mastaba shape—a series of recesses and protrustions. However, the roof he had omitted would have protected the pharaoh's body and valuables. Something had to substitute for it.

Some mastabas housed small, stepped structures beneath their roof. These structures may have been symbols of the primeval hill of creation or of steps to the sky or of the mound on which predynastic temples were built. The steps were directly above the place where the body lay. Inside Zoser's new enclosure was the mastaba that Imhotep had abandoned when he conceived his grander plan. Now Imhotep transformed the mastaba into one of those small, stepped monuments—inflated to gigantic proportions. All that was necessary was to build a smaller mastaba on top of the first, then another one still smaller on top, and so on. The final building stacked six mastabas. This was the first pyramid, called the Step Pyramid for its indented sides. Below it, Imhotep tunneled out rooms for the bodies of his lord, the queen, the royal children, and a vast quantity of supplies.

Ordinary mastabas also included a place outside where worshipers could pray and make offerings. With room to spare inside his walls, Imhotep made a separate temple for offerings beside the Step Pyramid. Egyptians believed in magic, especially what is known as sympathetic magic, in which an image or model can replace the real thing. So Imhotep placed a statue of Zoser in the temple to receive offerings. Imhotep erected other buildings in the enclosure to take advantage of this magic. He built storehouses of solid stone. He built another series of solid-stone buildings to represent original reed structures that were used in a pharaonic rejuvenation ceremony called the Heb Sed. If a pharaoh was fortunate enough to have a long reign, he periodically performed the Heb Sed ceremony (of origins lost in the distant past) to revive his powers. Imhotep reproduced such shrines so that his master could rejuvenate himself for as long as stone endures.

So pleased was Zoser with all this work that he had his faithful servant's name carved on one of the pharaoh's own statues, a singular honor then. The pyramid shape matched Egypt's soaring aspirations perfectly. The great ones among succeeding pharaohs all followed Imhotep's basic plan.

Zoser's immediate successors built on a smaller scale until, suddenly, the first pharaoh of Dynasty IV, Sneferu, performed an incredible feat. He built the first true pyramid, with the straight side familiar to us, and followed that by building two more. Each of the three is more than twice the mass of Zoser's one Step Pyramid.

The pharaoh Sneferu initially planned two pyramids. There was an old tradition that pharaohs have two tombs, a real one and an empty model, representative again of two countries united by one king. Early pharaohs built mastabas at Abydos in the south and another at Sakkara to the north. Since so much energy had been invested in Zoser's massive pyramid complex, he had paid only lip service to this custom with a pit tomb just fifty yards north of his larger structure. But Sneferu had a grander vision. He began a pyramid 12 miles south of Sakkara at a place called Meidum. Then he began work on another, 15 miles north of this one, at Dahshur. From the first these were intended to be larger than Zoser's and with straight, triangular sides. Zoser's pyramid was 197 feet high. Sneferu's at Meidum would have been over 300 feet high if a catastrophe had not occurred just before its completion. The pyramid collapsed. It remains today as an example of experiment, an awesome residue, looking in ruin like a ziggurat from old Babylon.

Imagine the consternation of the architect working on the other pyramid, the one at Dahshur. His project lagged behind the Meidum pyramid, but work had progressed more than halfway to the top when he heard the terrible news. He figured that the sides of the pyramid at Meidum had been too steep for safety. He immediately altered his plan, lessening the steepness of the angle. The completed structure is known now as the Bent Pyramid because the angles change abruptly from 54° at the bottom to 43° from the middle on up. Even with this change lessening its height, the pyramid stands over 30 stories high at 336 feet. But Sneferu wanted two *good* pyramids, not one complete and one in ruins. He began construction of yet another pyramid a short distance north of the Bent Pyramid. This time a conservative plan was followed, for its angle is about the same as that of the less acute top half of the Bent Pyramid. Called the Red Pyramid for the color of its stone, it is almost as high—325 feet—as the Bent Pyramid, and its mass is enormous. Sneferu used nine million tons of stone to attempt three pyramids and to produce two finished ones. Altogether, his three buildings employed more stone than that what was used in the more famous Great Pyramid at Giza.

Adjoining each pyramid was a temple. A causeway once ran from the river to the pyramid for transporting the deceased and his equipment from funeral barges. The whole complex originally was enclosed by a wall, as in Imhotep's plan. These same elements were included in subsequent pyramid complexes.

Pity Sneferu's successor, the son of a father who had accomplished a wonder never done before. What could he do? He could avoid competition by directing his energy elsewhere, or with a large enough ego, he could try to outdo his father. Khufu (often written as *Cheops* because of a Greek misspelling) took the brazen course of competing with his great father. And he won. At Giza he raised the pyramid that has been known since ancient times as the Great Pyramid. It was one of the Seven Wonders of the Ancient World, the only one remaining today, and it is one of the Seven Wonders of the Modern World. It is big.

Originally it rose 40 stories, about 481 feet. (Today it is 30 feet shorter.) The base of the pyramid covers an area large enough to contain all of the following: the cathedrals of Florence and Milan, St. Peter's in Rome, Westminster Abbey and St. Paul's Cathedral in London. Roughly 2,300,000 separate blocks, each averaging two-and-a-half tons, comprise the structure. The precision of the building is awesome, as it had to be. To gain the great height he wanted, Khufu went back to the steeper 51° angle that had proved so dangerous. New methods of construction had to be employed for this to work. The blocks sloped inward in the early pyramids, directing all the stresses of the great weight of the structure onto a small area near the center. In Khufu's pyramid, the blocks were laid level with the ground so that all the stress went downward on the larger area of the ground on which it rests. This spreading of forces makes the structure less precarious, but it works only if the pyramid is absolutely level. Otherwise it would tumble like a child's blocks.

The ground was made precisely flat by turning it into a giant carpenter's level. Connected ditches were dug around the perimeter of the intended structure and filled with water. Water settled to the same level all the way around—since it was all one continuous channel—so the ground could be marked and dug to exactly the same level all over.

Much has been written about the precision of the Great Pyramid, often with claims of magic. Commentators often interpret the dimensions and the angles as indicators of years to make the Pyramid predict the future. But each pyramid (and there are more than 70) has dimensions and angles different from the others. No indication exists that such differences mattered to the Egyptians. What was involved was not magic but cleverness and hard work.

The most difficult task was to quarry and transport all the stone. Ancient records say that 20 years were spent on the building and that 100,000 men worked on it. The time seems right, but the number of workers is misleading. During that period each year when the Nile overflowed, farmland was buried under five feet of water. Most people in Egypt were out-of-work farmers during that season. Perhaps the 100,000 men joined in during inundation time, but probably the year-round work force was considerably smaller. The permanent crew could cut blocks all year preparing for the time when the larger gang could transport them to the site (on sledges since no wheeled vehicles appeared in Egypt until the Second Intermediate Period) and up a ramp (or perhaps just hoisted by ropes) to their proper position in the pyramid. Hard work, time, and willing labor was all it took—vast amounts of each. The men were thankful to work just for meals during the season they could not tend their farms. Their bonus was the hope of a god's favor for helping him go West.

After Khufu, an exhausted country rested for one genera-
tion. Then came Khaefra (often written Chephren) who
erected a pyramid just ten feet lower than Khufu's. Cleverly
he built it on higher ground to make it look larger. This was
the climax. Following a short intervening reign, the next
pyramid came as a rather minor structure. Menkaura (Mycerinus) yielded on the ultimately futile competition for size.
His comparatively modest pyramid is 215 high, though it is
coated in part with beautiful pink granite. Dynasty IV ends
with two pharaohs of short reigns who gave up on pyramids
altogether.

The pharaohs of Dynasty V built small pyramids, con-
centrating instead on large temples dedicated to the sun god
Ra. However, the last pharaoh of the dynasty made one
radical addition to pyramid design. The pharaoh Unis built a
pyramid at Sakkara and decorated the interior—no pyramid
before had contained anything but bare stone inside—with
magic spells. He had these spells carved on the walls of his
burial chamber to assure his arrival whole and safe in the next
world. Decorated interiors became the norm in Dynasty VI,
the last of the pyramid era.

The Old Kingdom ended because Pepi II, the last pharaoh
of Dynasty VI, lived too long. Pepi II ascended the throne at
the age of six and ruled until he died at 96, when he had
degenerated into feeble dotage. Lack of strong central authority enabled the governors of the nomes (states) that
comprised the country to increase their power until Egypt fell
apart into independent states. Then came the dark and
lawless days of the First Intermediate Period.

GODS, MAGIC, AND ART: Pictures and statues of a
multitude of ancient gods will confront you when you visit
Egypt. The very number bewilders. Clearly religion was of
enormous importance to the ancient Egyptians. With some
understanding of ancient religious principles, magic and art
in Egypt become clearer.

The fundamental difference between ancient and modern
religions is a difference of goal. For the last 3000 years, much
of humanity has endeavored to concentrate religious energy

into a single focus on one god. People do not agree who this one god might be, but at least many share the endeavor. Egyptian religion was the creation of an earlier time, before sacred scriptures, when religious feelings spread wider than today—over plants and animals and forces of many kinds. Diffusion increased further since the official religion practiced by pharaohs and the educated community grew out of concerns more intellectual than those of the common people. Then, too, this civilization lasted for thousands of years: nothing remains the same through such a large span of time. By separating the official religion from that of the people and considering changes over time—even though each of these separations distorts—we can see in an orderly way that everything influenced everything else in ancient Egypt. The pharaoh was the leader of the educated and of the common people too, and no civilization held on to more of its own past than did this one.

The official religion had certain monotheistic tendencies. A systematic religion, it had a highest god and suggestions that other gods were aspects of the great god rather than independent beings. But in their struggle to understand what perhaps could not be understood, Egyptians were willing to try several different explanations. We might call it inconsistent; they would say that each explanation held some truth and none held all truth. They were syncretistic, combiners of several gods together. For example, the gods Amun and Ra eventually became the one Amun-Ra.

In the Old Kingdom the great god was Atum, the Complete (or Perfect) One, whose visible manifestation was the sun. Through all the periods of Egypt, Ra (the sun) was venerated and shown riding through the sky in a boat, the best form of travel known to Egyptians. In the original creation myth Atum raised a mound to stand upon amid a formless sea; then he created the earth and the sky with air to separate them.

Egyptians tried to make the basic elements of life and the universe somehow personable by representing them in human form. The sky (Nut), for example, was portrayed as a woman arched above the earth touching ground with only her arms and feet. She wore stars along her body. Ptah represented the power of creation. Portrayed as a mummy with a skullcap on his head, he held a long scepter of power. Thoth, who stood for knowledge and the science of writing, was represented by an ibis, and later by a baboon as well. Hat-hor, a fertility goddess, also stood for the heavens. She wore lyre-shaped horns and was associated with a cow. We can only guess, but it seems that certain birds and animals exemplified the main function of a given god and in that way came to represent him. It was not the creature who was worshiped; rather, sanctity was transferred to the symbol—like the cross in Christianity.

Beginning in the Middle Kingdom, but especially from the New Kingdom on, the greatest god was Amun of Thebes. By then political power had gravitated south from Memphis. Nothing suggests that this new god was a revolutionary development. What was new was the emphasis, the way of conceiving the same phenomena and forces. *Amun* meant the Hidden One, a concept that gave artists a problem. They represented Amun as a man with a headdress of double ostrich feathers (for reasons known only to those of the time) surrounding the cone-shaped crown of the south.

One genuine religious revolution did occur during the New Kingdom. The pharaoh Akhenaten pushed implicit mono-theistic tendencies close to literal belief. He preached about a god called Aten. Not much was new in this, for *Aten* meant the sun—though not as an aspect of a higher being, just the sun itself. What certainly was different, however, was Akhenaten's insistence that one god should have one name and one image. He erased the names of all other gods, destroyed idols, and closed temples. But the common people had too many religious feelings to be contained in any single religion. Old ideas and priests die hard. Akhenaten's new idea did not survive the man. (For more on this unusual person, see the chapter on Middle Egypt, the place where his capital can still be seen.)

Beyond the palace the common people worshiped many gods and goddesses, the most important of which were those who figured in the fundamental Egyptian myth of Osiris.

According to the myth, Osiris was the first king on earth. He brought civilization to the world. But his jealous brother Seth raged with envy. Seth gave a party one evening, and after all the guests had drunk more than they should, he challenged them to a contest. The game proposed that all the guests try to fit into a box placed in the center of the room. It was a set-up. One after another, the guests attempted to get into the box and proved to be either too large or too small. Finally Osiris tried; he fit exactly. (This is one explanation of the origin of the human-shaped coffins in which Egyptians were buried.) Seth rushed over and sealed Osiris into the box, then threw it in the Nile to float out to sea.

Osiris's wife, Isis (shown in pictures as a woman with a steplike throne on her head), searched the earth until she found her husband, still in his coffin and dead. Through the efficacy of her love Isis helped Osiris father a son, Horus, the falcon. (This is a myth, after all.) Eventually Seth discovered Osiris in hiding and this time did a thorough job. He cut his brother into pieces before throwing him by the handful into the Nile once more. Isis, ever faithful, collected each piece— by then spread over the length of Egypt—and put her husband together again. Although he was dead and could not rule the living on earth, he now had life enough to rule the hereafter. Osiris became the symbol for life after death. The ruler of the West, he was portrayed as a mummy with a beard and green skin. All Egyptians desired entry into his Kingdom one day.

The story continues. Osiris's son determined to avenge his father and win his inheritance—dominion over the earth. Horus first sought satisfaction in a court case with all the gods as jurors (Egyptians were highly legalistic). Dissatisfied with their decision, he challenged Seth to a fight. A drama ensued in which Seth wins or seems about to win, but Horus triumphs in the end, thereby winning the throne of Egypt. In the course of battle, however, Horus lost one eye, which was later magically restored by the god Thoth.

This Osiris myth represented important ideas to the Egyptians. Each of their pharaohs *was* Horus. When he died, he became Osiris, and his son carried on as the new Horus, making the institution of the pharaoh eternal. The eye made whole again by magic stood for the hope of regeneration, with the help of the gods. The heroes of this myth all constitute one family who act on principles of fidelity. They form a trinity of father (Osiris), mother (Isis), and son (Horus). Often Horus was shown on his mother's lap suckling, which perhaps was the prototype for similar scenes in Christian art.

Egyptians were greatly concerned about death. Though they may appear to have been rather morbid, the truth is probably quite the opposite. Rather than loving death, they so loved life that they did all they could to make it continue forever. During funerals close relatives sat in the tomb and shared a feast. Crying, lamenting, and beating of breasts accompanied the funeral procession, in addition to bands, singing, and garlands of flowers. The survivors would miss their dear departed, but he was believed to be on his way to a pleasant existence.

Proper spells had to be said to enter the next world, and the heart of the departed would be weighed in the hall of the gods to determine that he had done no evil (credit from good deeds was not required). Egyptians did not have our idea of an abstract soul. For any future life the deceased needed his body, which magic would enliven. Thus, Egyptians took great pains to hide away and to preserve the corpse. Paradoxically, these two endeavors conflicted with each other because when pharaohs were hidden in a pyramid, or kings or commoners were secreted underground in tombs, the natural preservative process—in which heat dries the body—was impeded. So Egyptians invented mummification.

Mummification involved placing the body in absorptive salts (natron) until all its moisture was drawn out. They pulled out the brain through the nose and removed the liver, lungs, stomach, and intestines—those organs which most readily decay. The brain was thrown away; the other four organs were stored in separate jars. Then the dried body, its skin turned leathery, was wrapped in yards of linen and sealed with resin to fight the intruding dampness from the tomb. The bandaged body, packed in a coffin of human shape, was often placed in another coffin and in another still, and then the collection might be placed in a rectangular sarcophagus. Anubis, the dog-headed god, oversaw all these preparations; he had done the same for his brother Osiris.

Pharaohs had religious scenes and spells carved on the walls of their tombs. Commoners tended to include favorite scenes from life in the hope that sympathetic magic would continue these pleasant times in the hereafter. They carefully recorded all their offices and titles because they expected to be called for work and wanted jobs appropriate to their attainments in life. They even had a ploy for avoiding work altogether. Little servant statues, called *ushabtis* (answerers) were placed in tombs so that, when the gods called on the deceased to perform chores, these model servants could answer in place of the deceased.

Much of what survives from ancient times is of a funerary character, for life was believed to be a fleeting moment compared to one's time in the West. Most surviving art comes from tombs or from temples. In both cases, permanence was the guiding principle behind their creation. From tombs we have sarcophagi and coffins, often with beautifully written spells and a picture of the owner as Osiris on the outside lid. In case the body somehow was destroyed and for times when the body might be away on a journey, large statues of the deceased alone or of the family were stored in tombs as stand-ins (especially in the Old Kingdom). Such statues were not intended for admiration (they were buried out of sight); the goal was dignity and eternality, not liveliness. Keep this in mind, and you may see their peaceful, awesome dignity. The quality of such work varies greatly. Many are standard-ized versions of the same thing; the great works were unique projects commissioned by a person of high position. Quality, with notable exceptions, was higher during the Old Kingdom than later when standardization increased.

Temples abounded with statues of gods, including phar-aohs. A pharaoh made certain that any temple he commis-sioned was well-marked with his name, his picture, and his statue. In such sculpture the goal was to portray a man who was a god. Consequently, these stiff, formal works are often remarkable for their combination of beatitude and power. The faces, especially the mouths and eyes, can be haunting. Walls of temples offered convenient surfaces to show communion with gods, the celebration of ceremonies, and those exploits of which the pharaoh was most proud.

Much less secular material has survived—mainly jewelry left in tombs. Such treasures, however, greatly tempted robbers who achieved almost total success in their trade. Compare the one room devoted to jewelry in the Museum of Antiquities to the 20 rooms for temple and funerary objects. Yet Egyptians loved jewelry, and both men and women wore it indiscriminately. Both wore rings and bracelets, broad bead collars—at parties—and earrings. The quality of materials and labor, of course, varied with the position of the owner. During times when Egypt was rich, there was gold in abundance and carnelian, lapis lazuli, and turquoise. Gems survived better than furniture, little of which has lasted all these years, though you can see depictions in countless tombs. The most impressive furniture, now in the Museum of Antiquities, came from the tombs of the pharaoh Tutankhamun and of Hethepheres, the wife of Sneferu and mother of Khufu. Hethepheres's bed and litter in their elegant simplicity are especially exquisite.

Amulets are the one class of objects that does survive in quantity from the world of the living. These good-luck charms, worn as rings or on necklaces, came in the shape of all sorts of gods and symbols. By far the most common are the Udjet Eye, the symbol of Horus' rejuvenated falcon eye, and scarabs. The scarab, or dung beetle, represented creation to the ancient Egyptian. He watched this insect roll a ball of fecal matter (which resembled the shape of the sun) from which suddenly emerged scores of little dung beetles. The young had been incubating inside, but it looked like a miracle in which life had been created from inanimate matter. So Khepher (the beetle) represented and was the hieroglyphic sign for existence. With obvious symbolism, Egyptians carved beetle shapes and wrote wishes, gods' names, and their own names on the base, in the belief that whatever was written might come to be.

Without question the ancient Egyptian thought differently about life and about death than we do. The differences make him all the more fascinating. If you study his monuments and temples and reflect, you may catch a glimpse of his mind.

CHRISTIAN EGYPT

Egypt figures prominently in both the Old and New Testaments as would be expected for a country only fifty miles from the Palestine area. The Old Testament expresses the fears of a small country toward a more powerful neighbor. The oldest use of the word *pharaoh* occurs in the Old Testament in contexts that gave it the connotations of cold power which it still retains. The word actually came from two ancient Egyptian words—*per* and *aha,* which simply meant "great house." To use the actual name of the one who lived in this Egyptian palace would have implied a status comparable to his; the Hebrews were careful not to insult him in that way. One unfortunate effect of this forced humility was to deprive scholars of valuable information for dating events in the Old Testament.

Probably, Joseph visited Egypt during a brief period when Egypt was ruled by a Semitic people, called the Hyksos, before 2000 B.C. Moses lived most of his life in Egypt, much later, near the time of Rameses the Great at about 1200 B.C. Since Memphis, the capital of ancient Egypt was only 20 miles south of modern Cairo, Moses may have passed through Cairo, although no city stood there in those ancient times. Some scholars believe, however, that a kind of resort-palace for pharaohs did stand on the island of Roda. A legend, in fact, recounts that baby Moses was found by the pharaoh's daughter floating past the southern tip of that island. Ben Ezra Synagogue counters with its claim to be built upon the spot where Moses was drawn from the Nile. The Nile has changed its course since those times; it once ran closer to the synagogue.

Egypt's Christian heritage is as old as any other country's. Egypt converted to Christianity in the 2nd century from seeds allegedly sowed by St. Mark during visits in the 1st century.

By this time Egypt had passed through Greek and Roman rulers and had grown somewhat decadent.

When they became Christians, Egyptians did so with a vengeance, reacting in part at least to the excesses of Roman life. Egyptians took to the desert, away from sinful cities, to become hermits or establish monasteries—the start of this Christian tradition. But Egypt had been influenced by extensive earlier contacts with Greeks, which left her more philosophical than most Christian countries. Egyptians studied the Bible in cold, intellectual ways, producing theories that often gained adherents but as often were condemned by international church councils as heresies. The last straw was the heresy of monophysitism. Egyptians maintained that Christ had only one nature in which the human and the godly blended; church councils adamantly disagreed, maintaining that Christ combined two distinctly different natures. As so often happens with theological disagreements, this one turned ugly. Other Christians persecuted the Egyptians and excommunicated her church leaders. In response, Egypt turned her back on the rest of the Christian world which had abandoned her. Egypt then became a willing victim of the Islamic forces who arrived early in the 7th century.

Not all the Egyptians converted to the Islamic religion. About 15% remained Christian and that percentage remains today. In a sense these Christians became the heirs of ancient Egypt, for they continued to speak the ancient language when the rest of Egypt learned Arabic. Although the ancient language is no longer spoken, it is still the official language of Egyptian church services, much as Latin continued in Roman Catholic churches long after Rome fell.

Egyptian Christians are called Copts, a corruption of the Greek word for Egypt, *Aegyptos;* their liturgic language is Coptic. Much closer to Greek Orthodoxy than to Protestant sects, their religion is one of the most traditional, despite the accusations of heresy. Churches hold innumerable icons that are splendid, even if sometimes gaudy. The dutiful, in most churches, preserve the early practice of standing throughout services that can last for three hours. There are no pews, but crutches are available for the old or infirm.

While they were dominant, from the 2nd century to the Arab conquest in 641, Copts introduced quite special art. Best known are their textiles, produced by using every method of both weaving and sewing, with an excellence never surpassed. Copts also decorated their early churches with sculpture reminiscent of the Gothic style in Europe, though older.

Coptic and Gothic art both developed from the same Greek and Roman traditions. From the perspective of its origins, Coptic sculpture looks provincial, almost a folk-art imitation of Roman styles, but it has a life and charm that Roman art seldom attained.

ISLAMIC EGYPT

If there were no ancient monuments in Egypt, tourists would still come just for the Islamic buildings in Cairo. Cairo boasts one of the oldest mosques that still survives in its original form (Ibn Tulun), and another (Sultan Hassan) that is among the most beautiful of all Islamic buildings. One street (el Muizz) preserves the 13th century almost intact.

Egypt, condemned and abandoned by the rest of the Christian world, was one of the earliest countries to convert to Christianity and was the first to give it up for Islam. Egyptians readily took to the new religion of Muhammad when Arab cavalry came bearing his message with their lances. Before very long, more than 80% of the populace converted. The original Arab invasion, however, proved less tumultuous than the events that followed Egypt's enrollment in the Islamic world.

When Muhammad died he left behind a theoretical and political dilemma concerning his successor. The pillar of Islam is that Muhammad was a great prophet, but the last of many. (The others are those of the Old and New Testaments, such as Abraham and Jesus.) Under Muhammad's leadership, the Arabs had already conquered a good part of the Middle East and, before he died, had the potential for conquering a good deal more. The sword of Islam eventually reached as far as southern France and sliced through all of India, Greece,

Sicily, and part of Hungary, in addition to the Islamic countries of modern times. But who would direct the sword and what status would a successor have after the last prophet?

The issue was avoided for the first three successors, all of whom had been involved with Muhammad, either as a relative or close friend. When the third successor was assassinated, however, a conflict split the Islamic world and divides it still. Two groups each proposed a candidate to be the next leader. Ali, the husband of the Prophet's daughter Fatima, was one claimant. Against him was proposed a man who represented the most prominent and powerful family in Arabia. The issue centered on whether the leader of Islam should be a relative of the Prophet or whether he could be simply a worthy man without ties to Islam's founder. The Islamic empire was a political entity, although acquired by religious fervor: should its leader be religious or secular?

As it happened, the adherents of secular power were more powerful and won by a show of arms. The fourth leader, a member of the dominant Arabian family, chose the title of mere caliph, "successor." In turn, however, he passed that title on to another relative who generated a dynasty, called the Ummayids. But those who lost this argument never conceded; in the ensuing years, from time to time, their adherents gained the upper hand in various countries, including Egypt. In more recent days, the Aga Khan headed one sect of these *Shiites*, "partisans" (of Ali, Muhammad's son-in-law). Iran today adheres to this claim that a leader should be first a holy man and that his dictates are invested with the force of religion. The majority (90%) of Islamic people, then and now, follow the other side, where religious decisions are made through a consensus of a body of men— the *ulama*, "men of the pen." Political leaders are just that— political men. Those who follow this theory are called *Sunnites*, "of the tradition." Here we will trace the four great Islamic periods in Egypt, plus Saladin.

Ummayids: 7th to 8th Century. The rulers of the Ummayid dynasty were from pure Arabian stock. Islam began as an Arabian religion; its army comprised all Arab cavalry in the beginning. They were a dynamic people shut so long within a barren desert that when they finally burst out they exalted in sudden freedom and the chance to dominate their too-civilized neighbors. Except for their leaders who came from the only two cities in Arabia (the trade centers of Medinah and Mecca), they were nomads unused both to government and art, each of which requires some settled living. Government amounted to giving a conquered country to each victorious Arab general who in turn let natives do the actual work. Art was simply the work and style of each new country, infused with a wilder Arab spirit, often for the better. But an empire could not be ruled from the desert, so the Ummayids moved to Damascus, the center of their conquests.

The enormity of their initial success produced its own problems. The conquering Arabs dwindled proportionately as their empire grew larger. The Ummayids were fish out of water (or, better, camels out of the desert) in cosmopolitan Damascus. As it happens with any new religion after it first gains many converts, theological controversies came along with the diversity of adherents. With its better developed traditions of both religion and government, Persia—the most recent great Middle Eastern empire before the Arab conquest—evolved a theology and an army that usurped her conquerers.

Abbasids: 8th to 10th Century. The Persian movement rallied behind disgruntled Arab tribes who supported a descendant of one of Muhammad's uncles, Abbas. They defeated the last Ummayid and moved the capital to Baghdad. This was the era of *The Thousand and One Nights*. Rich in empire and products, the Abbasids developed delicate filigree art, especially in miniature, that epitomizes medieval Islam. They even had mechanical toys, as the stories say, such as waving reeds and lilies all in silver with metal birds that seemed to fly. For two centuries the Abbasids ruled the Islamic world, and for two centuries more they ruled in Iraq and played with toys, while pieces of the empire slowly broke away.

Fatimids: 10th to 12th Century. Egypt, just one province in an empire, became independent when conquered by the

Fatimids. Of the minority Shiite sect, the Fatimids had come to power in Egypt's western neighbor, Libya. Following the tradition of Ali, they believed in the sanctity of rulers, taking the name of their movement from Ali's wife Fatima. In A.D. 969 they conquered Egypt and built Cairo. Egypt seemed a better seat for their power than Libya. By this administrative change, Egypt turned from conquered land into the capital of an empire, for the Fatimids were energetic builders and fighters. They seized all of Palestine. They covered Cairo with buildings of a pure style and of rich materials for religious reasons and for pride of wealth, respectively. The old days returned for two centuries: Egypt ruled her ancient empire again.

Saladin: 12th Century. In A.D. 1096 the first Crusade set out to seize the Holy Land for European Christians. This expedition, as much as anything, was the outgrowth of medieval chivalry: fighting was the highest goal in life and the only interesting business. Islamic forces were riddled with dissent, split into sects, and easily routed; thus Palestine became a European country for a time. But Jerusalem was as holy to Muslims as to Christians. The Seljuk Turks, with the pure fervor of new converts, were able to rally most of the Islamic countries for a *jihad*, a countercrusade. However, Egypt did not throw herself wholeheartedly into the cause because her Shiite rulers were uncomfortable with the Sunni leadership. So the Turkish sultan (this new title simply meant "ruler") sent an ambassador to Egypt to encourage Fatimid aid. The agent was a Kurd from Iran named Salah el-Din, who proved to be one of history's great geniuses and the most honorable of men—on the field of battle. In political matters he was not above schemes. He soon seized control of Egypt for himself. His generalship so far outclassed that of the Crusaders that he defeated them again and again, while winning their highest admiration as a true knight. The Crusaders took home great stories of this man they called Saladin, in part to make their own defeats more honorable.

Salah el-Din built the Citadel in Cairo, which is still the city's most visible skyline feature. Although he began a brief dynasty, none of his genius was transmitted with his genes.

Fifty-seven years later his last heir was killed by his own palace guards. The next ruler was Shagarat al-Durr, the wife of the recently murdered sultan. She was, for a very short time, the rarest of things, a sultana. Wisely, she married the commander of the guards who killed her husband; unwisely, she later killed the commander in a rage of jealousy. The women of his harem then beat her to death with their slippers.

Mamluks: 13th to 15th Century. The dynasty of Mamluks was peculiar because it consisted of unrelated rulers, not a family. *Mamluk* means "owned." Salah el-Din's heirs had difficulty finding troops in Egypt, so they began buying children to mold into guards of unquestioned loyalty. The children were born to infidels, mainly Turks in the Crimea or the Caucasus Mountains in Russia, because the Koran prohibits Muslim slaves. This practice of literally raising troops, however, worked very poorly. For two centuries Egypt's rulers bought children and for their money received more revolutions than ever conceived by loyal troops of earlier times. As foreigners in a strange land, Mamluks banded together. In their arms they held real power which they used over and over to place one of their own on the throne Each Mamluk ruler bought more Mamluk troops who commonly killed the one who had bought them. Politically, it was the most violent time in Egypt's history. But the Mamluks only killed each other; the rest of the country enjoyed the prosperity of relative tranquillity. For all their violence, and probably to atone for it, the Mamluks built more mosques, *madrassas* (schools), and hospitals in Cairo than any rulers before or since. Nor was quantity their only contribution to the buildings of Cairo—Sultan Hassan built the most beautiful of all the Cairo mosques.

Mamluk rule ended when the Ottoman Turks conquered the Near East. So ended Egypt's independence. Again, Egypt became a province in another man's empire. This time she was ruled by pashas, the agents of a Turkish overlord.

And so Egypt remained until modern times.

5.

Cairo

Cairo is like no other city in the world. It is a delight to the senses, a variety show. It is a page from *The Arabian Nights* played out in once-magnificent mansions, aged pleasure palaces of the caliphs; it is secluded mosques, venerable and stately. Cairo is part Paris, part London. It is American luxury hotels and New York City billboards—in Arabic. The city is strikingly international, yet constantly and insistently Islamic. Purity is for cities like Paris—Cairo throbs with complexity.

Sprawling Cairo is the largest city in Africa, the largest Islamic city in the world, and may well be among the three largest metropolises on earth. Estimates put the population at nine million or more, but no one knows for certain because the city has grown too fast and too unsystematically for any proper census. Another million people are added every year by birth or through migration—although the death rate lessens the number a little. Nothing seems to affect the flow of people fleeing the poverty of rural areas for the hope of a better life in the capital. Many have no real place to live.

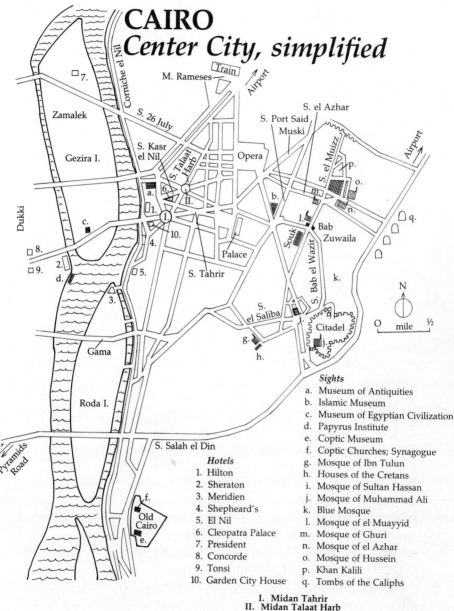

There are five people for every room in Cairo, which is why rooftops and building lots are packed with tents. On the road to Giza you will see families living in cemeteries and mausoleums.

When rural Egyptians migrate, they take their households and animals with them. Cairo has a quarter of a million cars, and almost as many horsecarts and donkey carts. Pedestrians, cars and buses, herds of camels and flocks of sheep all vie for the streets, with no particular priority given to motor traffic. Traffic lights can only blink futilely. The driver's best friend is his horn; the donkey rider's, his voice. The sounds of the city ring like exotic music to assure visitors that they have reached a different land. The streets of Cairo present intricate dramas—frustrating for Cairenes, but exhilarating for tourists. Even the brown dust that seems everywhere in this otherwise clean city becomes special when you realize that it is sand brought by winds from the Sahara.

Cairo will find a way to charm you, if not by the vibrancy of its street life, then with stately buildings of historical elegance or with museums like treasure chests or by the mystique of ancient monuments nearby. Who would not find fascination in a city that still preserves pieces of all its past—from the original Arab conquest to the Crusades to Napoleon and after?

In Egypt's long history, Cairo counts as new. When Arab hordes rode out of the desert in A.D. 641, they found only a Roman fort garrisoned by squatters where Cairo stands. Six miles east in Giza was an ancient necropolis of pyramids. Five miles north stood the ancient site of a center for sun worship suppressed by the early Christians. Here, beside the Nile, just before the river fans wide to form the Delta, was an inviting location waiting to receive the produce of the south flowing down the Nile and to collect the produce of the Delta as through a funnel. It was a fine site at which to erect the capital of a newly Arab country.

On the Roman ruins soon grew a city called Misr—a name still used by Egyptians for their country—but it was an imperfect start. Three centuries of internecine Arab struggles followed, during which the city was destroyed and rebuilt several times. The fourth rebuilding, in 969, proved permanent; modern Cairo is its direct descendant. This successful try occurred a mile away from the Nile where the original walls still encircle the great bazaar of Cairo, Khan Kalili. The story is told that on the day of laying this city's foundation, court astrologers warned that the planet Mars, an omen of war and ruin, was in the ascent. The emir decided to name his new town in honor of Mars to disarm its evil influence, so he baptized the city el Kahirah, from which we get Cairo.

The name seemed effective: at least the city grew rapidly. For a time during the Middle Ages, Cairo was the largest city in the world and today it sprawls for miles in all directions. Yet it is not a giant city; it never overwhelms with scale. Almost every part (except for a few suburbs from which the rich commute) is a neighborhood with businesses and markets. The heart, however, is the oldest quarter—a one-mile semicircle on the east bank of the Nile opposite the two islands of Roda and Gezira. The fancy hotels sit alongside these islands on both riverbanks. One block east of the river is the main square of Cairo, el Tahrir, distinguished by a raised pedestrian walkway around it. Fanning away from this hub run the streets of the business district and modern shops. By one side of el Tahrir Square stands the great Museum of Antiquities. One mile farther east is the old bazaar, Khan Kalili. All the main sights in Cairo lie within two miles of this center, and directly across the Nile, the Pyramids Road runs straight to the Giza pyramids six miles away.

Cairo, an exciting place to stay while making excursions, has splendid mosques and museums that have collected the treasures from all the eras of ancient Egypt and provide valuable background for visiting other cities and sites. Here your own feet are the best form of transportation whenever distances allow. Walking is the way to discover unforgettable details. On one stroll you can see a 14th-century *madrassa* (school) beside a 16th-century house with intricate wooden *mashrabiya* (harem windows) across from an 11th-century mosque where tourists never go. These exquisite charms come only with the slow pace of feet. You need not think of big-city dangers; the crime rate in Cairo is less by hundreds of times than that of any other city of comparable size.

Since street signs are almost never in the English alphabet, whenever possible our directions refer to distances and visible landmarks, but sometimes only the street names were feasible. If in doubt, simply ask a passerby; he will point for you. No Arabic is necessary—just pronounce the street name and put a questioning look on your face. "Street" in Arabic is *shari;* "square" is *midan.* Sometimes you may wish that the streets were less rambling, less confused, and more consistent in their names. Then you realize that Cairo is old and Middle Eastern, unsuited to the grand boulevards of other great cities.

A tourist's perfect stay in Cairo would last a year or so, but you can pack the essential sights into one full week. Though we have grouped separately the three excursions and the sights of downtown Cairo, for a change of pace we recommend a day of traveling alternating with a day in town. Use one half-day for the Giza pyramids. The trip provides no feeling of leaving the city until you climb the plateau on which the pyramids sit; the city is gone. Plan on one day for Memphis and Sakkara; two miles apart, they constitute a single trip. It takes a day to drive through the lush oasis of the Faiyum to the special pyramids, very different from Giza, at Meidum and Hawara. The distance is not great to any of these three out-of-town excursions—about an hour to the farthest. You can easily join any of the many tours formed by travel companies—all are pretty much the same. Brochures are available and arrangements can be made at your hotel. If you prefer the freedom and privacy of your own conveyance, we recommend hiring a car with driver over driving a rented car yourself. Not only is Egyptian traffic a problem handled best by those who are used to it, but also the roads (not the best, but not the worst either) are poorly marked, and in case of engine trouble or an accident you would be helpless not speaking Arabic. The hired driver is a kind of insurance, one that costs next to nothing because he, together with his car, will cost about the price of renting (about LE 15). Your hotel desk will have lists of recommended drivers with cars. For the brave, Avis has an office in the Hilton and in the Meridien hotels as well as at the airport. You will need an international driver's license. A Datsun or Fiat costs LE 8, plus 7 pt. per kilometer (about 18¢ a mile); another LE 3 hires a driver.

The afternoon of your Giza pyramids day you might spend on a leisurely walk through the town center or strolling among the Egyptian families who walk in the garden and zoo on the west bank over the Gama Bridge off Roda Island. The Museum of Antiquities requires at least half a day (you can always make discoveries, however often you go), followed conveniently by the activity of nearby Khan Kalili bazaar. And save one day at least for mosques and the Islamic Museum. Visits to the 5th-century Coptic church of St. Sergius and to the ancient synagogue of Ben Ezra logically follow the Coptic Museum. You should see Alexandria, but if you are short of time consider a day's excursion instead of an overnight stay there. At the end of your week you will need a day for small events: the Papyrus Institute, the Egyptian Civilization Museum, and a walk through a historic part of town with marvelous old buildings, such as el Muizz Street. If a week in Cairo is impossible, whatever you omit, let it not be the Giza pyramids or Sakkara (with the Luxor tombs these constitute the three greatest attractions in Egypt) or the Museum of Antiquities. They, by themselves, justify a trip to Egypt. Be prepared to be overwhelmed by splendor and monumentality—whether it be the ancient, the Christian, or the Islamic culture.

THE SIGHTS OF ANCIENT EGYPT NEAR CAIRO

The best introduction to our oldest civilization are the ancient Egyptian monuments that stand on the outskirts of Cairo. Egypt lives in an earlier age beyond the city limits. Years roll away with the miles; traffic dwindles to an occasional vehicle; houses become mud shacks; people dress and work in just the ways their ancestors did some thousand years ago.

MEMPHIS

Memphis was the original capital of ancient Egypt, founded by the first pharaoh (Narmer/Menes). Unparalleled
throughout the Old Kingdom, it gradually yielded first place
to Thebes in the south. As the first capital of the first nation
in the world, its historical importance is enormous, but the
importance must be all in your mind, for there is little left to
see. Memphis was built amid fertile, sometimes marshy land
that fosters the decay and dissolution of ancient buildings.
Wherever on the black soil you can pick out gray earth
shaped like large bricks, you are seeing the remains. Go for
the associations and for the one colossal statue and the
sphinx that remain.

If you do not join a tour or hire a car and driver, you can
hire a taxi for the day—but settle the price before you leave; it
should cost about LE 15, about the cost of a hired car.

If you drive, take the Pyramids Road to Giza. One mile
before reaching the pyramids, just after crossing a canal
where a large sign advertises the Sound and Light show at
Giza, turn right. Stay on this road for ten miles (18 kilometers). When you have passed the sun temples of Dynasty V
and the Bent and Red pyramids at Dahshur (off limits
because of military installations), you will see the Step
Pyramid of Sakkara on a hill. Continue to the first bridge on
the left for Memphis. For Sakkara, turn right. The round trip
covers 40 miles. Admission to the museum at Memphis is 25
pt. The sights at Sakkara cost 85 pt.

Egyptians called their original capital the Balance of the
Two Lands. The ancient Greeks, confused by such Egyptian
names, passed their confusions down through the ages when
they wrote the first history books. For example, they could
not understand how a single country could be called the Two
Lands. They had heard about a famous temple in the capital
dedicated to the god Ptah, whose name sounded like *Hi kaew-
ptah*. Somehow they confused the temple name with the
name of the country, and in their spelling it came out
Aegyptos, from which we get the word "Egypt." As to the
capital, they confused the name of a famous pyramid at

Sakkara called Men-nefer, "well-established," with the name of the city. That is how it became known as Memphis.

Memphis, the largest city in the world during its days of glory, was five miles square, filled with brilliantly colored temples, and held a population of over half a million. Even after Thebes took over first place, Memphis remained important. As long as pharaohs ruled, they were coronated in this city, a holy place of pilgrimages. In a sense, this sanctity was Memphis' undoing. When religion changed—when Egypt turned Christian—Memphis lost its importance and more: Christians destroyed the temples of gods they hated and avoided the city.

Uninhabited, its buildings untended, Memphis fell prey to nature, which finished the destruction. The city was built from mud bricks which do not survive dampness like that around Memphis. During the last 1500 years, the bricks have returned to the mud from which they came.

Today Memphis consists of only an unusual museum that houses one object. Two immense statues of Rameses the Great were excavated in Memphis—one now resides in the square in front of the Cairo train station; the larger one lies on its back in this museum. Originally, it would have stood over 40 feet high, all one piece of limestone. Now it has no lower limbs. On its right shoulder and at the center of its belt is Rameses's name in a cartouche that represented universal dominion. A son stands between what is left of the legs; Rameses's tiny wife embraces his right leg. The statue was meant to awe with its colossal scale; consequently, the details take second place to overall conception. It must have been much more impressive upright than in its present condition flat on its back.

Outside sits an alabaster sphinx, 25 feet long. It was found nearby on its side partly eaten away by the ooze in which it lay. From the good side you can sense the power of a sphinx: the strength and dignity of the lion merge with the beneficent wisdom of a pharaoh's face. He wears the ancient "nemes" headdress surmounted by a cobra, now damaged. (The "nemes" headdress was the standard crown of the Old Kingdom.) The name of the pharaoh is not known, but the style seems to indicate the New Kingdom, perhaps Dynasty XVIII. In the bushes, another pharaoh lies on his back wearing the cone crown of the south. Again, no clue identifies this fallen king. The lush setting that frames these attempts at immortality through size breeds sad thoughts about those who now have no identity at all.

SAKKARA

On a desert rise that makes it visible from Memphis, and less than two miles away, waits Sakkara (see directions from Memphis, above), the cemetery of Memphis and a holy place for thousands of years. Here repose some of the oldest and most beautiful surviving relics of Egypt. Here you most certainly will find opportunities for your eyes.

In all the world Sakkara has just one competitor—the necropolis of Thebes. No other place can compare with the quantity of tombs, the richness of decoration, and the span of time encompassed. Sakkara is far older than Thebes. Tombs date from Dynasty I to XXXI and later, but most are from the Old Kingdom. Sakkara covers four square miles, hardly one foot of which lacks a tomb. What is visible above only hints at the maze of burials below. At Sakkara, you stand on 5000 years of history.

The site, chosen for the drama of its height, showed off mastabas and pyramids to good effect. It also used desert land away from the living and from farmland too precious for use as tomb space. It grew holy because it was ancient even in ancient times—distant Egyptian ancestors were already there, including some with the status of demigod. There was space at first from which to select a good site for a tomb, but as people through the ages continued to take places near earlier pyramids and tombs, a jumble developed. Early tombs abut later ones above and below the ground, along with temples and houses for priests. Dominating the necropolis is the great Step Pyramid of Zoser.

The name *Sakkara* comes from the name of the god of the necropolis, the hawk-faced Seker. He shared power over death with Osiris, but came out of a different tradition.

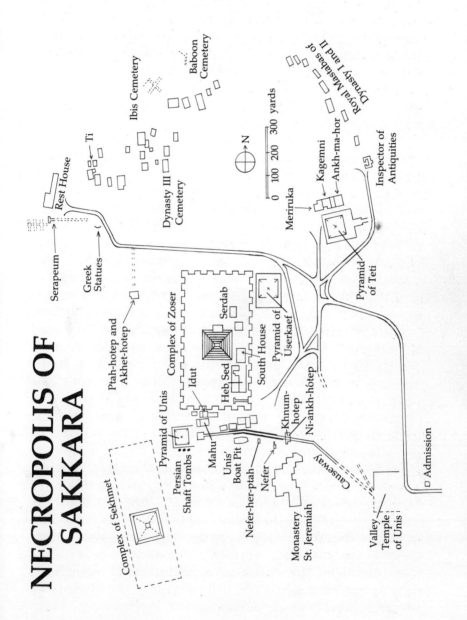

NECROPOLIS OF SAKKARA

Complex of Sekhmet

Pyramid of Unis

Persian Shaft Tombs

Mahu

Unis' Boat Pit

Nefer-her-ptah

Nefer

Monastery St. Jeremiah

Valley Temple of Unis

Causeway

Admission

Ni-ankh-hótep

Khnum-hotep

South House

Pyramid of Userkaef

Pyramid of Teti

Idut

Heb Sed

Serdab

Complex of Zoser

Ptah-hotep and Akhet-hotep

Greek Statues

Serapeum

Rest House

Ti

Ibis Cemetery

Dynasty III Cemetery

N

0 100 200 300 yards

Meriruka

Kagemni

Ankh-ma-hor

Inspector of Antiquities

Baboon Cemetery

Royal Mastabas of Dynasty I and II

Always tolerant of religions, Egyptians eventually combined the two into a composite and added Ptah, the god of Memphis, to get Ptah-Seker-Osiris. They produced endless wooden statues of this hawk god with mummy body, often hiding magic spells in secret compartments.

Not all of Sakkara can be seen on any single day. Sights are listed below in priority order. Stop when you get tired; come back on another day if your time and appetite allow. Everyone should try to visit the Step Pyramid complex, one pyramid with texts inside, and the magnificent mastabas of Ti and Meriruka.

ZOSER'S STEP PYRAMID: The world's first monumental building in stone, erected in 2650 B.C., is large indeed. The enclosure wall, a mile in circumference, surrounds an inside complex which covers 37 acres. A paneled and bastioned outer wall reproduces an adobe fortress in stone, complete with parapet and catwalk to protect the funerary monuments inside. The whole complex was an experiment with stone. Lacking knowledge of its special properties, workers used stone as though it were a more familiar material, copying adobe, wood, reeds, and palm trunks. Of the 15 gates in the wall, all are false entrances except the one in the southeast corner. The wall near the real entrance has been reconstructed to its original height of 21 feet. (Reconstruction of the walls and of the buildings inside has been the lifework of Jean-Phillippe Lauer since 1926.)

Beyond the narrow entrance stands a double door—of immovable stone—with both sides open. Across this foyer another open door leads into a colonnade hall. Probably these are the first stone columns in the world—a tentative first effort, for they do not stand free but engage the wall behind them. Forming a series of niches, they may have held statues representing the nomes (states) of ancient Egypt. The ceiling copies wooden logs. At the hall's end is a roofed chamber carried by four piers of paired columns, moving closer to our free-standing columns. This chamber exits to a great courtyard with a view of Zoser's pyramid across the flat terrain.

Two altarlike structures in the courtyard played some role in an ancient rite—perhaps in the Heb Sed ceremony.

To the right a series of buildings forms the court of the Heb Sed rites. In this ceremony of the Tail Festival, the powers of the pharaoh were rejuvenated after his duties had drained him. The idea may have originated from a much earlier time when kings were killed if their strength weakened. Later, rejuvenation by magic developed as a more practical solution to the need for vigor in a leader. Two times the pharaoh ran (some say he danced) along a set course while carrying sacred implements. The ceremony involved special reed buildings representing the Delta and the south. Symbols counted for the real thing, for the eternal rejuvenation of Zoser. Here the buildings are stone and dummies—steps lead to doors that do not open, fronting solid structures. Buildings line both sides of the course; those on the left are especially fine. Notice all the ways stone was used to represent other materials—for example, the stone leaves at the top of columns. Near the end of this aisle of buildings, on the left, is a platform with a double staircase—a throne (once covered by a canopy) on which the pharaoh was robed and anointed for the Heb Sed. At the end of the courtyard a niche holds four sets of feet belonging to lost statues. It is tempting to think that Zoser and his family once were portrayed here.

After the Heb Sed courtyard come two houses. First is the House of the South, shaped like the prehistoric shrine of that area, followed by the House of the North fronted by columns with papyrus capitals (the earliest known example of this order of column, which become so popular later). Now you are behind the pyramid and face the *serdab*, consisting of three small structures. The front two represent doors that open to the rear structure—the *serdab* itself. Two bored holes allow you to look inside and see an imposing statue of the pharaoh for whom all this building was done. The true purpose of the holes, however, was so the statue could look out. By great luck the original statue of Zoser was found inside in 1924, still watching the affairs of men and waiting patiently for prayers and offerings. The original was taken to the Museum of Antiquities; a copy now resides in the *serdab*. Even the copy is haunting, faithfully reproducing the cavernous dark eyes of the original (not quite original, because the true eyes of crystal had been pried out by ancient thieves). Beside the *serdab* stand the ruins of Zoser's mortuary temple where priests prayed for his soul.

The pyramid itself shows evidence of revisions in its plan. On the north side, where the *serdab* is, you can see the first stage where stones have fallen off. The first plan called for a typical large tomb of the time, a low rectangular mastaba. Then came the vizier Imhotep's great idea of a stepped structure, though the first attempt consisted of only four steps. Success led to the final monument of six levels. Local limestone blocks mortared for binding strength form the pyramid's mass. Outside is a casing of fine limestone imported from Tura, in the hills south of modern Cairo (also the source of the casing for the Giza pyramids). Finished, it stood about 200 feet tall on a base 411 by 358 feet.

Permission to enter the pyramid is all but impossible to obtain, so a description will have to serve. Under the pyramid a maze of corridors was chiseled through solid rock. The central element is the tomb chamber, ten feet by five and one-half feet, lined with pink granite from Aswan. Galleries run to the four points of the compass. Their walls, covered with small blue tiles, suggested dyed reed matting that hung in palaces and homes. Corridors fan off from the galleries. In one corridor two alabaster coffins were found, one with the remains of a child inside. Evidently Zoser planned to rest with his family.

In ancient times robbers plundered the entire area including the burial corridors (probably during the First Intermediate Period when central authority gave way to lawlessness). But they missed a few rooms. In one room alone, modern excavators found 40,000 beautiful stone vessels which suggest what riches were interred with Zoser.

PYRAMID OF UNIS: (*Leave Zoser's entrance, walk around the near corner of his wall, follow the enclosure wall to the next corner.*

*To the left is a mound of rubble. Only the line of people waiting
indicates that something is worth seeing.)*

Unis was the last pharaoh of Dynasty V. By walking 200
yards from Zoser's entrance you have moved three centuries
to a time when pyramids no longer were built on a massive
scale. His pyramid would have been about 60 feet tall before
it fell to ruin. The interest lies underground in the chambers
of the tomb, for this is the first pyramid with carving inside.
Beautiful hieroglyphs cover the rooms; these are spells, called
Pyramid Texts.

Watch your head in the uncomfortably low descending
passage.

After leveling out, the passage widens slightly where three
massive slabs of granite once sealed the tomb. Soon after, you
enter the first room. Following the confinement of the
passageway, the sudden space is a relief. Dramatic white
limestone walls are covered with columns of beautiful blue
hieroglyphs.

The hieroglyphs secured a safe journey and stay in the
hereafter. Egyptians firmly believed in the efficacy of magic,
that proper words could make a desired goal real. Funerary
complexes included houses for priests, so they might recite
desired spells aloud. By the time of Unis, however, enough
years had passed to prove that priests were not entirely
reliable. The legacy that funded them could run out or could
be appropriated by others, and the spells would stop. So Unis
had his spells carved in stone for reliability.

The hieroglyphs do not form a continuous discourse; each
column is a separate spell. Some ensure supplies of food or
drink; some protect Unis from dangerous gods and demons;
some make his body healthy again. So powerful was the
magic of words that they had to be used carefully, especially
in the case of hieroglyphs which, being drawings as well as
representing sounds, might become the things pictured.
Signs that represent dangerous creatures, therefore, sometimes are omitted or replaced by more benign signs of the
same phonetic value. Hieroglyphs of humans, animals, and
birds might run or fly away, it was feared, so they were often

carved without legs or wings, or else in two halves to make them less real.

Left of the first room is a narrow room with three niches that originally held statues. Little of interest remains. To the right is the burial chamber, complete with sarcophagus. The far wall and adjoining parts of the near walls are of alabaster carved in the design of a palace with a false door in the center through which Unis's soul could pass. The rest of the burial chamber continues the spells. The roof, like that of the first room, is a corbeled arch of limestone covered with stars. The sarcophagus is basalt. The first excavator was not the first person to enter the pyramid after it had been sealed—as with all the other pharaonic pyramids, this one was empty.

Outside, by the entrance to the pyramid, a causeway begins that runs for more than half a mile. It connected the mortuary temple and the pyramid to a temple in the valley below. Parts of the causeway have been restored to show what it looked like when new. The side walls, carved with lovely low reliefs, balanced slabs on top leaving a space between them for a strip of sunlight to illuminate the way. Various scenes still remain along the causeway walls. Boats laden with stone columns on the way from Aswan travel to these very temples. Desert scenes show violence and tenderness, as a collared hunting dog attacks a gazelle and an antelope licks her calf nearby. Goldsmiths blow through pipes to raise the temperature of their fire, while others beat sheets of metal. A market scene presents products for sale, including a baboon. Strangely, because pharaohs seldom show misfortunes, there are fifteen starving people with skeletonlike ribs.

OTHER TOMBS: Before leaving this part of Sakkara, if you have energy beyond what you will need for the remaining two or three best mastabas described below, you may wish to tarry to see two smaller tombs.

Exactly midway and alongside Zoser's south wall (the walk you followed to Unis's pyramid) is the Tomb of Idut. She was a princess of Dynasty VI who usurped an earlier tomb. Only the first two rooms on the right are special; the second especially so. See the acrobatic dancers on the near wall, the wall where the mummy is shown on a pilgrimage. On the opposite wall, just below a large scene of the princess riding in a papyrus boat, is a dramatic vignette—a hippopotamus screams while giving birth to her calf, whose head is just emerging; a crocodile waits behind with open mouth.

The second extra is the tomb of Nefer (Dynasty V) with its mummy still inside. The single-room tomb lies just beyond the reconstructed part of Unis's causeway to the right (if walking away from the pyramid). On the left as you enter is the mummy. Each limb is wrapped, and on the whole it is very lifelike—too much so for some viewers.

For the insatiable tourist, this list includes other interesting tombs near the causeway: Mahu (beside Idut mentioned above) for excellent colors; Nefer-her-Ptah (two tombs back toward Unis's pyramid from the tomb of Nefer) for delicate sketches still uncarved; Khnumhotep and Ni-ankh-Khnum (both in one tomb just past Nefer) for a simply lovely tomb.

MASTABA OF TI: *(Ti's mastaba is almost one mile from the entrance to Zoser's complex. Follow the old road that gradually leads away from the enclosure. Turn left at each of two forks in the road. The route follows Zoser's long east wall until it passes a small ruined pyramid (of Userkaef from Dynasty V), then goes left along the northern wall. Continue to the rest house, a large tent on a hill. Walk or take a carriage or a camel 200 yards down the path to Ti's mastaba. The Serapeum (discussed after Ti) is less than 100 yards in the opposite direction from the rest house.)*

By general agreement this is the finest tomb in Sakkara (other than pyramids, which are a different sort of thing). Certainly the delicacy of carving and blending of details into an overall conception earns it a very high place. As added benefits, this tomb lies near the Serapeum, which most people want to visit, and close to the rest house, which may be welcome by this time.

Ti (linguists argue correctly that the proper spelling is Tjey—but who can pronounce that?) was an important personage in Dynasty V. The hairdresser of two pharaohs, he married well, to a woman with royal connections. His tomb, carved in elegant low reliefs, shows life as it was in the time of the Old Kingdom.

Enter through a vestibule. Two pillars here show Ti carrying a staff of authority and dressed as a lord with the prissy triangular apron that made active work impossible and was a sign of class. On the left wall women who represent the estates controlled by Ti file past carrying food for his tomb. In the doorway that leads to the pillared courtyard, we find Ti again—asking that visitors do not desecrate his tomb. Unfortunately, the reliefs in the courtyard are much the worse for the years. The left side of the near courtyard wall portrays the butchering of cattle. A *serdab* lies behind. The right wall shows the fattening of geese and cranes. All are appropriate scenes for this room which was intended for offerings. From the center of the courtyard, a shaft leads to the undecorated burial chamber which houses a plain sarcophagus of relatively little interest.

The wonders begin beyond an opening in the end wall of the courtyard, on the right. A corridor points the way. More bearers of offerings, this time with priests, line the right side of the corridor along with a false door dedicated to Ti's wife. Another doorway (a real one) leads to a short corridor with still more pictures of sacrifices and statues of Ti being dragged to his tomb. On the right, ships are drawn in admirable detail. A door leads to a side chamber with fine reliefs that makes one begin to understand the fame of this tomb.

But the jewel is the last room, the Chapel. Two painted pillars and the ceiling resemble costly red granite, the real thing apparently beyond Ti's means. The left wall shows Ti in shade, his wife at his side, inspecting a variety of harvest operations. Farther along this wall shipbuilding scenes show the step-by-step stages of construction. The end wall is too rich for coherent description. A *serdab* on the left holds a statue of Ti (a copy). All over are scenes of workmen— carpenters, coppersmiths, sculptors, leatherworkers. Animals of many species from Ti's various estates are being led to him. On the right side of the end wall Ti sits before a table heaped with food, while servants bring more. Below a band of musicians plays while Ti reaps the choicest parts from a slaughter of desert animals.

The right-hand wall is extraordinary. Below, more women representing Ti's estates bring more offerings. Above them on the left, look for the dwarf and the figure that may be a hunchback. Two rows of cattle scenes appear next. Notice the cow calving and the precise depiction of the mother's pained face and hanging tongue. Another cow is milked while a herdsman holds her calf to prevent it from running to its mother. Cattle are driven across a river. The words above say: "Hey, herder, put your hand over the water" (i.e., make a protective sign against crocodiles). The herdsman in the boat on the right makes the required sign. Water is depicted by a clever device—what is under the rippling water is only painted while the rest of the scene is carved.

The central scene, in which Ti sails through the Delta marsh, is one of the great works of ancient art. Ti hunts hippopotami. The pattern of lines forms papyrus stems—a risky device that succeeds. It dramatizes the variety of birds above (stalked by a civet cat and mongoose) while it separates the scene below and still conveys the denseness of a swamp. It is wonderful.

To the right, boatmen quarrel while men fish below. Three agricultural scenes at the end of the wall follow: plowing, tilling, and sowing; rams trampling the seed into the ground; and the Nile overflowing to water the land.

These scenes show the gods what Ti enjoyed in this world so the gods would allow his enjoyment to continue after death. Therefore, we have pictures of life as it was in 2450 B.C. The same might be said for some other tombs, but Ti found artists of elegant taste at a time when art was generally exceptional. He left a singular monument.

THE SERAPEUM: On the other side of the rest house lies a series of bizarre tombs that hint at the excesses of Egypt in later times. A massive underground cavern runs the length of almost two football fields—a cemetery for sacred bulls.

Serapeum is a corruption of the word "Osiris-Apis." Apis, a special bull sacred to pharaohs, had a star marking on its forehead and tongue that proved its divinity. In the twilight of Egypt, the times of the Ptolemies, these subterranean chambers were dug to house the mummies of dead bulls, each of which had reigned as a god until death. A crude place of crude excess, the underground tunnel is still mysterious, and the sarcophagi carved from single pieces of black basalt are impressive in size and polished finish.

MASTABA OF PTAH-HOTEP AND AKHET-HOTEP: (*Go back about 300 yards along the road you took to the rest house to a path on the right going up in the general direction of Zoser's pyramid.*)

Some consider this mastaba an equal of Ti's. Unquestionably, one wall is very fine. From the same period, it was a tomb for a father and son, relatives of a great vizier of Egypt. Enter by a corridor dedicated to Akhet-hotep, the son. To the right lies a large undecorated hall with pillars, and across is the entrance to an offering chapel. These two rooms are communal, for father and son. Left from the hall with pillars waits the corridor belonging to Ptah-hotep—with the one wonderful wall.

In the first room after entering, a large figure of Akhet-hotep is carved on the right wall. Above him are his titles—the high priest of three pharaohs' (see the cartouches) pyramids. Behind his hand that holds a folded piece of cloth (for some unknown reason, a traditional sign of authority), you can see the successive stages of carving reliefs. Closest to the hand are lovely finished cattle; farther away the scene is only blocked out. The opposite wall holds the now familiar scene of estate women bearing offerings.

Through the pillared hall and left, enter the room of Ptah-hotep, the best in the mastaba. Note the ceiling carved to resemble logs—wood usually was represented with red color; traces remain. The left wall inspires our pilgrimages to this tomb. We start from the far end and work back to the entrance.

The deceased walks magisterially, preceded by his small son Akhet-hotep, who holds the bottom of his staff. They watch the delivery of fowl and cattle. The Egyptians observed the oxen in wonderful detail. Note the bad leg of the herdsman leading the ox with the lyre-shaped horns. On high are two lovely registers of a desert hunt. Notice the lion biting the muzzle of a wild bull which defecates in fear. At the right end, panthers and wolves mate. Farther toward the entrance Ptah-hotep contemplates country diversions. A marsh scene rests on top. Boys play below, followed by two rows depicting each stage of grape growing and wine production. Finally, the juice is pressed by tightly winding grape-filled sacks twisted on long poles. Note the man spread-eagled to keep the twisting sticks apart. Below more boys play, some engaged in a peculiar spinning game. (Hair braided in a sidelock is a convention for youth.) Under the boys, people build papyrus punts. Marsh scenes follow. Note the large birding nets. In the lowest register, a man in a boat to the left receives a drink from a boy. Titles call this man "sculptor-in-chief." Perhaps the artist tried to immortalize himself. If so, he deserves it for this one wall.

The end wall carries the familiar scene of the deceased at an overflowing table. A similar scene on the other long wall boasts the usual stream of bearers and priests. Around a false door, farther toward the entrance, Ptah-hotep rides a litter and then sits in a chapel.

MASTABA OF MERIRUKA: *(Retrace the road back to Zoser's wall. Where it first turns right around the corner of Userkaef's pyramid, continue straight. Go 100 yards to a four-way intersection and turn left. At the end of the short road is Meriruka's mastaba.)*

The carving in this tomb is not as fine as that of Ti and Ptah-hotep: Dynasty VI begins an artistic slide downhill. Yet the overall impression of this tomb is somehow very striking both architecturally and emotionally. The feeling of a presence provided by a life-sized statue of the deceased pervades the structure. Because the tomb is large enough for leisurely browsing it is impressive.

Meriruka's mastaba stands at one end of what is called the Street of Tombs. All these tombs belong to various officials of the pharaoh Teti, whose pyramid they face. Their entrances warn that those who enter must be pure or else the deceased will suffer tortures in the next world. Meriruka was a vizier to Teti; his wife was the pharaoh's daughter. No wonder his mastaba has 30 rooms.

Wander as your fancy wills. In general, you see scenes like those mentioned before in other tombs, but spread over the space afforded by more rooms. Meriruka interred his wife and his son with him, reserving a suite of rooms for each. Left of the entrance is the suite of rooms for Meriruka's wife. The first room is especially lovely. At the end of the largest room in the back, the one with the statue, rooms were added for his son. That the son's body was an unexpected addition to the tomb is shown by the fact that the decoration was disrupted to make a door to his rooms.

(The tomb next door, of Kagemni, is also impressive. Ankh-ma-hor, next down the "street," depicts a circumcision operation in the first room.)

GIZA

"The Pyramids" always means the three at Giza, though in the vicinity of Cairo alone stand more than 70 other pyramids, seldom written about, seldom photographed. Those at Giza so completely exemplify the perfection of the form that the others are ignored. These three pyramids are virtual symbols of ancient Egypt. Their elegance, massive size, and sense of power summarize the aims of this ancient civilization.

However, there are dangers. So often photographed and so often described in glowing hyperbole, the pyramids can hardly meet our expectations; yet we want them to amaze us. Try to break away from your preconceptions. Spend some time just sitting or walking while your gaze wanders over their sides. Watch clouds pass along one face; see the colors change with the lighting; follow the line of the slope to its pinnacle. Tourists could once regularly climb to the top of the Great Pyramid. The ascent, not terribly difficult, offered a magnificent view of Cairo, the Delta, the Nile ribbon, and the pyramid next door. The climb encouraged a feeling of kinship with the pyramid. Now it is illegal (though still done). Even without the climb, given time, the pyramids unfailingly impress. After all, there are reasons for the photographs and hyperboles.

(Nowadays the area at the base of the Great Pyramid especially is crowded with insistent hawkers of souvenirs and persistent dragomen [guides], the worst in Egypt. They buzz around like flies and become just as annoying. Be firm and stern with the first few or you will never be left in peace. If the distractions get too severe, consider a ride through the desert. Mention the desire to anyone and you will soon be led to a fine Arabian steed.)

The Giza plateau was selected as the site for these pyramids because its altitude helped elevate the structures and because it is a solid hill. Though sand from the adjoining desert forms the top layer, rock lies underneath—necessary to bear the tremendous weight of the pyramids. Khufu (Cheops) built the first pyramid here, the one we call the Great Pyramid. His grandson built the second and *his* grandson built the last, the smallest of the famous three. Their queens raised miniature pyramids near their husbands (one of these little ones dates from a later period), nobles built tombs near their king, and Giza literally grew into a city of the dead, with orderly streets spreading over hundreds of acres.

You may enter all three pyramids, but the interior of the Great Pyramid is far more dramatic than the others. Walk and you will see more—the Sphinx, the boat pits, and the Valley Temple of Khaefra.

The pyramids lie a quick six miles from the center of Cairo. Take a taxi, after agreeing on a price that should be near LE 3, to the Mena House Hotel at the foot of a short but steep hill to the pyramids. Cabs are always waiting at the Mena House to take you back, so don't pay your driver to wait.

Camel drivers will pester you to ride their beasts up the hill. If you desire this exotic transportation, set the price before you mount and be prepared for an argument, nonetheless, before you are let down again. A brief camel- (or horse-) ride in the desert on top of the plateau would be more interesting than one up the road. There are plenty of animals to ride on the far side of the Great Pyramid.

Admission is 50 pt. Open from 8 a.m. to 4:30 p.m. A rest house, a former mansion of King Farouk, is to the left of the Great Pyramid. Refreshment stands are down by the Sphinx.

THE GREAT PYRAMID: It was called the Horizon of Khufu. It is the largest tomb ever built and probably the most massive monument of any sort. Raised over the course of a 20-year period and completed by about 2575 B.C., it stands over 40 stories high at 481 feet. (The iron pole on top shows the original height.) With precise accuracy, each side—756 feet long—faces one of the four cardinal points. The entrance, on the north face, points to the polar star, which (being unmoving) represented eternity to the Egyptians. About 2,300,000 yellowish rectangular blocks weighing about two-and-one-half tons comprise this pyramid. Each, quarried on the Giza plateau, was then dragged on a sledge by gangs of men pulling ropes, while one man oiled the runners. Probably the blocks were hauled up ramps to their position in the structure, though one ancient historian claims that "machines" (perhaps hoists) were used. The blocks fit into place on a thin layer of mortar—more to ease the way than to bond the structure. Originally, fine white limestone ferried across the Nile from the Tura hills covered the outside, so the structure would have seemed perfectly smooth, glistening brightly. This outer casing, stolen over the years to build houses and mosques in Cairo, still remains at the top of the second pyramid and at the very bottom of the Great Pyramid below the entrance.

The entrance, once concealed behind the limestone casing, is easily seen now that the casing is gone. Below is a large hole, through which you enter today, made by Caliph Mamun (the son of the caliph in the *Arabian Nights* stories) in his search for treasure in this tomb that had been robbed clean 3000 years before his effort.

Inside, the first 100 feet is cramped. The corridor, less than 44 feet high, is steep as well. At its end the Grand Gallery opens wide, and to the right is the so-called Queen's Chamber. The entire pyramid was intended for only one person. Originally Khufu's burial room, this misnamed Queen's Chamber represents a change in the architect's plan. Later it was decided to make Khufu's burial chamber higher up instead. The Grand Gallery that leads to the final burial chamber seems infinitely high after the low corridor. The walls angle, forming a corbeled arch that is covered by enormous blocks 30 feet overhead. Ramps run along either side on the floor with small rectangular pits at regular intervals. Some say that the pits supported wooden stakes anchoring massive granite plugs until the time they were knocked loose to slide down and seal the entrance shut. Others say the pits were for poles to support an overhead platform.

A short corridor at the top of the Grand Gallery leads to the real burial chamber. Three sets of shallow grooves in the corridor walls once secured granite slabs that sealed the doorway. The chamber itself is beautifully proportioned, with a hard lining of polished pink granite. At its end is Khufu's unadorned sarcophagus. One inch wider than the door, the sarcophagus must have been placed inside while the pyramid was being built. Three feet above the floor two holes for ventilation lead all the way to the outside of the pyramid. Over the roof, in the core of the pyramid, a series of relieving slabs spreads the weight of the structure away from this chamber. If not for them, the weight above would crush this open space. On several of the relieving slabs, Khufu's name was scratched by quarrymen. These scratches are the only personal marks still remaining of its one-time owner in the largest mausoleum ever made.

THE OTHER PYRAMIDS: The next pyramid belongs to Khaefra (Chephren). Although it is ten feet shorter, it stands taller because it is built on higher land. The mass is a good deal less than that of the Great Pyramid because the angle of the sides is more acute.

The third pyramid, that of Menkaura (Mycerinus), seems small, although it reached almost 220 feet when new. The casing is its special feature. The upper part was cased in limestone, but the lower third of the pyramid was covered with pink granite, a harder, more expensive stone. Only in parts was the granite given a smooth finish—evidence that this pharaoh died before his tomb was finished.

People like to think that magic permeated the pyramids, that the measurements which were so accurate had mystical meaning. The fact that each of 70 pyramids had different angles and bases and that all the corridors and tomb chambers are different should give pause to such theories. Still, some people go so far as to claim that pyramids were not meant to be tombs. They have to explain away the sarcophagus in the Great Pyramid and the one found in the pyramid of Menkaura (though subsequently lost at sea on its way to England). In 1968, further proof of the funerary nature of pyramids was found in a text carved in the granite casing of Menkaura's pyramid (below the entrance to the left). It gives the date when the pharaoh was buried inside. Though the year is obliterated, enough can be read to know that he was buried on the 23rd day of the last month of the winter season.

THE SOLAR BOATS: Walking around the Great Pyramid, on the side to the left of the entrance (farthest from the other two pyramids), you pass tombs cut in the rocks across from the modern road. You also pass two narrow elliptical pits, each 100 feet long, that once held buried boats. A third pit is between them, farther away. For years archaeologists knew of the tradition of burying boats outside a pharaoh's tomb. The tradition goes back as far as Dynasty I. The three pits belonging to Khufu were opened years ago, as were five others associated with the second pyramid. Of course, all were empty except for fragments, since wood is not likely to last 4500 years.

Passing around the corner to the back face of the pyramid, you see a flimsy modern structure with scaffolding around it. Inside is one of Khufu's "solar" boats. It seemed to be a miracle when, in 1954, a new pit was discovered that contained a boat perfectly preserved. A second pit was also found along this face of the pyramid with a second perfect boat inside. By far the oldest boats ever discovered, they had been dismantled to fit into their pits, but the pieces were arranged to give the proper appearance. All the ropes were there, coiled, as well as mats on which to sit. Oars lined the deck.

One of the boats is currently being reconstructed inside the flimsy shed, though permission to see it is difficult to obtain (a bribe sometimes buys a peek through a window). The boat, about 135 feet long (25 feet longer than the pit) and about eight feet wide in the center, is composed of nearly 700 pieces of wood fastened by tenons, wood pegs, and copper staples. Almost all the wood is the famed cedar of Lebanon. Ebony (from the Sudan) and locally grown sycamore were used for details. Although these vessels are known as "solar" boats, their purpose is not clear. It may indeed be that they were meant to carry a pharaoh through the sky like the sun. On the other hand, it may be that their use ended when they ferried the pharaoh's body and funerary materials from Memphis to his pyramid, that they were buried just because objects associated with a funeral were considered too sanctified for reuse.

Wisely, the archaeologists decided to leave the second boat in its pit while reconstructing the first. The excavated boat is dying. Atmospheric changes, the sun, and humidity destroy the wood as the experts work on it. Under stone slabs sealed tight with plaster, the second boat stays safe, it is hoped.

THE SPHINX: Each pyramid has a funerary temple (Khufu's is between the two newly discovered boat pits) where priests made offerings and prayed. All are too ruined now to offer much worth seeing. Separate causeways (like that of Unis at Sakkara) led from these temples to valley temples down the hill. From behind the second pyramid, Khaefra's causeway leads straight down to his valley temple but takes a sudden turn at the Sphinx. It seems that, while building the causeway, work was blocked by a mass of tall rock. Construction went on around it, but someone decided to make use of a hill that otherwise would intrude on the view. A sphinx was carved from this living rock.

Countless sphinxes survive from ancient Egypt, but only one is called "The Sphinx." In general, sphinxes combine the head of a pharaoh with the body of a lion to represent power, although some use a ram's body. Somehow the Greeks got the idea that a sphinx represented a female, but the ones in Egypt (except those for the rare female pharaohs) are males.

The Sphinx—its head is that of the pharaoh Khaefra whose causeway it guards—so impressed ancient Egyptians of later times that they worshiped it as the god who watched over the pyramid necropolis. A small temple was built in front of the paws. At some time the figure of a god, now very indistinct, was carved on the chest. Limestone blocks were added to reform the recumbent lion shape after weathering distorted it, mainly in Roman times. The nose was shot away by Arab vandals, not by Napoleon's army as many stories claim.

The sand deals harshly with the Sphinx. Lying in a depression it rested under sand during most of its history. Now the sand erodes it severely (the neck was not always so scrawny). The stele (a commemorative stone) between its paws records how Thothmoses IV, a pharaoh in the New Kingdom, came to excavate the Sphinx. It says that while yet a prince, Thothmoses grew tired after hunting in Giza and fell asleep on the sand. In a dream the Sphinx spoke to him saying that it was buried where he slept. If he would free the Sphinx, he was promised the throne.

The Sphinx still has that mysterious smile hinting of secrets, though it is actually just the standard mouth of most Old Kingdom statuary. The headdress represents a striped "nemes" cloth, worn by pharaohs as a type of crown in the Old Kingdom. Originally a cobra coiled on the brow; the cobra head was a separate piece of stone, long gone, that fit into a socket still visible. The head of the Sphinx rises 66 feet above the base. The length from forepaws to tail runs about 200 feet, and the mouth is seven feet, seven inches from corner to enigmatic corner.

THE VALLEY TEMPLE OF KHAEFRA: Beside the Sphinx, left of its temple, stands the beautiful Valley Temple of Khaefra in a good state of preservation. It probably served to prepare the mummy of the king or at least to provide a hall for performing final purification rites. Remains of basins and tent-pole holes were found on portions of the temple roof. In ancient times a canal ran in front and a quay received boats laden with funeral effects.

The temple, built of massive limestone blocks covered inside and out with polished pink granite slabs, boasts alabaster floors. Two doorways, each carved with the titles of the king (some still visible at the bottom), have indentations on either side that probably held statues—likely, small sphinxes. You enter through a narrow vestibule. To hide it from thieves, a statue was buried in a well in the center of the vestibule. It was the famous seated statue of Chephren, with a falcon spreading its wings around the king's majestic head, that is now a great showpiece of the Museum of Antiquities. Pass through a doorway and enter a T-shaped hall. Notice the fit of the massive slabs of pink granite: they meet in angles, not perpendicular lines, to strengthen the joints. The square granite pillars that once supported a roof are elegantly plain. Depressions in the alabaster floor show where 23 statues once stood, presumably of the pharaoh. Each was originally lit by rays of sunlight streaming through small windows that were arranged around the tops of the walls.

In back of the hall, on the left, a corridor leads to six storerooms on two levels. On the right, a narrow passage leads to the exit where the causeway to the pyramid begins. Halfway along this passage sits a small chamber lined in alabaster, and opposite, a ramp runs up to the roof. The temple, now lacking all adornment, is all the more powerful for its monolithic design.

THE FAIYUM AND MEIDUM

Here is a day trip through the Egyptian countryside that offers a visit to the first true pyramid, an imposing ruin, and a visit to a Middle Kingdom pyramid surrounded by a maze that influenced the myth of the Labyrinth.

Few tour companies include the pyramid of Meidum in their visits to the Faiyum, though they pass right by it. That means your choices are a taxi for the day (pay no more than LE 20), a hired car and driver, or your rented car.

If you drive yourself, it is a bit of an adventure. The road is not paved for part of the route and directional signals are scarce. Take the Pyramids Road to Giza, turning right at the Mena House Hotel onto the road to Alexandria. In two miles turn right on the main Nile road to Upper Egypt (south). In 43 miles (76 kilometers) the road forks. The left branch goes to Meidum. The right fork (which soon becomes a sand and gravel track) runs to the Faiyum.

MEIDUM: Though it is just a pyramid that collapsed, the sharp lines of the structure here remind some people of a modern building and others of a ziggurat from ancient Mesopotamia. Situated in a flat desert landscape so it can be seen from miles away, the pyramid never fails to be dramatic. For some reason, sightseers seldom make the effort to visit; the site is guaranteed to be peaceful and meditative.

Around the pyramid lies a hill of debris and beside it are a series of ancient mastabas. The famous fresco known as the Geese of Meidum came from one of these, and from another came the magnificent statues of Rahotep and Nofret with perfectly preserved paint—all stars now of the Museum of Antiquities.

Controversy surrounds both the shape of the Meidum pyramid and the builder. Some claim that the present shape was intended, though the top was never finished. The heap of rubble, however, is wholly out of character, given the flatness of the surrounding terrain. Others claim that the rubble is the outer casing of a collapsed pyramid, that what we now see is the interior of the first true pyramid. According to this latter theory, a step pyramid, like Zoser's but with eight steps, preceded a pyramid in which the steps were filled in to make straight faces—but the filling fell in a landslide, leaving the rubble hill.

Entry is a little precarious. After descending nearly 200 feet, you reach ground level and enter a series of two small antechambers. A shaft leads up to the burial chamber, requiring a climb up rickety ladders. You pass wooden beams cut almost five millennia ago. The burial chamber has a corbeled roof but is otherwise simple and plain. The silence is awesome. If you extinguish all lights, you will experience how it feels to be in a tomb.

Behind the pyramid and opposite the entrance is a small temple with two uninscribed stelae above. Once inside, notice the ancient graffiti from the New Kingdom, which tell of a pilgrimage here to the pyramid of Sneferu (and pretty much settle the question of who built this tomb). A limestone causeway runs down to the former site of a valley temple that sank into the marshy soil.

HAWARA, THE LABYRINTH: Amunemhat III, a great pharaoh of the Middle Kingdom, built a pyramid here. By then, pyramids were built by less time-consuming methods: the adobe interior, manufactured quickly from mud, lay under a thin limestone casing. The structure would look finer and more permanent than in truth it was. Amunemhat III developed the Faiyum—building towns, irrigation systems to increase fertility, and temples to the local god, the crocodile Sobek. Amunemhat III had a 46-year reign, during which he had time to prepare a rich and complex funeral monument.

In his pyramid he constructed a puzzle of secret passage-ways and invisible doors, misleading corridors leading to solid dead ends, and a chamber for his coffin hewed from one of the largest pieces of rock ever quarried. All these devices were designed to save his body from tomb robbers. The entrance was hidden on the south side—though pyramids traditionally were entered from the north. A passage led down to an apparent dead end, but a stone in the roof slid away to reveal another passage filled with rubble that made it difficult to enter. Anyone misled into believing that this rubble filling protected valuable remains would painstakingly burrow through to find a dead end. The real passage was invitingly open although it led to a blank wall.

A stone that seemed cemented in place slid open to another corridor that led to another apparent end, and on and on. Finally came the quartzite burial chamber. Harder than granite, the chamber was a single stone hollowed to 25 feet by 8 feet and almost two feet thick, weighing over 100 tons, roofed by massive slabs of the same material, only one of which was movable by a hidden slide. All these tricks and labor worked well enough to fool modern excavators. In desperation they finally tunneled from the top of the pyramid all the way down to the tomb. (A metal plate on top covers their hole.) They discovered an empty tomb with evidence of a fire. As to the ancient robbers, it seems that all Amunemhat's efforts at concealment served merely to make them angry. When, despite all the tricks, they reached his tomb, they burned the pharaoh's body.

The entrance is now blocked; the adobe structure is dangerous to enter. Climb the pyramid only if you are prepared for some dirt slides. The view over the surrounding farmland is lovely.

From above you also get a feeling for the size of the strange surrounding structures. No one is certain what purpose they served. Herodotus, the world's first historian, visited in 270 B.C. and considered this complex more amazing than the pyramids. He claimed, with typical tourist's exaggeration, that the building consisted of 3000 rooms, half above and half below the ground. The Greeks believed that the buildings might be the fabled Labyrinth that formed a maze in which you could lose your way. Most likely, the building was a new kind of complex mortuary temple, grown gigantic. It must originally have been 1000 feet long and almost as wide, as large as both of the largest surviving ancient Egyptian temples combined. Finished by the successor of Amunemhat III—his daughter Sobek-neferu (the last ruler of the Middle Kingdom and one of the rare female pharaohs)—the temple has served for thousands of years now as a convenient quarry for people living nearby. Like ants at a picnic, they have slowly taken away the pieces. Not one wall now stands.

THE SIGHTS OF ANCIENT EGYPT IN CAIRO

THE MUSEUM OF ANTIQUITIES: *(Located behind the Hilton Hotel a short block from the Nile, beside el Tahrir Square. Open daily from 9 a.m. to 4 p.m.; closed between 11:15 a.m. and 1:30 p.m. on Fridays only. In summer the museum closes at 1 p.m. and 11 a.m. on Fridays, but opens a half-hour earlier than in winter. Admission is 75 pt.)*

Not a normal museum, this building houses the most wonderful art ancient Egypt produced. Most other large museums try to show objects from as many periods of as many countries as have produced art. This museum has only one goal—to present ancient Egypt. With overwhelming quantity and quality, it puts all other collections of this art in a minor league.

The present building dates from 1902. In terms of display, it may be the worst great museum in the world. Over the years the collection has grown until it now fills the basement and spills outside into the courtyard. There are pieces outside for which curators elsewhere would happily build special rooms in their museums. Inside, some strange numbering system baffles modern man, while priceless objects lie stuffed in cases with glass so dusty that we advise you to carry a rag and a flashlight. Several years ago the inside was painted; many of the large statues still bear the yellowish spots. Total remodeling is now under way and eagerly awaited.

Walk around to find the best angles; you must search for the objects. The potential reward makes the difficulties worthwhile. You can get an education just by looking at masterpieces culled from 2500 years of a great civilization and arranged by period. You can see the arts develop (not always for the better) and learn the characteristics of the various periods. If you return at the end of your visit to Egypt, after reading and after seeing all periods of temples and tombs, then you may bind your experiences together to form a composite picture of Egypt.

Before entering the museum you pass a fountain surrounded by tall papyrus, which no longer grows naturally in

CAIRO
Museum of Antiquities

Ground Floor

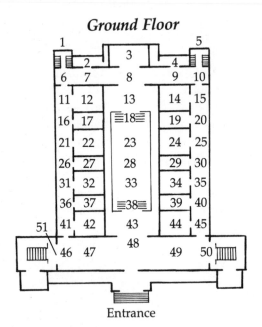

Entrance

Second Floor

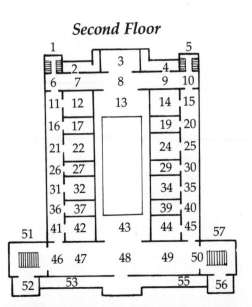

WALKING TOUR
Ground Floor

Room 48. Large Statuary, various pharaonic periods
Room 47. Old Kingdom Statuettes
Room 46. Old Kingdom Miscellany
Room 51. Fragments from the Sphinx
Room 41. Old Kingdom Miscellany
Room 42. Old Kingdom Masterpieces
Room 36. Old Kingdom Statues and Temple Reliefs
Room 37. Early Coffins
Room 31. Old Kingdom Miscellany—Panels of Hesi-Ra
Room 32. Old Kingdom Masterpieces
Room 26. Middle Kingdom Miscellany
Room 27. Closed
Room 21. Middle Kingdom Royal Sculpture
Room 22. Middle Kingdom Funerary Material
Room 16. Probable Middle Kingdom Works
Room 17. Closed
Room 11. Statues of Hatshepsut, Senmut, and Thothmoses III
Room 12. Dynasty XVIII Sculpture Masterpieces
Room 6. New Kingdom Stelae
Room 1. Stairs and Large Papyri
Room 7. Hatshepsut and Others
Room 2. Closed
Room 8. Miscellany
Room 3. Akhenaten and His Era
Room 13. Dynasty XVIII and XIX Large Sculpture
Room 18. Large Pharaonic Sculpture
Room 23. Large Sculpture
Room 28. Pavement from Akhenaten's Palace
Room 33. Colossal Sculpture
Room 38. Sarcophagi
Room 43. Middle Kingdom Ships and Statues
Room 9. Dynasty XVIII and XIX Sculpture
Room 4. Coins
Room 5. Stairs
Room 10. Rameses the Great
Room 15. Rameses the Great
Room 14. Rameses the Great
Room 20. Rameses the Great and Rameses III
Room 19. Closed
Room 25. Late Period
Room 24. Late Period—Alexander
Room 30. Late Period
Room 29. Closed
Room 35. Foreign Material
Room 34. Greco-Roman Statuary
Room 40. Pre-Christian Nubia
Room 39. Pre-Christian Nubia
Room 45. Pre-Christian Nubia
Room 44. Pre-Christian Nubia
Room 50. Late Sarcophagi and Large Statues
Room 49. Late Sarcophagi and Large Statues

WALKING TOUR
Second Floor

Room 57. Stairs and Priests' Coffins
Room 50. Furniture, various periods
Room 49. Furniture, various periods
Room 55. Prehistoric Material
Room 48. Statuettes, various periods
Room 43. Early Dynasties
Room 53. Prehistoric Material
Room 47. New Kingdom Royal Coffins
Room 46. New Kingdom Royal Coffins
Room 51. Priests' Coffins
Room 52. Royal Mummies
Room 41. Coffins, various periods
Room 42. Early Dynasties and Old Kingdom Treasures
Room 36. Coffins, various periods
Room 37. Middle Kingdom Coffins and Models
Room 31. Coffins, various periods
Room 32. Models
Room 26. Coffins, various periods
Room 27. Middle Kingdom Models
Room 21. Coffins, various periods
Room 22. Funerary Materials, various periods
Room 16. Coffins, various periods
Room 17. Funerary Materials, mainly New Kingdom
Room 11. Coffins, various periods
Room 12. Royal Tomb Material
Room 6. Scarabs, various periods
Room 1. Stairs
Room 7-8. Tutankhamun's Shrine
Room 2. Royal Furniture
Room 3. Jewelry, various periods
Room 13. Material of Tuya and Yuya
Room 9. Tutankhamun's Canoptic Chest
Room 4. Tutankhamun's Jewelry and Gold Coffin
Rooms 10, 15, 20, 25, 30, 35, 40, 45. Tutankhamun's Equipment
Room 14. Greco-Roman Funerary Material
Room 19. Amulets of Gods, various periods
Room 24. Ostraca, various periods
Room 29. Written Material and Writing Equipment
Room 34. Tools, various periods
Room 39. Greco-Roman Material
Room 44. Architectural Material, various periods

Egypt. Inside, at the ticket booth, you may buy a guidebook to the collection. The book was confusing to us, but it was inexpensive (LE 1). Cameras must be checked along with packages and umbrellas at the free checkroom on the left.

From time to time the museum presents special shows of indeterminate duration. By all means go, despite the extra fee, because the exhibits usually include some of the finest objects in the museum. Such shows, along with loans to other countries, however, remove objects from their normal locations.

You enter a vestibule lined with large statues. Facing you is a pink-granite head (two feet high) of the pharaoh Userkaef from Dynasty V—the first instance of the colossal statuary that later became almost a trademark of Egypt. To the right is a wing for Greek and Roman artifacts; to the left, ancient Egypt.

Ground floor: Starting left, move around the rectangle of the building, passing from early to later works. The arrangement is by period—Old Kingdom, Middle Kingdom, and Late Period, though no particular chronology is followed within the periods. Afterward, go upstairs to special rooms for jewelry, Tut's treasure, and the mummies.

In the corridor, you can admire various Old Kingdom pieces in passing—except for the beautiful "reserve heads," which are worth a pause. Unpainted limestone heads, they are extremely well modeled, most with ears broken and a slash on the top of the skull. All, found in Dynasty IV tombs near the Pyramids, have necks smooth on the bottom, which allow them to stand. Why, no one knows. Nothing like them exists in any other period. This corridor, too, holds charming small statues of people working—washers and brewers and bread makers, several with deformities. On the left wall is a fine green shist statue of Menkaura (Mycerinus) with two females. The cow goddess Hat-hor holds the hand of the king, who wears the crown of the south, while beside him stands a woman representing a nome (state), designated by the strange collection over her head. Her hands and one of Menkaura's wrap around objects that appear over and over in Egyptian sculpture. Do they represent a baton of office, a bundle of papyrus, a deed, or some other thing? At the end of this gallery are fragments from the Sphinx. Then the passage turns right to another long corridor.

Here lie some nice tomb reliefs of craftsmen and of country scenes, but join the crowd for greater works in the room marked #42. Back and to the left are two veritable master-pieces. One is a large, dark-green (diorite) seated statue of Khaefra (Chephren). On the sides of his throne two plants tie around the sign of unity—lotus and papyrus, south and Delta, two countries in one. Behind his head a falcon embraces the king with his wings. Every pharaoh was Horus, the falcon, as the unknown sculptor of this piece so artfully shows us in symbols. Majesty has seldom been better portrayed. Beside stands a wooden statue of Sheikh el Beled. Not really a sheikh, he was just an official from Dynasty V who looked so human and so much like the chief of their village that the workmen who found this statue were sure it was their sheikh. Usually the statue of Zoser, originally found in his *serdab* at Sakkara, is in this room. (Sometimes it is at the very end of the corridor outside.) Heavy-headed and mysterious, he does look like the sort of man who could start new traditions. Beside him is the mere base of a statue, which is here amid much more impressive objects because it bears the name of Imhotep, Zoser's genius architect. Nearby is the most extraordinary of many wonderful statues of scribes. He sits cross-legged with a roll of papyrus open in his lap, ready to write. Crystal eyes stare into eternity. The eyes become almost frighteningly real, especially if a light shines in them.

In the corridor again, before entering the next room, #32, inspect the elegant wooden panels of Hesi-Ra. The hiero-glyphs are exquisite. Left of the door as you enter room #32 stand two larger-than-life copper statues. Before these were found, archaeologists thought copper work of this scale was impossible in such early times. The focus of the room, however, are the life-sized statues of Rahotep and Nofret toward the rear. By some miracle their paint remains as fresh as the day it was applied. He, the son of Sneferu, is a dandy with moustache (extremely unusual). His many titles sur-round his head. She, with the delicate painted band around her hair, is merely an "acquaintance of the king." (Notice the depiction of her real hair peeking out from under her wig.) Left, just before Rahotep and Nofret, is the dwarf Seneb and family. Dwarfs, esteemed in Egypt, frequently were made jewelers and goldsmiths. Seated compositions such as this one are common—the wife placing her arm around her husband. A dwarf, however, would be too short to balance the full figure of a normal-sized wife. Cleverly the sculptor obtained balance by placing Seneb's two children where the man's legs normally would be. This room also houses two life-sized statues of the priest Ranefer, side by side. One shows the man in the vigor of youth, the other in old age. Here, too, is the statue of Ti found in his *serdab*. On the right wall hangs the painting called the Geese of Meidum, so accurately rendered that all the species are recognizable. It is the oldest surviving example of Egyptian painting. Before leaving, notice the bent statues of humbled prisoners.

Move along the corridor to the Middle Kingdom. No longer elegant, the art is at first crude and heavy (like the statue of Montuhotep with black face, i.e., as dead). Later the art becomes vigorous. By the end of the Middle Kingdom, with the statuary of Amunemhat III and of Senusert (Sesostris) III, veritable portraits appear again. For the first time care and concern is etched in the faces of the pharaohs. Especially note the sphinx of Amunemhat III and the head of Senusert (Sesostris) III in room #21.

At the end of the corridor the New Kingdom begins. Note the painted sphinx of Hatshepsut, the female pharaoh. Nearby is a gray, legless statue of her ward and rival, Thothmoses III. His face, the typical Thothmosid pharaoh's face of the New Kingdom, has a serene countenance with small chin and large nose. Off the corridor again, in room #12, you will find many of the best works of this period. The kneeling pharaohs, Amunhotep II in gray granite and Thothmoses III in white marble, convey solemnity. The enormous painted statue of the Hat-hor cow with the suckling Amunhotep II suggests devotion. Two large granite statues of Hatshepsut depict her beneficent dignity. In general, New Kingdom sculpture aimed less at accuracy of portraiture than at mood, at conveying a quality.

Around the turn of the corridor awaits more and similar New Kingdom sculpture. Detour, again, into room #3 on the left. Here is the art of a strange time in Egypt when Akhenaten (Amunhotep IV, before he changed his name) endeavored to make religion monotheistic and art realistic. Sometimes realism became grotesque, as with the colossal statues inside the entrance and with most of the reliefs. In the case of the small statue of Akhenaten holding an offering tray—in the glass case on the left (the blue crown does not belong to this piece)—the art is "cute," not grotesque. The unfinished statues of Nefertiti (his wife) and of a pharaoh with a child on his lap (not kissing, as the label says— Egyptians probably rubbed noses) are lovely. Near the end of this short period, as you see in the lovely canopic jars (used for the viscera of the deceased) and in the pieces for Smenkara, the art turns delicate, leading to the next pharaoh, Tutankhamun. The atrium opposite this room contains the original, almost impressionistic, painted floor from Akhenaten's palace. Think how it would have felt to actually walk on water scenes so sensually real.

At this stage in your visit, a decision is in order. On reaching the atrium you have gone halfway around the ground floor. The second floor will take again as much time and concentration as you have already spent. If you continue now to the end of the first floor you will see Late Period artifacts that borrow more and more Greek and Roman features as you move through the corridor and the years. Down the long corridor, just before the halfway point, are a number of striking portrait statues of priests in dark stone. But it might be wise to save the later periods for another visit, or you could just run by them on your way to the second floor. For the best route, go down this corridor to the front of the museum and up the stairs on the left.

Second floor: At the top of the stairs you first pass coffins, then furniture and basketry, before reaching an open space on the right leading to the balcony of the atrium. Head toward that balcony, but before you turn, study the case of small masterpieces from various periods. Prehistoric material fills a case to the right; and to the left, on the balcony itself, are relics from the very first dynasty. Look for room #42, where you can see the treasures of the first two dynasties. Here hangs the famed "Narmer Palette," which shows in pictures how the first nation was created. Notice that on each side Narmer wears a different crown—the tall cone of the south and the peculiar flat crown of the Delta with spike behind and curl in front. Never before had one person been in a position to wear both. This palette is a small object that holds infinite historical significance.

Continue down the hall you walked along after coming up the stairs. This is the time to see mummies. The real thing, unwrapped for your delectation, welcomes you at the far end of the corridor. The Mummy Room waits by the west stairs (you walked up the east stairs). It is eerie enough to be worth the LE 1 extra charge.

Continue along the atrium corridor from where you left off. The next three rooms—#37, #32, and especially #27—are noted for their models. Magic inspired these models. Egyptians believed that a replica could become the real thing. Those who could afford them placed these models in their tombs, expecting them to bring pleasure in the next world.

Moving along, approach the last room in this line, #12. Inside you'll find material gathered from royal tombs, a piece from here and one from there, overlooked by thieves. Then Tutankhamun's "treasures" begin; they run along the end corridor, around the corner, and down the length of the corridor parallel to the one you just traced. Before you begin, though, take the time for two other wonderful rooms.

Directly across the corridor from Tutankhamun are two small connected rooms. Both called #2, the first contains material belonging to Sneferu's wife from an almost intact royal burial of Dynasty IV. This woman, Khufu's mother— Queen Hethepheres—lived 1000 years before Tutankhamun, when art was more simple but of surpassing elegance. The small adjoining room displays equipment from an unrobbed

pharaoh's tomb. No, Tutankhamun's was not the only pharaoh's tomb that escaped thieves; there was this one too. Its
equipment shows the decline of Egypt—500 years after
Tutankhamun—in the cruder workmanship and the use of
silver rather than gold.

Don't miss the room next door, #3: jewelry from all periods
of ancient Egypt is crammed in case after case. The gold
falcon in the farthest corner is special, one of the very few
surviving temple idols—a gold Horus from the Old Kingdom.
The finest jewelry of all seems to be that of the Middle
Kingdom, Dynasties XI and XII. Our favorites include the
gold diadem of Sit-Hat-Hor-Yunet and the airy, gold, star
crown of princess Khnumet.

Now for Tutankhamun. Most visitors to Egypt plan a visit
to Luxor to view Tutankhamun's tomb. After seeing how
small the tomb is (the area of many living rooms), they
appreciate how things were heaped and crammed inside.
This was a king whose name was hardly known to specialists
before the discovery of his tomb, so minor was he and so
short was his reign (seven years). In fact, his insignificance
was what saved him. Ancient Egyptians even forgot where
his tomb was, so that a pharaoh from 150 years later built his
tomb near enough that its refuse covered Tutankhamun's
tomb. Only Tut's tomb really shows us what a king's burial
was like. The artifacts you may have seen in the small room
#2 (adjoining Hethepheres's) came from the only other
known, undisturbed, pharaoh's tomb, but its contents were
far poorer. Dating from a period after the glorious New
Kingdom, it lacked the spectacular wealth of Tut's tomb.

Tutankhamun reigned immediately after the religious revolution conducted by monomaniacal Akhenaten. In Tutankhamun's time the old gods were restored and the temples
reopened, but Egypt suffered from the confusions and the
abrupt decline in power caused by his predecessor. Egypt
had been more powerful and wealthy before and would be
again after Tutankhamun. His valuables gleam with gold, but
more often in the form of coatings rather than as solid metal.
Glass often replaced valuable stones for decorations. If we

had the remains from a truly great pharaoh, like Thothmoses III, they would be solid and real rather than veneers and imitations.

Past the atrium is room #4, where Tutankhamun's most valuable objects are displayed—the jewels and the coffins. The famous, solid-gold mask that joined the Tut exhibit to tour the world along with 56 other objects was hardly missed with so much still remaining. Tutankhamun had four coffins, inside one another. The outermost—with mummy intact—still resides in his tomb at Luxor. The next one sits in this room along with the last—450 pounds of solid gold. In the corridor outside, look for the four shrines that nestled inside one another to protect the chest that held Tut's viscera in miniature gold coffins. Four lovely female statues of Isis and her sisters, with their hieroglyphic signs on their heads, protect the gold-leafed sled that transported all this. Note, too, the three large funeral beds with hippopotamus, cow, and lion heads.

On and on it goes, object after object, around the bend and down the long corridor. For a change of pace, step into the second, third, and fourth rooms after the turn into the long corridor. Room #19 contains hundreds of amulets and other material picturing the various gods and goddesses of ancient Egypt. Room #24 holds ostraca from the New Kingdom. On pieces of limestone, or even broken pottery, Egyptian artists practiced their craft with charming sketches. The haste of their execution makes them more lively than formal finished work. Room #29 is devoted to the craft of writing. You can see scribes' equipment and lovely papyri.

Congratulations, you've just completed a very compact visit. On your way out stop by the shops—one in the lobby for postcards and books, and one outside and to the left for inexpensive reproductions.

THE MUSEUM OF EGYPTIAN CIVILIZATION: *(The museum stands on the Society of Agriculture grounds on the island of Gezira. Shari el Tahrir is the street that runs out of el Tahrir Square; passes the Hilton Hotel, upstream; crosses el Tahrir Bridge; then continues through Gezira and beyond. The Society of Agriculture* *grounds are along this street at the end of the island, about a half-mile in all from the Hilton Hotel. The museum is open most of the year from 10 a.m. to 4 p.m.; in the summer it closes at 1 p.m. Closed Fridays.)*

An hour spent here is the best preparation for a trip up the Nile. Not a typical museum, it offers dioramas of various ancient occupations incorporating real ancient objects to show how they were used. Displaying such objects in a typical museum shows off their beauty, but abstracts. They exude an altogether different aura when placed in replicas of their past environment.

THE PAPYRUS INSTITUTE: *(The institute is in houseboats on the far bank of the Nile, a short distance upstream from the Sheraton Hotel. You can walk—or ride—as you would to the Museum of Civilization, turning left along the Nile after crossing the island of Gezira. For a more interesting route, hire a small sailboat—with its captain—and float across the Nile. Numerous faluccas wait by the banks upstream from the Hilton Hotel. After the usual bargaining, the fee should be about LE 3. The institute is open daily from 9 a.m. until 7 p.m., one of the few places open in the early evening. Admission is free.)*

Begun as a research center to explore the ancient process of papyrus manufacture, the Papyrus Institute now is a kind of museum that illustrates the steps of this process—one that sells actual papyrus, newly made and painted. This is the source for all the papyrus you may see in the stores.

THE SIGHTS OF ISLAMIC EGYPT IN CAIRO

What follows describes six tours of Islamic monuments, plus the Islamic Museum which is as fine as any in the world. If time is a problem, follow the first tour which covers the greatest mosques, include the Islamic Museum, and join the life in Khan Kalili bazaar. Anything less would be a loss; whatever else you can include will be your treat. Wise men argue over whether the Islamic Museum is better seen before or after the mosques. We place it first only because no one should miss it.

THE ISLAMIC MUSEUM: *(From el Tahrir Square walk straight away from the Nile along Shari el Tahrir. Continue across the square—Midan el-Falaki—on the other side of which the street becomes Shari el-Bustan. At the next intersection turn right onto Shari Muhammad Farid; cross that street and enter the large square—Midan el-Gumhuriya—which fronts the palace and grounds of the president. Follow around the left side of the palace grounds. The museum is one block away, at the next intersection— Midan Ahmed Maher—after leaving the palace grounds. The walk is less than half a mile. In winter, the museum is open from 9 a.m. to 4:30 p.m.; closed from 11:15 a.m. to 1:30 p.m. on Fridays. Between May and October, the museum closes at 1 p.m., on Fridays at 11:15 a.m. Admission is 50 pt.)*

Do not forget the walls in this museum. Magnificent "Oriental" carpets hang in every room.

The first room displays recent acquisitions, followed by four rooms showing the four Islamic periods in Egypt. In room #2 the artifacts of the Ummayid period (7th to 8th century), crude but lively, are mixed with some later things. Room #3 contains delicate Persian work from the Abbasid period (8th to 10th century). The great and rich Fatimid period (10th to 12th century) is represented in room #4 especially with carved panels and lovely textiles. Notice the lovely 17th-century windows in the corridor on the way to the Mamluk room (#5). A stunning door covered with intricate bronze work, a mosaic fountain still sending peaceful water sounds through the room, and a wonderful chandelier in the center characterize the Mamluk period (13th to 15th century). Four rooms follow that display all sorts of wood carving, seldom surpassed. The last, room #10, contains the components of a late 17th-century room—fountain, timber ceiling, and *mashrabiya* (peek-a-boo windows—so harem women could look out without being seen by visitors). Room #11, for metalwork, complements room #12 which collects exquisite metal weapons. Four rooms of pottery follow. Room #13 (Egyptian) and #14 (Turkish) display pieces that are especially lovely in their color and design. Islamic textiles from all over the world fill room #17. Illuminated manuscripts, as wonderful as you will ever see, are the subjects of room #19. The Korans in Kuftic (angular) script and the Persian miniatures that decorate other books will stand comparison with the finest collections in the world. Save some energy for the last room, #22, devoted to Persian objects—magnificent carpets and elegant pottery (reminiscent of China, a strong influence on the potters of Persia).

IBN TULUN MOSQUE: *(Take a taxi to the Ibn Tulun Mosque— on Gabal Yashkur. Or take a taxi to the Citadel, if you wish to save your legs and follow this itinerary back to front. In either case the fare should be about LE 2. Ibn Tulun is open daily from 8 a.m. to noon and from 3 p.m. to 6 p.m.)*

This mosque can be combined in a walk that covers the other great mosque of Cairo (Mosque of Sultan Hassan), the two wonderful old Houses of the Cretans, and one decadent mosque in Saladin's Citadel, all described below. The historian and art critic want you to start at the Ibn Tulun Mosque and walk toward the Citadel; the practical tourist, who thinks of tired muscles, points out that the reverse order goes downhill—a very steep hill. You make the decision; the sights will be there whether you go forward or in reverse. The walk is less than half a mile.

Whether Ibn Tulun is the finest or the second finest mosque in Cairo depends on how much you favor sober purity over delicate ornateness. Unquestionably, however, this is the oldest mosque that survives substantially intact. Built by Ahmed Ibn Tulun in A.D. 879, it follows the simple plan of the earliest mosques: an open square inside enclosing walls. Around the courtyard, cloisters open to arcades with porticos pointing in four directions. One cloister, the special one with a *mahrib* (prayer wall) at the end, points to Mecca. (This whole design replicates the most holy place of Muslims, the Mecca Kaaba.) Various parts of the mosque were reconstructed in 1297–1300. This building, then, needed restoration at the time that Europe first began to build cathedrals. Most of its decoration is long gone. Do not expect to be overwhelmed by brilliant colors; look instead at the elegance of the plan.

Since the mosque no longer offers services, don't worry

about your shoes. Enter through the wall, pass an outer space, cross the doorway of the mosque proper, and come into a vast courtyard. What a glorious space—a football field square, open to the sky! The pointed arches that open the cloisters are the earliest instances of this Islaic trademark.

Around the top of the walls wood beams are inscribed with texts from the Koran. By legend, this wood came from Noah's ark, discovered on Mount Ararat by Ibn Tulun. The *mahrib*, in the cloister opposite the tall minaret rising above the portico, is a lovely mosaic and a masterpiece of Fatimid stucco carving. As you approach the *mahrib*, look for the 13th-century wood pulpit. This was one of the first mosques with a fountain inside for washing one's feet; before, the devout had to purify themselves outside the mosque. The present fountain dates to reconstruction at the end of the 13th century. Overall, the complex recalls Byzantine buildings interpreted by purer Islamic hearts.

Built before the invention of minarets, the heavenly spires from which the faithful are called to prayer, this mosque added one in the 13th century as part of the reconstruction. Not at all like the pencil-thin minarets of most mosques, this very early one was modeled on a Roman watchtower. Climb to the top via a twisting stairway; the view is worth the effort.

HOUSES OF THE CRETANS: *(These two houses wait directly across from the entrance to Ibn Tulun Mosque on Shari Tulun.)* Called the Gayer-Anderson Museum (after the last owner who collected furnishings) and Kritliya (Cretans), they date from the 17th century. Here is a rare opportunity to see actual houses from early Islamic times. In fact, parts come from the 16th century, and the remainder copies that style. See the basic atrium design and the maze of curious rooms. The often lovely furnishings are eclectic (French, English, and Islamic).

MOSQUE OF SULTAN HASSAN: *(Walking back toward the entrance to Ibn Tulun Mosque, take the right fork in the small square in front that will follow the mosque wall north. This narrow street soon—about 75 yards—meets a larger one that crosses it. This is Shari el Saliba. Turn right and follow this street toward the square* *in front of the Citadel—Salah el Din Square. Just before reaching the square, you pass a marble fountain and two mosques facing each other on opposite sides of the street (built by Emir Sheikhum of the 14th century). Here the street continues but its name changes to Shari Sheikhum. A little farther—on the right—is a group of old houses; then comes the large square of Salah el-Din. The Citadel is ahead. On the left side of the square are four mosques. The first is your goal—the mosque of Sultan Hassan. You will have to cover your shoes with slippers provided by the caretakers for a nominal fee. The mosque is closed to visitors during prayer times, off and on from noon to 4 p.m.)*

If you see only one mosque in Cairo, this should be the one. It contains the characteristic features of all mosques, but with an elegance that many lack. Sadly, it needs much restoration. Your imagination must make the walls splendid again.

Outside, it may seem like a fort (which it was in times of unrest), but the intricate cornice and pinnacles balance this mass. The entrance (on the far side, on Shari el Kalaa) is monumental, 100 feet to the half-dome above. The minaret is the tallest in Cairo. Through a vestibule, then down steps to an angled corridor, you enter the court. Small compared with Ibn Tulun's mosque, it is 100 feet square. Off from each of the sides run four halls with lofty barrel-vaulted ceilings. The rooms formed by the halls each held a *madrassa* (school), now ruined. The hall opposite from the entrance is as large as most mosques; it contains the *mahrib* with an elaborate inscribed Kuftic frieze all around. In the rear *mahrib* wall a fine door inlaid with gold, silver, and bronze leads to the mausoleum of the builder—the Mamluk, Sultan Hassan—the earliest mausoleum in a mosque. In the early days of Islam there was a prejudice against conspicuous tombs. The dome is impressively large to make the severe simplicity of the sarcophagus more dramatic. Sultan Hassan, assassinated before his mosque was finished, never rested in the mausoleum. The workmen laid their tools down forever on that day.

Sultan Hassan's mosque is stone, in contrast to the brick mosque of Ibn Tulun. The structure, grown more complex, somehow fits together in a balanced whole. The mosque next door, designed on the model of this one, fails miserably; the difference is called art.

THE CITADEL: *(On Salah el-Din Square.)* The original fort, built by Saladin, began in 1176 with stones taken (it is said) from the small pyramids at Giza. Nothing much remains of the original structure except the wall at the back and a few towers inside where visitors may not go. Still, it captures the feel of a medieval fortress (it is a fortress in a sense today, since it serves mainly as a barracks for troops). Even murders happened here. On March 1, 1811, Muhammad Ali stabbed the pasha and his relatives (near the place where you entered), for they stood in the way of his ambition.

The ramparts provide a splendid view of Cairo and time to think of the mosque. Muhammad Ali wanted it to be magnificent, but the alabaster walls were poor quality stone. He built it high, above all the other mosques in the city, because he wanted to outshine them—yet he hired a non-Muslim, a Greek who lacked the proper understanding. Maybe so much gilt is simply out of place and eyes get no rest, but the depths of inappropriateness are reached by the French clock tower, donated by King Louis-Philippe. If the story is true that Muhammad Ali traded it for the obelisk now in the Place de la Concorde in Paris, that surely ranks among the worst trades in history.

KHAN KALILI BAZAAR: *(If you take a cab, pronounce* Khan *as though it were "cane" and watch for overcharging. The distance is less than a mile from the Hilton Hotel area, but drivers have been known to wind through streets for over an hour, as though it were miles away. If you wish to walk, follow the directions to the Islamic Museum. The museum sits in an angle where two large streets meet. Take the larger street, the one on the right—Shari Port Said—north, which is downstream. In 250 yards where Shari el Azhar crosses, go right. In about 150 yards the road forks, sending out a smaller street on the right. The smaller branch leads to el Azhar Mosque in two short blocks. The larger left fork, after two short blocks, leads you to* *a large mosque on the left—the Mosque of Hussein. Head for it because Khan Kalili lies on its left.)*

The oldest and busiest bazaar in Cairo was founded in 1400 as an import depot where caravans could unload. It began as a collection of warehouses, but sales shops soon sprang up to satisfy the desires of visiting camel drivers. The market, not as exotic now as the souks in Fez, Marakesh, or Istanbul, does quite nicely falling short of those. Just walk. It is impossible to describe a route through the maze of streets that were once winding animal paths. Original tents became permanent small shops which no one in the intervening years could move to make modern streets. In a souk, each type of business groups together in a single area: perfumes in one area, jewelry in another, rugs and brasswork in others still. (Though the main street lately has become quite a mixture.) You must keep one eye and one ear attentive while you walk—look out for the carts that hurl by and listen for the shout *khali bellak,* which means roughly, "watch your back."

Many of the goods are rather shoddy, but prices are reasonable by our standards. You can buy kaftans *(gallabiyahs)* here, but Luxor eases the chaos at no extra cost. Some shops are obviously designed for tourists, usually with higher prices. Try to go in at least one shop deep inside the bazaar (those near the entrance are like places in America) if for no other reason than to experience the complex ceremony of gentle bargaining, superb salesmanship, and tea. Most of the "antiques" are fakes (see "Shopping" in Chapter 1). Look for the colorful cardboard calendars sold along the street for 50 pt. or less; there are no nicer, more inexpensive, souvenirs.

EL AZHAR MOSQUE: *(See directions for Khan Kalili Bazaar, above.)* This is agreed to be the most important of Fatimid monuments. Begun in A.D. 970 and extensively remodeled over the years, it is still a living, intricate mosque. Built to combine religion with education, it became the heart of the greatest university of the Middle Ages.

Elaborate polychrome (Persian) doorways lead through a vestibule to the oldest part of the mosque, a court smaller than those in the mosques described earlier. Ahead is a large prayer room filled with eight rows of arches standing on various types of columns collected from earlier buildings in Cairo. In the center, a long hall leads to two *mahribs*. Halfway down is the older, Fatimid (probably 12th century) *mahrib*, preceding the new 18th-century one. Off the vestibule (to the left as you leave) is a small *madrassa* (school) with a lovely *mahrib* of its own. Watch for the three minarets outside—the most graceful in Cairo.

OLD EL MUIZZ STREET: *(Follow the route to Khan Kalili. At the place where Shari el Azhar split, where one fork leads to el Azhar Mosque, the other to the bazaar, turn left onto Shari el Muizz— there is a fountain and a pedestrian overpass where you make the turn. By taxi, tell the driver you want the intersection of Shari el Muizz lidin Allah and Shari Gawhar el Kaid ["Kah-eat"].)*

If an entire city has one concentrated essence, Cairo's can be found along this half-mile stretch of street. Bustling, overcrowded, filled with beggars, schoolchildren, and businessmen, the street is littered with rubbish and bordered by ancient gateways, ornate house facades, marvelous *madrassas*, mosques, and the gates of an 11th-century city.

The first lane on the right is one entrance to Khan Kalili. Farther on the right stands the 18th-century mausoleum of Sultan Ayyub with a lovely doorway. Then you pass three fine buildings on your left, side by side. The *madrassa* and mausoleum of Sultan Kalaoun from the late 13th century come first. Especially fine are the doorway leading from the *madrassa* to the mausoleum, and also the tomb chamber and the *mahrib* inside the mausoleum. Next door, the *madrassa* built by Kalaoun's son has a lovely stucco *mahrib* inside and an unusual porch outside. The porch—pure Gothic—was stolen from a Crusader church in Palestine. A slightly later *madrassa* follows, also with a fine but grimy doorway and doors.

Down the lane on the right is the facade of a 14th-century palace, under restoration inside. The center of the street boasts a graceful 18th-century public fountain, above which stood a small elementary school. Try the view of the teeming street from the terrace on the upper level of the fountain. Continuing on, you will soon see the facade of a truly old mosque on the right—el Akmar Mosque from 1125. The street then widens into a square (where in May there is an onion and garlic market) surrounded by crenellated walls—defense against a Turkish attack that never came. Adjacent to these 11th-century fortress walls stood an even older mosque. Now ruined, its two, massive, early minarets still stand. On either side rest the ancient fortified gates (*babs*) to the city; enter on your left through the Gate of Conquests to the parapet walls leading to the Gate of Victory on the right. You may see indistinct hieroglyphs on some of the rampart stones.

THE BLUE MOSQUE: *(Follow the directions to el Muizz Street above, this time turn right onto el Muizz. The same taxi destination mentioned above.)*

Now follow the other half of el Muizz Street to slightly later buildings. The walk covers about one mile of varied sights. On the right side, as el Muizz Street begins, is the *madrassa/* mosque of el Ghuri (early 1500s), with its imposing minaret. Walk across the street to this builder's lovely mausoleum. Proceed to a teeming market. From the left runs Shari Kushkadam; you may enter the 17th-century house of Gamal el Din ez Zahabi here. Turn back to Shari el Muizz and come in 300 yards to Bab Zuwaila, the only surviving southern gate from the old fortification of Cairo. You may notice the offerings nailed to the gate doors; a holy man once lived here. (Nearby an ancient Christian enclave dates from the 9th century. Only with a guide can you manage the maze of streets.) By the gate on the right side of the street—opposite a fountain—is the mosque of Sultan el Muayyid with a remarkable bronze door ("borrowed" from the older mosque of Sultan Hassan). Beyond the gate, look for the covered souk, a market arcade. Artisans make colorful patchwork tents used for marriages and funerals.

Past the gate turn left along the large street, Darb el Ahmar. By the fork 100 yards farther is a charming mosque built by Kigmas el Ishaki. Continue by the right side of this mosque, where the street becomes Shari el Tabbana, until you reach the second mosque on the right with a lovely doorway and courtyard in front. Constructed for el Mardani in the 14th century, the mosque contains a rich *mahrib* inside. Three hundred yards ahead waits the lovely Blue Mosque. Cross the X-shaped intersection and continue in the same direction (though the street becomes Shari Bab el Wazir) until you reach the Blue Mosque, on the left side of the street beside a smaller mosque farther along. Built by Aksunkir, the mosque receives its name from the color inside: walls are tiled in lovely shades of blue with plant designs.

THE TOMBS OF THE "CALIFS" CEMETERY: *(Take a taxi— it is too easy to lose your way walking—to the Tombs of the Caliphs to Sultan Barkuk's mausoleum. If the driver looks blank at these instructions, try "Kait Bay"—another name for the cemetery.)* Although we expect only the dead in a cemetery, Cairo's population problem leads to strange combinations—mobs of people inhabiting acres of otherwise serene mausoleums. The architecture is well worth the visit, but let one of those who approaches you be your guide. You will stumble through the maze by yourself. At the very least, make sure you see the mausoleums of Sultan Barkuk, with its elegant court; of Kait Bay, with its grace; and of Sultan Bar Bay, less lovely but with limestonelike filigree on the dome. The lovely sarcophagi are empty; Muslims bury the deceased directly in the ground or in a vault.

THE SIGHTS OF JUDEO-CHRISTIAN CAIRO

The oldest part of Cairo contains the most interesting Judeo-Christian sights. A Roman fortress provided the foundation for the original town. "Old Cairo," less than a quarter-mile square, lies just opposite from the southern tip of Roda Island. A maze of tiny streets, it is small enough that you will not be far from your destination even if you get lost. Because the few sights attract many visitors, most of the local people know exactly where you are aiming for, and they will keep you on the proper track.

You reach Old Cairo by walking along the Nile Corniche for about a mile and a quarter upstream from the Hilton Hotel. Turn left away from the river. On the street beyond the trolley station, Shari Mari Giris, is the Coptic Museum, famed for its textiles and housing art treasures from Christian Egypt. Three lovely Christian churches are just north. Only one synagogue remains, but it is inspiring for its great age and its historical associations.

THE COPTIC MUSEUM: *(On Shari Mari Giris, directly opposite the trolley station. Open 9 a.m. to 4 p.m.; closes at 1 p.m. in summer. Admission is 50 pt.)* Decorated with fine pieces of wood and furnishings from old Coptic houses, the buildings that form the Coptic Museum are themselves antique. It is a wonderful museum spotted with little gardens for quiet rest.

The ground floor is replete with carved stone—capitals of columns, friezes, niches, statues, and tombstones. Note the frescoes in room #7. The second floor displays mainly textiles, of wondrous variety and of quality seldom equalled. Paintings and ivory fill room #13, while room #14 contains wood carvings; #15 and #16 exhibit jewelry, much of which hearkens to ancient Egyptian motifs. Don't miss the manuscripts in room #17. Room #17 also contains some ceramics and glass, neither of which is exceptional. In its own different style, this museum equals the Islamic Museum; the setting is so right, so peaceful.

COPTIC CHURCHES: Directly behind the Coptic Museum, within the museum's garden, you'll find the entrance to **el Mallaka** (Church of the Virgin). It is called the Hanging Church because it is suspended between two bastions of old, Roman, fortified wall.

After leaving el Mallaka, turn right (downstream) to the second Roman tower. To the right of the tower you'll find **Abu Sargah** (St. Sergius). This church, begun in the 5th century, expanded with additions in the 10th and 11th centuries. Tradition claims that the Holy Family once rested here while in Egypt. The standard Coptic plan of the church includes a basilica with three domes over the sanctuary at the far end. Notice that there are no chairs (see Chapter 4). A lovely, carved wooden iconostasis (partition) inlaid with ivory icons separates the sanctuary from the congregation.

From Abu Sargah, walk right to the first intersection; on your left is **Santa Barbara,** one of the finest and among the largest of all the Coptic churches. The plan is the same as Abu Sargah, but the existing parts are older. Keep an eye out for the fine marble work (notice the steps) and some fine icons and frames.

BEN EZRA SYNAGOGUE: *(On the opposite side of the intersection from the Church of Santa Barbara.)* This, the oldest synagogue in Cairo, recently discontinued its services. Built in the 12th century by Abraham Ben Ezra—a great rabbi from Jerusalem—the synagogue claims that Moses prayed on this sanctified spot before leaving Egypt. Evidence that a much older synagogue existed here was discovered buried on the grounds—a Torah from 587 B.C. If the rabbi is present, he will proudly show you this priceless work written on gazelle skin.

AMENITIES

COMING AND GOING: CAIRO AIRPORT

Your first adventure in Egypt is negotiating the Cairo airport. You step from your flying cocoon into Eastern chaos: exotic people spin in all directions. No one looks official except soldiers with ominous guns. Signs are unreadable—beautifully penned scribbles; speech is incomprehensible—a babble of pitches. You stand feeling very small and wholly out of place, lost in the cavernous terminal.

Most people call this helpless time their worst moment in Egypt. Treat it like a dizzy spell. Stop, take a deep breath, and get your bearings. Soon things begin to sort themselves into understandable forms. A flow becomes discernible in the only direction it can go, for you are at the end of the terminal building. Go with the crowd, and feel free to ask the nearest passerby for help. The line between the official and the unofficial is drawn differently in Egypt; anyone, however casual his dress, is as likely to assist you as anyone else. He will probably take you under his wing with grace and smiles or search out another person who will.

If you are on a tour, wait for your leader to reach you; if you are on your own, this next section is for you.

Arriving: First find your luggage, then follow the crowd. The main terminal building will stretch ahead of you after a left turn from the arrival area. You will face a row of booths, usually preceded by lines, where passports and visas are checked. If you want duty-free cigarettes and liquor from the shop along the left-hand wall, stop before going through these booths. Any form of currency is accepted. Most customs inspectors speak enough English to ease customs formalities. After your passport is stamped, the terminal still waits for you; you have to walk to the far end for transportation, but officially you are now in Egypt.

Leave the terminal from the exit marked "International Arrivals." Find the taxis and limousines waiting outside, along with a jostling crowd eager to hire them. The Misr limousines fix prices at about LE 4 to central Cairo, LE 5 to Giza. Taxi drivers often "forget" to turn on their meters, which will mean an expensive charge or a long argument; so negotiate a price for your destination before getting in, using the limousine rates as your bargaining chip. You may save LE 1 or 50 pt. under the price of the limousine for your effort. Figure on an hour to Cairo, unless you travel at night.

Departing: By your return visit to the Cairo airport, what seemed shockingly unfamiliar will seem orderly and sedate—just Cairo people in Cairo clothing in Cairo crowds. Enter from the end where you left on your arrival. The check-in counters face you and are clearly labeled "Egyptair" for inter-Egypt flights (to the far left) or "TWA," "Air Maroc," "Pakistan Airlines," etc., for departures from Egypt, in lines moving right. One thing you must not forget when finally leaving Egypt is to keep LE 3 in Egyptian currency—this, the exit tax, must be paid in Egyptian pounds.

CAIRO TRANSPORTATION

When a Cairo bus goes by with twice the complement of passengers it was designed to carry, draped from windows and riding on bumpers, you will probably decide that another form of transportation would better suit you. The confused mass of laneless traffic should remove any ideas about driving a rented car. Taxis and your own feet are the best forms of transportation.

Cairo taxis have meters, and they continue to pick up passengers until they are filled. However, when *you* hire a taxi, it will not pick up extra passengers, and the meter will not be turned on. Things work differently for non-Egyptians. The driver, naturally, expects to make at least as much from your one fare as he would from having the car full. How much the fare will be, since the meter is off, is anyone's guess. If you let the driver do the estimating, he will aim high. If you wait to discuss money matters until the ride is over, he will have all the power. State your destination and settle on the fare before getting in. The driver expects it. This is a bargaining situation. For destinations described in this chapter, we have indicated the approximate taxi fare; you may have to pay more or less, depending on your bargaining skill. Tipping is not a rule in Egypt. The driver may expect some tip from a non-Egyptian, but the promise of a tip (say, 10%) can be used as part of the bargaining. A driver will be happy to agree to wait for hours while you take in the sights and then meet you when you are ready to continue. He makes more, or at least works less, with you than with Cairenes. Even so, the fares are extremely low—LE 5 to LE 10 buys the use of a cab for half a day or more.

To hire a taxi, you must find one; that will be your greatest problem. Those on the street usually have passengers already. For the best odds, look at a hotel or beside any favorite tourist attraction. The more empty taxis there are, the stronger your bargaining position.

HOTELS

Cairo has many fine hotels, also many tourists. Right now the two balance better than they did a few years ago because visitors who used to come in quantity from other Middle Eastern countries stopped when Egypt began to pursue peace with Israel. For as long as the Arab boycott lasts, American and European visitors have the opportunity of choosing a hotel, rather than the necessity of taking whatever is available. Try for the downtown area, convenient for sights, or else try the quiet of Giza, convenient for excursions and just 25 minutes away from downtown. Our list covers the better downtown hotels, followed by two hotels in Giza.

Nile Hilton. *Deluxe.* (The Nile Corniche and el Tahrir Square.) No hotel is more central—on the Nile, Tahrir Square in back, one block from the Museum of Antiquities. Bustling, opulent, an American oasis in which Egyptians love to hold weddings, this is an easy first hotel for us foreigners. Clean and efficiently, if impersonally, managed. Dining rooms are grand; although food is good, we find it expensive; free views over Cairo. This is the most heavily booked hotel in Egypt. Singles start at LE 32, doubles start at LE 35.

Cairo Sheraton. *Deluxe.* (El Galaa Square, on the west bank of the Nile opposite the Nile Hilton.) Comparable in every way to the Hilton except for being the width of the Nile less convenient in location. We think the Aladdin restaurant offers the best hotel food in the city (for about LE 40 for two). A single room costs LE 32, a double room will be LE 35 and up.

Hotel Meridien-LeCaire. *Deluxe.* (On the north tip of Roda Island, in the Nile.) A few blocks less convenient than other hotels, it offers grand views and a special feeling because of the island location. At least as attractive and clean as the American-run hotels. In our view, the food at this French-owned hotel is better than most, and the Kasr el Rachid restaurant serves perhaps the best Middle Eastern food in Cairo (about LE 20 for two). The single rooms rent for LE 30, double rooms cost LE 33.

Shepheard's Hotel. *Deluxe.* (The Nile Corniche, two blocks south of the Hilton.) This hotel takes its name from, and models its decor after, an earlier Victorian institution in Cairo which was burned during the revolution of 1952. Instead of instant charm, what happened was instant old. We rank Shepheard's as a good class below the other deluxe hotels and musty-dusty. But the service is willing, the location is good, and tea in the lobby is a 19th-century experience. The food does not earn our praise. Singles cost LE 25, doubles go for LE 28. Egyptian Hotels Company.

El Nil Hotel. *First Class.* (The Nile Corniche and Ahmed Ragheb Street, two blocks south of Shepheard's.) As we see it, a distance separates deluxe from first class, a gap of vinyl, of appliances that do not always function, and of furniture that shows repairs, not to mention dust. There is also a distance of price. Singles cost LE 14, doubles cost LE 15. Egyptian Hotels Company.

Cleopatra Palace Hotel. *First Class.* (No. 2 Shari el Bustair, one block east of the Museum of Antiquities and to the north side of Tahrir Square.) We rate this a touch better than the el Nil, but the location is too good—noisy. Singles rent for LE 18, doubles cost LE 19. Egyptian Hotels Company.

The President Hotel. *First Class.* (No. 22 Shari Taha Hussein, in Zamalek.) This hotel stretches the desire for convenient location, but it offers the quiet of a middle-class residential area at the north end of the large Gezira Island. The hotel is modern and clean. Single cost LE 15.5–17, doubles cost LE 21–23.

Hotel Concorde. *First Class.* (No. 146 Tahrir Street, in the Dukki—west of the end of Gezira Island.) Closer than the foregoing hotel to the center of sights, with rooms as modern. Single rooms cost LE 17, doubles cost LE 18.50.

Hotel Tonsi. *Second Class.* (No. 143 Tahrir Street, in Dukki, across from the Hotel Concorde.) An older hotel, but with newly renovated rooms which soon will raise its category and prices. The layout is a little peculiar: only the 1st, 2nd, 16th, and 17th floors of the building belong to the hotel. Prices for singles will be about LE 17; nice doubles start at LE 20.

The Garden City House. *Fourth Class.* (No. 23 Kamal el Din Salah Street, the south end of the Hilton.) First-class location for those whose budgets allow few such luxuries. This hotel has a loyal following which keeps it full. Even the food is good. Write several months ahead for reservations. A single with bath costs LE 5, a double with bath costs from LE 8.

Mena House Oberoi. *First Class.* (End of Pyramids Road in Giza.) Originally constructed so the Empress Eugenie would have a place to stay during the festivities marking the opening of the Suez Canal, it is now entirely remodeled inside and has added blocks of new rooms around the garden. Rooms are larger in the original building than those in the garden quadrangle and you can see the majestic pyramids from the windows. Public areas look Moorish-modern, the way one expects a hotel to look in Cairo, though few hotels actually carry it off. To be sure, we saw problems with the cell-like garden rooms, with untrained and uncaring staff, and with boring food (the Indian dishes are exceptions), but such mundane matters hardly detract from the beauty of the hotel and its splendid neighbors—the pyramids. Singles in the garden rent for LE 33, doubles for LE 36; for rooms in the original building, add LE 7 and LE 8. Oberoi International Hotels.

Hotel Jolie Ville. *Deluxe.* (The Alexandria Road, one mile left of the Mena House, in Giza.) Food here, we think, is better than at the Mena House, and the Jolie Ville shares the Giza quiet, but to be a mile from the pyramids is not like being next door. Rooms, in prefabricated rows spread around a garden, are new but not altogether solid. Single rooms cost LE 20, double rooms go for LE 22. Movenpick Group Hotels.

RESTAURANTS

For hotel cuisine, the **Sheraton's Aladdin Restaurant** (at LE 40 for two) has the best reputation, challenged by the evening buffets at the **Meridien's Kasr el Rachid Restaurant** (for about half the price). The **Hilton** may be more posh (at posh prices). The **Mena House al Rubayyat Restaurant** (about LE 25 for two) does Indian dishes quite well. Otherwise, hotels mainly serve vaguely conventional food. Exceptions are the Hilton's and the Sheraton's Italian restaurants and a fine French restaurant in the **Meridien's Palm d'Or** (LE 40, at least). All deluxe hotel specialty restaurants require reservations, as they are popular with Cairenes as well as foreigners.

Cairenes, however, are not generally in the habit of dining out. Cairo has no luxury restaurants outside of hotels. What Cairo offers instead are many medium- to low-priced opportunities to sample Egyptian culinary talents. The following suggestions are arranged by style of food.

Medium-priced restaurants will run LE 6 to 7 per person; inexpensive restaurants will be substantially less. Twelve percent for service will already be included on your bill, so a five percent extra gratuity is plenty. None of these restaurants require a trip out of the center of town, except those in Giza.

DOWNTOWN RESTAURANTS: For Continental food, the four best restaurants lie within a short block of each other, near the square north of el Tahrir, called Midan Talaat Harb. From the Museum of Antiquities walk due east on the street called Kasr el Nil. At #4 stands the **Arabesque Restaurant**—new and perhaps the best of this group, though it pushes past medium priced to LE 30 for two. **Caroll's Restaurant** is at #12, costs half as much, and is extremely popular; reservations are necessary. The American Express office is on the opposite side of the street and just past it is an alley containing the **Estoril Restaurant,** genteel but faded, with hearty "specials" at slightly less cost than the foregoing restaurants. **Groppi-Cafe and Restaurant** is in the square of Talaat Harb. Go, it is an institution. Try ice cream and pastries for snacks in the cafe or go to the restaurant part next door for lunch or dinner, and do not forget the soup.

Middle Eastern restaurants are spread around town. The most convenient kebab place is **Coin Kabab.** Continue on Kasr el Nil past Midan Talaat Harb to a passage beside #28. This restaurant is through the passage. Kebab restaurants we like better, however, are a mile away. Take a taxi north to **el Hati Restaurant** at #8 Midan Halin for the best. You will like the atmosphere, anything you order, and the inexpensive prices. Also good is **Abu Shakra Restaurant** one mile south of Tahrir Square. It is located at #69 Shari Kasr el Aini, which places it on the first main street back from the corniche near the intersection of the road leading to the bridge over Roda Island. Good Lebanese food at modest prices is served at **Sofar** at #21 Shari Adly, four short blocks north of Midan Talaat Harb.

Varied and very inexpensive Egyptian food exists in the area of el Tahrir Square. **El Domiati** is best, in the Midan el Falaki, the square east of Tahrir on Shari Tahrir. **Fataran el Tahrir** at #166 Shari Tahrir (one block east of the square) is the best place for *fiteer* pastry stuffed with cheese, meat, or sweets, as you elect. **Filfilia,** on Shari Huda Sharawy (off Shari Talaat Harb just before the square), is very popular.

For something different, try dining in an environment designed to appear Egyptian to tourists, in a houseboat in the Nile. The **Omar Khayyam Restaurant** offers limited choices of fairly good food, plus a Middle Eastern band and an intimate atmosphere. The boat is anchored of the eastern side of Gezira Island, and north of the Cairo Tower.

Desperate cravings for familiar foods can be satisfied, more or less, in Cairo. The best pizza is served at the **Baffo,** next door to the President Hotel on Taha Hussein in Zamalek. Hamburgers, of a sort, are served at **Wimpy's,** whose most convenient location is on Shari Talaat Harb near the Filfilia Restaurant. Yes, there is even Kentucky Fried Chicken, with all the ingredients imported, and on the road to the pyramids you will pass the familiar red-and-white design with the Colonel's face.

GIZA RESTAURANTS: Since even those who do not stay in Giza pass through on the way to the pyramids, dinner or lunch in Giza is of general interest. Giza boasts of several enjoyable restaurants. For grilled seafood, the medium-priced **Seahorse Restaurant,** just over the river in Giza, on the west bank of the Nile toward Maadi, is probably best. Start with *mezza*, assorted hot appetizers. Pigeon is an Egyptian delicacy and truly tasty. The **Casino des Pigeons** on the Nile in Giza obviously specializes in this dish, at moderate prices. Nearer the pyramids, is the well-known **Andrea Chicken Restaurant.** Watch the birds roast over wood on your way to seating in the rustic "barn." Andrea's is opposite the road to Sakkara, to the right from the Mena House. Look for the big painted chicken. **El Dar Restaurant,** on the same road, has Egyptian food at moderate prices served in an Arabian setting. **Stereo des Pyramids,** just west of the Mena House, has been recommended for both food and the view of the pyramids.

SHOPPING

Gold remains a good buy in Egypt. Workmanship is so inexpensive that precious metals are sold by their weight, with only a small surcharge to cover the manufacture. This means that bargaining is not as necessary as it would be for other articles. One nice purchase is a gold cartouche with your name inside in hieroglyphs. Gold products are sold in numerous small shops in **Khan Kalili** bazaar.

Hammered brass and copper, especially in the form of trays for end tables, are also good buys in Khan Kalili. Camel saddles in leather and wood are popular purchases from the bazaar, costing about LE 45.

Perfumes, incense, henna, and kohl are very inexpensive if bought in the spice market. The best shops are located in the market west of Khan Kalili, called the **Mouski.** Both Shari Mouski, which runs east out of the Opera Square, and Shari el Muizz, which runs along the north end of Khan Kalili, have scores of perfume shops.

Downtown, one can buy leather and cotton goods. On **Kasr el Nil,** which runs east from the Museum of Antiquities, shops sell one or the other of these products. The leather is not, in our opinion, the best quality, but copies of French and Italian handbags and shoes sell for less than half of what the originals cost. Fine Egyptian cotton done into linens are never cheap but are good buys for the quality. **Senouhi,** a fascinating shop, filled with jewelry—both antique and modern—tapestries, and a thousand curios is located on the fifth floor at #54 Abdul Khalek Sarwat, which crosses Shari Talaat Harb four streets north of Talaat Harb Midan.

If you are willing to travel 40 minutes for exciting shopping, hire a taxi to take you north of Giza to the village of **Kerdassa.** Here you will find tapestries and rugs as well as intricately embroidered antique bedouin dresses.

AT NIGHT

You can watch a Sound and Light show at the Giza Pyramids. Ignore the saccharine dialogue, but enjoy the opportunity to look at the lighted pyramids and Sphinx while wondering about people and projects from four millennia ago. The show starts at 7:30 p.m., but go early because seats are not reserved. Do the trip yourself by taxi and save compared to what tour companies charge. The show costs LE 2.

Cairo has casinos in the Hilton, Sheraton, and Meridien hotels, but only for foreigners—who must show passports and buy chips with foreign currency.

If you want belly dancing, each hotel has a cabaret. You will also see trained bird acts and magicians rejected by Ed Sullivan. For a more exotic show, but very touristy, take a cab to Sahara City beyond the Giza pyramids. Here you see whirling dervishes, dancing horses, and acrobats inside a tent. There is a minimum of LE 10 which covers dinner but not drinks. The show starts at 10 PM.

Do not expect eroticism from belly dancers. This is an art form that deserves appreciation for the virtuosity of muscle control, not for the dancer's shape or lack of clothing. In both of the latter regards, you would be in for large disappointments. Many of the dancers are hefty women, by our standards, and Egyptian law requires that a body stocking cover even the midriff.

A thousand discos have sprung up in Cairo, mostly lining the road to the pyramids, but we found them more noisy than exciting. Stick to hotel discos if in the dancing mood.

LEAVING CAIRO

TO ALEXANDRIA: A round-trip tour to Alexandria and back to Cairo that takes in the sights of Alexandria can be purchased from a travel company suggested by your hotel concierge for about LE 25. A hired car and driver will cost a little more but can carry several people at the price.

Alexandria is close enough to Cairo that flying takes as long or longer than the train, once travel to and from airports and check-in times are added in. The trains take just over two-and-a-half hours and are clean and comfortable. They leave Cairo at 8:00 a.m., 9:30 a.m., 11:20 a.m., 12:20 p.m., 2:00 p.m., 3:50 p.m., 5:50 p.m., and 7:00 p.m. A first-class ticket in an air-conditioned compartment costs LE 2.60; in second class, which is more crowded but is also air-conditioned, the ticket costs LE 1.50. The train station is eight blocks northeast of the Hilton Hotel at Midan Rameses.

TO LUXOR: Although trains are old and the trip is long (ten hours or more), the sleeper compartments are charming, and you can arrive in Luxor in the morning, saving one night in a hotel. Express trains leave at 7:30 a.m., 10:00 a.m., 7:00 p.m., and 7:35 p.m. First and second classes are both air-conditioned, but first class is private. A first-class sleeper costs LE 14.25, a second-class sleeper costs LE 8.40. Reservations should be made several days in advance. The train station is eight blocks northeast of the Hilton Hotel at Midan Rameses.

Planes leave for Luxor almost every hour, costing about LE 29. Check with your concierge for further information. Egyptair has offices in the Hilton Hotel, at #9 Shari Talaat Harb, at Midan Opera, and #6 Shari Adly.

TO HURGHADAH: Planes leave every day at 7:00 a.m. and land 50 minutes later. The cost is LE 31.50. (See Chapter 14 for information about Hurghadah.)

TO MINYA: Minya is a drive of less than four hours by hired car and driver, and should cost in the LE 20 neighborhood. By express train, the trip takes as long and costs LE 6 for first class.

TO ABU SIMBEL: Flying is the only way. Planes leave frequently—almost every hour. These are the same planes that go to Luxor and continue to Aswan before Abu Simbel. A ticket costs LE 57.

STEP PYRAMID AT SAKKARA, NEAR CAIRO. *Raised c. 2650 B.C. to provide eternal life for the pharaoh Zoser, mankind's first monumental stone structure overlooks two buildings in its ceremonial court of rejuvenation.* (Photo courtesy of Ira Meistrich)

PYRAMID AT MEIDUM, NEAR CAIRO. *An ancient catastrophy probably created this intriguing structure which was designed as the first pyramid with plane triangular sides. It sloped too acutely and collapsed in a landslide to form the mound of rubble at the base. What now stands is the interior from an earlier stage of construction—a partial step pyramid.* (Photo courtesy of Barbara Benton)

SECTION OF THE EAST WALL OF TOMB #2 AT BENI HASSAN, MIDDLE
EGYPT. *The top three rows depict unexpectedly lively looking wrestling
holds. For some reason hundreds of such contorting figures cover walls of
tombs at Beni Hassan, dating to the start of the second millennium* B.C.
*Rarely were figures drawn so lively elsewhere in ancient Egypt. In
contrast, stiff Egyptian figures in the lower rows display the traditional
"frontal" style—side silhouettes with shoulders turned toward the viewer.*
(From Beni Hasan by P. Newberry)

VALLEY OF THE KINGS, NEAR LUXOR. *Barely six acres in area, the valley is utterly barren. Here the most powerful pharaohs of ancient Egypt buried treasures beyond calculation. Due to the aridity of the valley, carvings in the tomb survive with paint still miraculously fresh; but the only treasure to be found was of the teen-aged pharaoh Tutankhamun.* (Photo courtesy of Ira Meistrich)

HATSHEPSUT'S TEMPLE AT DIER EL BAHRI, NEAR LUXOR. *Built to match the grandeur of a mountain backdrop, this unusual temple, among the most elegant of all buildings, was commissioned by a female pharaoh. Her ward and successor, the great Thothmoses III, so despised Hatshepsut that he erased her name and pictures throughout the temple.* (Photo courtesy of Nana Koch)

SCENE FROM THE SOUTHEAST WALL OF TOMB #55 IN THE VALLEY OF
THE NOBLES, NEAR LUXOR. *Ramose, mayor of Thebes and vizier of Egypt,
and his wife sit at a banquet. The above scene was never completed—left
unpainted, except for black outlines. Other walls were painted hurriedly to
save the time of carving; yet every detail is exquisite. Ramose commissioned
this tomb at the very peak of artistic excellence in ancient Egypt.* (Photo
courtesy of Ira Meistrich)

SCENE FROM THE CHAPEL OF OSIRIS IN THE TEMPLE OF SETI I AT ABYDOS, SOUTHERN EGYPT. *Pharaoh Seti I offers an idol of the goddess Maat, symbol or **order**, to the god Osiris (out of view). This temple preserves many of the finest reliefs from ancient times.* (From A History of Egypt by J. Breasted)

HALL OF COLUMNS IN DENDERAH TEMPLE, SOUTHERN EGYPT). *The massive columns of this well-preserved temple from the era of the Ptolemies are topped by capitals in the shape of a woman's face with cow-ears to represent Hat-hor, goddess of love and the celestial sky.* (Photo courtesy of Ira Meistrich)

The rightmost colossi of Rameses the Great from the Temple of Ra-Horakhty, Abu Simbel. *The small statues below and between Rameses' feet are larger than life-sized. Behind four such colossi, in what originally was a hill of solid stone, Rameses excavated an underground temple.* (Photo courtesy of Ira Meistrich)

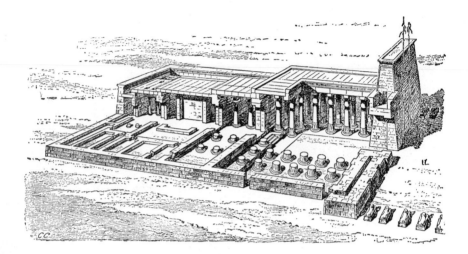

DRAWING OF AN IDEALIZED ANCIENT EGYPTIAN TEMPLE. *Half of the roof is cut away to show the three principal parts of ancient temples. After front pylons (right), an open court with columned sides forms the largest section of the temple, where commoners could worship. Steps lead up to a hall of columns supporting a high roof (usually much higher than shown by this drawing) for the nobility. The rear third of the temple, the Holy-of-Holies, is raised another step and carries a lower roof to create an atmosphere of dark intimacy for priests and pharaohs. Here, in the center, is the chapel of sacred boats for transporting the temple idol; behind is the sanctuary of the idol; surrounding rooms hold temple equipment. The temple would be called the "house" of the god whose statue resided within.* (From A History of Egypt by J. Breasted)

6.

Background for Middle Egypt

Two ancient dramas that took place in the middle section of Egypt draw visitors today. The earlier of the two events was Egypt's reawakening about 2000 B.C.—the Middle Kingdom—when civilization rose again from its own ashes like the Phoenix (a myth originally derived from ancient Egypt). Splendid tombs at Beni Hassan in Middle Egypt illustrate this era with the most vivid pictures that Egypt ever produced. The second drama encompassed the tragedy of history's first monotheist, the heretical pharaoh Akhenaten. He moved his court to the center of Egypt to find peace in which to adore his god. For a decade he did find peace, but those whom he loved died one by one, and then he died too. His successors destroyed the hated city of Akhenaten in Middle Egypt, cursing the spot. No one since has built upon this desecrated ground which, by history's perversity, makes this city the only one of its era that survives.

THE MIDDLE KINGDOM

We left the history of Egypt at the end of the Old Kingdom when the country had lost its central authority and dissolved into pieces, each controlled by local strong men. Although it took about 150 years for Egypt to collect herself again, when she did she was stronger than ever. Egypt needed strength, for as each century passed other civilizations grew as her competitors—Minoa, Babylon, and others less well known. At her best Egypt could stand against any country. She surpassed them all during the Middle Kingdom, Egypt's renaissance, a rebirth of power, art, science, and religion. But with competitors all around, a moment of weakness may be fatal. In Egypt such a moment ended the Middle Kingdom.

Like the European Renaissance, the Middle Kingdom in ancient Egypt grew out of a dark age. Prosperity and productivity, whether material or intellectual, leave signs. Dark ages are characterized by the absence of information left for history. During Egypt's First Intermediate Period great buildings were not raised, writing decreased, and extensive tombs were no longer prepared for the dead.

The ancient Egyptians believed in a single cause for this unhappy era and claimed in their writings that the times were desperate:

> When the Nile is in flood, no one plows, everyone says: "We do not know what may happen in the land."

> Lo, the women are dried up, none can conceive . . . because of the state of the land.

> Poor men have become possessors of treasure, even he who could not make himself a pair of sandals.

> The dead are buried in the Nile, the river is a tomb.

> Nobles lament while the poor rejoice.

> Dirt is everywhere, no clothes are white.

Barbarians have come to Egypt.
Really there are no people anywhere.

The problem, as the ancient Egyptians saw it, was that *maat* had been lost, the proper order of affairs had been replaced by disorder. Since the pharaoh was the guardian of *maat*, its defender and agent, if *maat* had been lost, then the pharaoh was not right. In ancient Egypt, this conclusion was a revolutionary idea that led in turn to an actual revolution.

The seeds of anarchy and then of revolution were sowed in the Old Kingdom by administrative decisions. To manage the country, pharaohs divided Egypt into 40 departments, called nomes. Each nome had a separate bureaucracy, headed by a nomarch who was responsible for collecting taxes, administering work projects, and conscripting troops for Egypt's army, if needed. Because originally pharaohs appointed nomarchs from their own family, since more males were produced in royal harems than could sit on one throne, loyalty to the pharaoh was initially familial. But blue blood did not always nourish administrative abilities and royal jealousies often erupted, so this practice soon ceased. Instead, pharaohs selected commoners of proven ability to administer each nome. Their loyalty was assured by their debt to the pharaoh who appointed them and by their fear of replacement.

The danger of this system lay in the fact that nomarchs were direct overseers of their area, while a pharaoh's power was only indirect. He had to deal through his nomarchs to acquire the goods or the troops he needed. These dangers surfaced when the Old Kingdom ended in a series of weak kings, just the circumstances under which nomarchs could increase their power. To satisfy their own needs, pharaohs had to offer concessions to the nomarchs. The favorite concession allowed the present nomarch to pass his office down to his son. Soon nomarchs formed a hereditary caste. Then one nomarch, in charge of an especially rich nome, seized the throne. By the force of his personality, he imposed some order on the country. But this change did not solve the more fundamental problems, and now the pharaoh was illegitimate.

Three times in its ancient history Egypt lacked cohesion—in the beginning, in the Second Intermediate Period, and in this, the First Intermediate Period. Each time a savior came out of the south to reunite the country. Perhaps southerners were more warlike by nature. Perhaps the constraints there of the narrow ribbon of fertile land promoted greater cohesion among its population. Proximity to the Sudan, just below southern Egypt, lent undeniable advantages too. Egypt traded more with the Sudan than with all other countries combined at this time, and the southern nomarchs controlled the commerce. These nomarchs had easy access to Sudanese troops bought with Egyptian wealth.

By conquest and alliances, one southern nome soon attracted all the power of the southern area—the nome of the scepter Waset. Its capital was a town formerly of no great political distinction but of great beauty in its setting—facing pastel mountains of infinite configurations across the Nile. Later the Greeks called the town Thebes. Its special god was among the very few in ancient Egypt associated with war, the fighter Montu. Waset (Thebes) would make its god proud.

To head the southern confederation, there came a warrior, Montuhotep, the second bearer of a name that meant "Montu is satisfied." The proximate cause of war, by now inevitable, was a struggle for possession of Abydos, the ancestral home of the first pharaoh, Menes. Before Montuhotep II gained control, the south already had attacked, won, and added Abydos to its collection of territories; but the pharaoh in Memphis tried to regain it while Montuhotep II governed the south. Montuhotep II defended Abydos successfully; then, having gathered an army for defense, turned it to attack. He marched north, never stopping until he reached the Delta, overthrowing the pharaoh on the way.

In 2040 B.C. Montuhotep II thus became the first pharaoh of a new age, the Middle Kingdom. He ruled for 51 years, 20 of those years as pharaoh of Egypt. He cleaned up the borders, reasserted Egyptian superiority in the Sudan, and generally made Egypt strong again. However, he did nothing to dissipate the potential dangers of the nomarch situation. Power remained dependent on the character of the pharaoh. After Montuhotep II died, his son, who was already middle-aged, ruled briefly and without distinction. The next pharaoh also lasted only a short while. Another turn of fortune was in the air.

All the glory of the Middle Kingdom, except for the honor of beginning it, came from a single family—the amazing Amunemhats. With the weakness of the fourth and last Montuhotep, opportunity presented itself for a man of ability. In this circumstance the vizier of Egypt, Amunemhat, gathered more power for himself than for his nominal lord.

Little is known of Amunemhat's family origins; only two facts are clear. The vizier's father, Senusert, possessed not one drop of royal blood, although his descendants would make his name famous. The family, it seems clear, came from the south. Their name means "Amun is foremost." Amun at that time was an unimportant god from a town two miles north of Thebes, called Karnak. While rising in power, this family elevated their favorite god, until both became first in Egypt.

The greater the pains taken to hide something, the more suspicious the concealed event looms. The Amunemhats took great pains to hide the steps that brought them to the throne. Was an assassination involved, or perhaps a putsch? All we know is that history was rewritten after the event. A document purporting to be from the Old Kingdom, but which clearly dates from these later times, foretells of a man called Ameny (the familiar form of the vizier's name) who would come to save Egypt. In advance of the actual writing, the prophecy came true. Amunemhat I began the mighty Dynasty XII, after the Montuhoteps of Dynasty XI. Amunemhat, no young man, spent all his time on the throne extinguishing rebellions. He made a son co-regent in case he should die; then he was assassinated. For the remainder of the dynasty, pharaohs alternated two names: each Amunemhat was succeeded by a Senusert. In most cases the reigns were long and successful. These pharaohs' work concentrated on the Sudan, where they sent in armies to gain territory. They constructed a series of eight colossal forts in the heart of the Sudan to guard their southern territories.

The greatest of the family were Senusert III and Amunemhat III. Much of the fortress construction was due to the former, and the latter earned fame for his work in civil engineering. Senusert III finally solved the problem of the nomarchs' autonomy. He decreed that the office henceforth would be filled through appointment, thus placing nomarchs under a pharaoh's control. He replaced all the nomarchs who questioned this decree; those remaining were beholden to him from then on. Amunemhat III constructed a 17-mile-long dam to break communication between the Nile and the large lake in the Faiyum. With the Nile no longer replenishing the lake's water, natural evaporation shrank the lake to free 17,000 new acres of fertile land.

When these two powerful monarchs died, the end of the dynasty and era came with astonishing rapidity. Amunemhat IV reigned for less than ten years, followed by a pharaoh who survived for less than four years; then the Middle Kingdom ended. The abruptness of the end suggests some evil doings, some mystery, but all that is known is the name of the final pharaoh, Sobek-neferu—and her sex.

The political theory of ancient Egypt required a male ruler, he who married the most royal woman. That a woman became pharaoh is evidence of a total lack of royal males. Even more, since Sobek-neferu was the sister of the last male pharaoh, probably there were no other royal females either. Otherwise, a princess would have married a commoner male to satisfy the rules of succession, and this commoner would have become pharaoh. Sobek-neferu's reign suggests a barren predecessor, that no one else had lived to carry on the line.

Although the Middle Kingdom lasted only two centuries, by far the shortest of the three great Egyptian "kingdoms," it was a Camelot time. During this era the greatest writing was produced—the language, Middle Egyptian, remained the model ever after for fine literature in Egypt. Indeed, all the arts flowered. Extraordinarily fine jewelry was crafted in sensitive styles that ranks with the best productions of any other time or place. Architecture enjoyed a renaissance which resulted in temples more elegant than those before or after. Few of these temples have survived, but one has been reconstructed from its blocks, dismantled by a later pharaoh to use for a massive pylon at Karnak. Archaeologists recently reconstructed the earlier temple. Compared to later temples, this one is small but elegant in shape and carving, with delicate hieroglyphs.

While the poor people of Egypt have always lived in mud huts, during the Middle Kingdom the higher classes lived in wonderful mansions. Houses were situated at the back of a rectangular enclosing wall to leave space in front for private gardens. In the garden, limestone pools held water cooled by the shade of a canopy or trees. Half of the first story of the house was an open columned portico, and the remainder was a living room; the second story held family rooms. Two ventilation scoops on the roof caught whatever breeze was available and funneled it through the house. Thousands of homes of this type were constructed during the Middle Kingdom for people of moderate means. The wealthy inhabited 20-room estates, amounting to small villages.

In the field of sculpture, the two dynasties of the Middle Kingdom divided into two stages. Dynasty XI, the Montuhoteps, made crude statues thick in torso and legs, with very swollen feet. These evolved into fine and accurate portraiture in Dynasty XII, though with the common element of large ears. The statues of Senusert III and Amunemhat III stand with the finest ancient art, especially since pharaonic sculpture rarely took the form of portraits. Senusert's statues show a homely man with large ears and a triangular face lined with care. The statues of Amunemhat III are equally fine, though most are sphinxes that unfortunately suggest the face of the Cowardly Lion from Oz. During this era a new form of statuary developed, called block statues. They represent a gowned man with knees drawn to his chest so the whole forms a cube from which only the head, hands, and feet emerge. The flat planes created space for long inscriptions.

Of the very little painting that survives, by far the best is in caves at Beni Hassan. Amid ordinary Egyptian paintings in these caves are some remarkable scenes. Through all the periods of Egyptian art, figures are stiff, almost always in one pose—striding, with shoulders turned toward the viewer, but head and legs in profile. The walls at Beni Hassan are covered with hundreds of contorted figures—acrobats, wrestlers, dancers—arranged in a series like cartoon strips. These were unique even for the Middle Kingdom.

Burial practices were partly innovative, partly decadent. Although pyramids continued, they were now constructed of adobe; stone was used only for an outer casing to present the appearance of greater solidity. Innovations, however, were made in the equipment of burials. Charming wooden models of soldiers, ships, houses, servants, and workshops, seldom produced in other periods, were characteristic of this era.

From the distance of historical perspective, the Middle Kingdom seems a minute long. To the ancient Egyptians, it was a time of grandeur, remembered for a thousand years after it ended.

AKHENATEN AND NEFERTITI

Once in ancient Egyptian history events paused in their march up and down. The drive of political forces was thrown out of gear by a man and wife who worshiped a single god. It was a strange time, an out-of-place time, called the Amarna Age.

Leading up to the Amarna Age was Dynasty XVIII of the New Kingdom, a time of heroes and riches when Egypt conquered the Middle East. After the Amarna Age, at least after its repercussions ended, came a period with emphasis on the colossal under Rameses the Great and his Dynasty XIX. In between, the armies stopped, the pharaoh showed himself as sensitive instead of as heroic, the official religion changed, old temples emptied, and the old capital fell quiet while Akhenaten built new temples and a capital for his new god. By Akhenaten's side—not behind him, nor in any degree smaller in scale—stood the immortal Nefertiti.

The single clear fact about Akhenaten is that he was different. He showed the public things that omnipotent rulers never display—in carvings children play on his lap; he caresses his wife; he mourns a daughter's death. Statues of Akhenaten shock—looking like bubble gum stretched at the ends with a blob for belly, with breasts (on a man) and voluptuous thighs. His brooding thin face is haunting. An arrow of a nose announces his eyes so long in advance that their slits become mysteries. Bulbous lips, chisel chin, swan neck—nothing in Egypt was ever like these statues. Surely he exaggerated his physiognomy to publicly display what others would have hidden.

He saw a different reality, a universe created and governed by a single god. As the first monotheist known to history, he was remarkable; but his was not a familiar monotheism. Not simply did he give himself over to a greater being; he combined worship with egomania. Modern thinkers consider this strange idea a step forward in intellectual history. They wonder if Hebrew tribes were in Egypt during this time and if they might have formed their religion from Akhenaten's ideas.

Certainly Akhenaten was different, but he was also Egyptian with roots anchored in Egypt's past. His father, Amunhotep III, was known principally for his love of luxury. More important for the understanding of Akhenaten, his father took the first steps during the New Kingdom to become a god. He constructed temples to himself, though these were not inside Egyptian territory. Further, he celebrated a long neglected Egyptian god, the Aten. The Sun, worshiped as far in the past as anything is known of Egypt, was given many names. Atum, "The Complete One," was favored in the Old Kingdom; Amun, "The Hidden One," took precedence in the New Kingdom. These refer to invisible aspects of the sun, its regularity and its power. Aten referred to the visible sun, the "Sun Disk."

Amunhotep III baptized his son—the one we call Akhenaten—Amunhotep. Since he was not the first in line for the throne, perhaps he received a different sort of education from the warfare and statecraft which a potential king would need. He may have been pointed toward the priesthood, which would explain his consuming religious interests. However, his elder brother, the heir apparent, died, moving Akhenaten to the head of the line. Behind him were sisters (at least two are known) and younger brothers named Tutankhamun and Smenkara who later ascended the throne.

When he reached 17, his father coronated him as co-pharaoh. A wife was needed. Ordinarily, for Egypt, he would have married a sister so he would have a royal wife. In this case, he married a commoner who was probably his mother's niece. Her name was Nefertiti, "A Beautiful One Comes."

As soon as he was coronated, Akhenaten began a temple dedicated to the god Aten behind the Temple of Amun at Karnak. Even in this first work, immediately after his kingship and marriage, the peculiar style of art appears which was unique to his reign. The new pharaoh and his wife are shown with pointed skulls and sinuously curved bodies, as attractive in his wife's case as it is surprising in the king's. The two are difficult to distinguish, except for different crowns.

The desire to honor his new god, the Aten, grew more insistent as the first years of his reign passed. It was not sufficient to build a temple for his god in the religious precinct devoted to Amun. Every other god had a home, a location in Egypt consecrated entirely to that god and his source—but not the Aten. The young king searched Egypt until he found a place suitable for a town, one which no other god had claimed. He found that place in the middle of Egypt and determined to raise a great city and temple there for the Aten. In person he laid out the boundaries for the city and construction began. Today the area is called Tell el Amarna, after a tribe of Bedouins who lived nearby when the first archaeologists arrived. In ancient times the city's name was Akhetaten, "The Horizon of the Aten." By the sixth year of his reign, enough of the city had been completed so Akhenaten could take residence with his queen and court. He had changed his name by this time, from Amunhotep (which labeled him as one who "Pleases Amun,") to Akhenaten (which meant either "The Beneficent Aten" or "The Spirit of Aten").

When completed five years later, the new city was among the largest metropolises then existing. It stretched for five miles, with quarters for workers and for upper classes, plus several palaces and temples. The palaces were splendid, and the temples were unlike all those for other gods. There was no roof, no mysterious inner sanctum, just a large courtyard filled with altars for offerings, all blindingly bright—thanks to the Aten's rays. For six years Akhenaten and Nefertiti enjoyed an idyl in this world they had created. Six daughters blessed the marriage. But outside, the world was changing, becoming increasingly violent as the Hittites disrupted the *Pax Egypti*. Allies sent a stream of letters begging for troops as every petty monarch began attacking his neighbors. Akhenaten took his family on chariot rides.

Sealed from the world in his own fairy tale, Akhenaten's only problems were family problems. The fairy tale turned into tragedy during, or soon after, the twelfth year of his reign when catastrophe followed catastrophe. First his father died, then his favorite daughter, still a child. And then Nefertiti died.

Only after these blows did Akhenaten display unequivocal signs of monotheism. He may have held such beliefs before— we do not know. Certainly he had claimed before that his Aten controlled all that happened in the world, and Akhenaten worshiped only him. But such a theory was not new. Egyptians as far back as the Old Kingdom claimed that Ra was all things, the one true god, though they tolerated other gods as alternatives for other people. So did Akhenaten before his tragedies. He was a henotheist before—believing in one god, but not condemning all other gods as false. Only later did he add the intolerance that distinguishes monotheism. For the remainder of his reign, he ordered his agents to destroy statues of other gods, to hack out the names of all gods except Aten, and to erase all plural endings from the word *god*. A person's name, if it included a word for a god, had the offending portion rubbed out. The word for mother happened also to be a goddess's name; the spelling was changed. His agents did not stop at Akhenaten's own father, Amunhotep III, who lost the first part of his name even in the tomb where he had so recently gone.

Five years of life remained for Akhenaten. To replace Nefertiti, he married his eldest daughter and produced another child. However, concerned about the succession, he made his brother Smenkara co-regent and gave him his own most recent wife. Then he married another of his daughters, we assume, because she too bore a daughter. This wife, Ankhesenpaaten, later married Tutankhamun. In the seventeenth year of the Amarna Age, the co-regent Smenkara died. This death may have been altogether too much for Akhenaten, because the pharaoh too died that same year. He was about 35 years old. His body has never been found, nor will it be, for his successors considered Akhenaten a vile criminal and obliterated all his traces. No ancient list of kings includes his name.

Akhenaten's legacy is a collection of enigmas. The strange art of his era has never been explained. Some people do claim that the grotesque statues accurately reflect Akhenaten's physiognomy. They point out that Akhenaten himself stated that his life was devoted to *maat,* whose meaning some Egyptologists extend to include artistic truth. But if Akhenaten actually possessed the body portrayed by his statues, it was abnormal and had a pathological cause. Thus arises the modern theory that Akhenaten suffered from a glandular disease, called Froelich's Syndrome, which creates similar abnormalities. This disease makes the victim impotent, however, and Akhenaten had six first-generation daughters and two second-generation children. It is doubtful, in any case, whether the word *maat* meant "truth" in the sense of a faithful copy.

Maat had to do with order and rules. Further, all the people in scenes with Akhenaten are shown with the same abnormal features. Rather, this was an art drawn by new principles. The chief artist of his reign credits Akhenaten as his teacher. Since Akhenaten concentrated on his religion to the exclusion of everything else, one would expect that this new art came in some way from the religion. How, is unknown.

The new religion was unusual for Egypt in having no idol; however, it had an iconography. The Aten was shown as a disk radiating straight lines that terminated in hands. Some of these hands hold the *ankh*—the cross with circle—to the noses of Akhenaten and Nefertiti. Egyptians believed in the "breath of life," that life originally entered through the nose. The *ankh* was also a hieroglyphic symbol that meant "life," so the symbolism was simply that life comes from the sun, the Aten. Akhenaten wrote a hymn that makes this point poetically.

> Thou appearest beautiful on the horizon of heaven,
> Thou living Aten, the beginning of life!
> When thou art risen on the eastern horizon,
> Thou hast filled every land with thy beauty.
> Thou art gracious, great, glistening, and high over
>   every land;
> Thy rays encompass the lands to the limits of all
>   that thou hast made:
> As thou art Ra, thou reachest to the ends of them;
> Thou subduest them for thy beloved son.
> Though thou art far away, thy rays are on earth;
> Though thou art in their faces, no one knows thy going.
>
> When thou settest in the western horizon,
> The land is in darkness, in the manner of death.
> They sleep in a room, with heads wrapped up,
> Nor sees one eye the other.
> All their goods which are under their heads might
>   be stolen,
> But they would not perceive it.
> Every lion is come forth from his den;
> All creeping things, they sting.
> Darkness is a shroud, and the earth is in stillness,
> For he who made them rests in his horizon.
>
> At daybreak, when thou arisest on the horizon,
> When thou shinest as the Aten by day,
> Thou drivest away the darkness and givest thy rays. . . .
> All beasts are content with their pasturage;
> Trees and plants are flourishing.
> The birds which fly from their nests,
> Their wings are stretched out in praise of thy *ka* [soul].
> All beasts spring upon their feet.

Whatever flies and alights,
They live when thou hast risen for them.
The ships are sailing north and south as well,
For every day is open at thy appearance.
The fish in the river dart before thy face;
Thy rays are in the midst of the great green sea.

This poem continues with the statement: "And there is no other that knows thee save thy son [Akhenaten], for thou hast made him well versed in thy plans and in thy strength." Perhaps only one god lived in heaven, but he had a special agent on earth.

Akhenaten was more than chief priest in his religion, he was the self-appointed god's son. Prayers were made to him and he received offerings. Many stelae were found in excavations with pictures of Akhenaten and Nefertiti, whose worship replaced the earlier worship of humanlike gods. One aspect of the new religion, often noted but seldom discussed, suggests some of the process by which the new religion may have evolved toward this complete monotheism. The mark of a pharaoh was the enclosure of his name in an oval cartouche; Akhenaten did the same for his god. This idea made sense, for it marked the Aten as special and superior, but it had not been done with other gods. Before, there had been many gods, yet never had there been more than one legitimate pharaoh (co-rulers are a complex case—Egyptians viewed each as sole ruler). If, then, the Aten were a kind of pharaoh, there could only be that one god—suppressing other gods would be the equivalent of removing pretenders to the throne. To view a god as a pharaoh would lead to appreciating his uniqueness, but the analogy had another direction as well. If god were a kind of pharaoh, the pharaoh must be a kind of god. He had been so in the Old Kingdom—"the son of the Sun"—but had not stood so tall after the turmoil of the First Intermediate Period. Akhenaten's father then began a cult for himself outside the borders of Egypt which Akhenaten brought home and made his. Successors destroyed the religion of Akhenaten but not that one principle—they too desired divinity.

7.

Minya: Middle Egypt

Most tourists skip the middle third of Egypt, leaping from Cairo to Luxor in a single bound. They do not know what they are missing. This section of Egypt is seldom included on tours, seldom pictured in brochures, and almost never covered by documentaries on Egypt. Naturally, people get the impression that hardly anything worthwhile exists in the middle third of the country. It is not true.

Middle Egypt does not have hotels suitable for groups, most of which travel first class. Thus, tour companies cannot offer trips here. A vicious circle results in which few visitors come, and no pressures exist for changing the situation by providing better amenities.

Such problems did not bother the ancient Egyptians. They lived in the middle of Egypt as well as in the Delta and the south, and left monuments here as worthy as those elsewhere near modern hotels. Near Cairo you can explore the Old Kingdom; in Luxor you can see the New Kingdom and view relics of later times on the way to Aswan. But for the best of the Middle Kingdom, a great and special period, go to

Middle Egypt. By skipping the middle of Egypt you miss the Middle Kingdom tombs at Beni Hassan and the most charming of all the later monuments, Tuna el Gebel, guaranteed to revise your appreciation of Ptolemaic art. Last, but most important, you would miss Tell el Amarna, the former capital of the heretical pharaoh Akhenaten (see Chapter 6). Now it is ruined, destroyed by his successor, but it is the only city of the living that survived in any way from very ancient times. These ruins emit a special aura because Akhenaten was perhaps the only ancient Egyptian whose personality has endured. People make pilgrimages to his city, so great was his charisma.

Still, Middle Egypt is not for everyone. Accommodations verge on the crude. Companies to serve tourists do not exist here; you must make your own arrangements. Whatever you desire can be done, but initiative is required. The climate here is agreed to be the worst in Egypt (see Chapter 1). Though winter temperatures almost never reach freezing, 40° is cold enough when your hotel room is unheated. You will have an opportunity to try on the clothes you brought to Egypt—all of them—if you hope to sleep. Summer brings the contrary problem. Temperatures climb to well over 100° in the shade, and shade is hard to find—which explains why hotel rooms are dark and night is eagerly awaited.

Our intent is not to dissuade you. Middle Egypt is a very special place we would love to share, but you deserve to know the problems before making a commitment. Do not come if you require comfort to enjoy your trip. Do come if you are an adventurer who seeks an Egypt unadulterated for tourists' sakes and ancient monuments unlike those available elsewhere. Our bet is that you will remember the Middle Egypt part of your trip more vividly than the rest.

THE SIGHTS NEAR MINYA

Sights are conveniently located so they can all be seen on day trips while staying in Minya, the only city with tourist hotels. Minya, a quiet town of about 100,000 people, is the capital of its province, modestly bustling with a small importance. Unselfconscious, it is too preoccupied to make itself attractive. The main street, crowded with stores and shoppers, displays religious articles with Christian themes. The population is predominantly Coptic—Egyptian Christians.

The three important sights—Beni Hassan, Tell el Amarna, and Tuna el Gebel—can be covered in two days. Tuna el Gebel can be included in the day you spend at either of the other two sights, depending on your schedule and endurance. Tell el Amarna, however, needs more time than does Beni Hassan; ideally it should have a day.

To visit these sights you must coordinate several sorts of transportation the day before through the local Director of the Ministry of Tourism in Minya (your hotel will put you in touch), who also arranges the opening of monuments. Tuna el Gebel is, like Minya, on the west bank of the Nile, and so can be reached by hired car. The other two sights are across the Nile; since there are no bridges for miles, you must cross the river by boat and then ride a donkey to Beni Hassan or a tractor-powered flatbed trailer for crossing the several miles of desert to Amarna.

TELL EL AMARNA

To get to Amarna you drive 25 miles south through Mellawi and then six miles more to the town of Dier Mawas. Turn left through this town to the river. A launch at the bank will take you across the Nile, almost a mile wide at this point. From the landing, a short walk brings you to the rest house where, one hopes, your transportation waits.

After Akhenaten died, he was so hated that later pharaohs razed his city. They wanted to remove all traces of the man they considered a heretic and worse—the man who tried to destroy their religion. It is not clear whether Horemheb, at the end of Dynasty XVIII, or, more likely, Rameses the Great, in the beginning of the next dynasty, did the razing. Whoever it may have been, he did a thorough job, knocking over every stone in the temples and hacking out the figures and titles of Akhenaten, Nefertiti, and their god from tombs. Overnight the city lost its population. Curses and a belief in evil spirits kept Egyptians away from the place for thousands of years thereafter. Not until the 18th century of our era did anyone move back, and then it was not Egyptians. Bedouins, of the el Amarna tribe, migrated here, built two tiny villages on the east bank and one on the west, and began farming. The modern name for the area comes from the name of this tribe and was wrongly applied by early excavators to the era of the ancient city. By now the name is too ingrained to change—the times and the art of Akhenaten are called "Amarna."

Be advised that these people—the Beni Amran—are determined people. Early excavators found four splendid painted floors buried under the debris of Akhenaten's palace. When these became great tourist attractions in the early part of the century, tourists often trampled the fields of the Beni Amran. One day the painted floors were found broken into pieces. The best parts were then removed to Cairo.

Children can be insistent in their begging if encouraged in the slightest. They may have a treat, however, when they meet the launch on the east bank. They sometimes offer small potsherds for sale. These are one exception to the rule that antiques offered for purchase will be fakes. In the reigns of Akhenaten and his father (and, perhaps, Tutankhamun for a while) a special pottery was produced with predominantly dusty-blue decoration in the form of stylized lotus leaves. Mounds of broken pieces from thousands of large wine and oil vessels still lie behind the ancient palace, where children root for fragments. (There is a fair chance, too, that Roman oil lamps, if offered, will be real as well.)

This ancient city is the best preserved for its age precisely because later generations did not live and build on the site. After the ancient destruction, only time added its erosions, but time has had 3330 years to work. With the exception of parts of the temples and small decorative elements in the palaces, all the building was in soft adobe. Not much survives, and nothing splendid. Wherever you see regular square or rectangular ridges of sand, there once was a building, reduced now to a foot or two of crumbled walls.

THE CITY: A strip of vegetation borders the Nile; then desert flows to a row of distant cliffs. The hills form a bay 12 miles long, two miles distant from the Nile in the center, curving closer to the river banks at the ends. The ancient city was situated in a long line along the river just where the desert begins—not closer or it would have occupied precious fertile land. It ran for five miles, only a few blocks wide. A thoroughfare, called the King's Road, connected one end to the other. This is now a dirt track.

The city had three sections, each separated by a dried stream bed. In the South City lived high government officials in mansions fronting the main thoroughfare. Here, too, was a peculiar temple with a lake inside and roofed kiosks for the queen and various princesses. Most official buildings were in the Center City. An immense palace with almost half a mile of frontage ran from the King's Road to the river. From this palace a covered walk spanned the road—with a window ("Window of Appearances") from which Akhenaten appeared in ceremonies—leading to a mansion for escape from official pressures. North of this mansion rose the Great Temple of the Aten, covering 200,000 square yards. Pieces of fallen granite columns still lie here and there. Government offices for foreign affairs, public works, and police also were on this west side of the King's Road, along with extensive storehouses both for feeding the populace and for religious offerings. At the north end of this central part of the city, German archaeologists uncovered the house of Thothmoses, the royal sculptor. They found busts of the royal family, discarded as useless when the city emptied. The Germans kept the immortal bust of Nefertiti despite later Egyptian protests. Half a mile farther north began the North suburb consisting of small houses for merchants beside the city port. Also here was the Northern Palace, a favorite resort for Nefertiti.

Isolated in the desert beyond the South City the workmen who dug tombs for high officials lived in a walled village patrolled by sentries. Evidence excavated here shows that common people continued the worship of their old gods even so near the house of the new Aten religion.

To see the city today, you must look closely to discern a faint trace of a house, a temple, or a palace. Walk and let your mind travel back to distant times of religious revolution. Listen for the murmur of 100,000 kilted men and simply gowned women who forgot their empire for a while in order to worship.

THE TOMBS: When he moved his court here, Akhenaten swore that he and his family would make their final rest in the Horizon of the Aten. He prepared a royal tomb in the bay of hills. Courtiers, those important enough to earn the right, also began their tombs. Eleven years later, Akhenaten and his city died. None of the tombs were finished or show evidence that they were used. (There is, however, a funeral scene of the death of the oldest princess in the royal tomb, and Nefertiti apparently died before Akhenaten. These two may have been buried in the royal tomb, though no remains were found.)

The royal tomb is through a wadi halfway in the semicircle of hills. Unfortunately, it has been closed to visitors for several years. However, tombs that may be visited are both north of this wadi and south. In these tombs you see more than just scenes of the new religion in the strange Amarna style; you see an act of history. You see genuine religious fervor in the monolithic theme of the Aten and his favorite family, the Akhenatens. You see the revenge of later generations who obliterated the family they hated—their names, their faces, and their god.

The decoration of these tombs is different from those of any other period. Instead of multiple vignettes, whole walls are devoted to a single scene. In other times, prominence was given to the owner of a tomb; his figure would be large and central. In Amarna tombs, Akhenaten and Nefertiti, with a daughter or two sometimes added, are the focus of events no matter who owned the tomb. When pictured, the owner appears as a small figure in a large scene. Even in iconography this principle of subservience to a greater being (or family) was followed.

The tombs begin with a large hall. Columns of rock left

standing help support the ceiling. Two or more chambers follow the first room, usually ending in a recess to hold a statue of the deceased with his wife. If sufficiently finished, a steep pit would lead to a lower chamber prepared for the body.

The best and largest tomb is that of Ay, father of Nefertiti and holder of numerous offices in Akhenaten's court. His is among the tombs in the southern hills, where Mahu's tomb is also worth seeing. In the northern group, a 15-minute ride away, are three tombs (#1, 4, and 6) also worth a visit. A flashlight is essential for these tombs, so deep that natural light cannot illuminate the carvings. A fall down one of the deep burial shafts would be dangerous indeed.

TOMB #25: AY: Ay's titles included Divine Father (father-in-law), Fan Bearer of the King, King's Secretary, King's Groom, Commander of Cavalry, Husband of the Royal Nurse.

He was important enough to have the largest of the nonroyal tombs at Amarna. Later he served as Tutankhamun's vizier, marrying his widow when Tutankhamun died, and then prepared another tomb in the Valley of the Kings. His tomb at Amarna was barely begun. A large hall was roughed out, enough to show that there would have been 24 thick papyrus columns. Only two sets of scenes were carved, but both are important.

The doorway to the tomb is flanked with scenes. On the left stands the royal family before an altar bathed in Aten's rays, which end in hands holding the ankh sign to their nostrils. Ay and his wife kneel below. On the right side of the entrance, Ay and his wife pray. The words carved above and beside are those of the famous Hymn to the Aten in its most complete version. Akhenaten wrote this most popular hymn to his god, it seems. Many scholars find strong similarities with Psalm 104 in the Bible, and they wonder.

Inside the massive room is one finished wall, the left one. It vividly depicts details of life in the city. The king, Nefertiti, and three daughters stand in the Window of Appearances. One daughter—Ankhesenpaaten, the future wife of Tutankhamun—strokes her mother's chin. The royal family presents gold necklaces and other gifts to reward their faithful servants—Ay and his wife. (The section of the wall with Ay on it is now in Cairo.) This wife appears to be Ay's second: she is not called the mother of Nefertiti although Ay is called her father. Above the honored couple charioteers bow, scribes (bent in homage) record the occasion, and lines of palace functionaries bow in respect. Behind Ay and his wife, servants dance their joy. Farther on the right the scene continues with subsequent events. Ay and his wife are congratulated by friends who admire the king's gifts. Sentries who cannot leave their station send boys to find out what great event causes so much excitement. Left, behind the Window of Appearances, is a plan of the palace which records details otherwise unknown. On three columns in this room, Ay and his wife adore the name of the Aten and the names of Akhenaten and Nefertiti.

TOMB #91: MAHU: We would call Mahu chief-of-police, for he commanded the garrison at Akhetaten. In his left doorway is an adoration scene similar to that in Ay's tomb. Below the royal couple and their daughter Meryaten (who married her father after Nefertiti died) is Mahu reciting the Hymn to the Aten. On the right, Mahu recites the hymn again.

Although scenes are preserved on all walls of the main room, some are only blocked out in parts. On the right wall by the entrance, Mahu displays his duties. He arranges provisions for his men, hears reports, tours outposts on his chariot, and brings prisoners to the vizier. On the right side wall, after a stele, and continuing on the rear wall, is a scene of Akhenaten and Nefertiti on a chariot visiting troops. Because Akhenaten initiated no wars, some Egyptologists claim he was a pacifist. Scenes such as this one, however, show that he did not disapprove of soldiers or their duties. Akhenaten may have been a man wholly consumed by his religion rather than a pacifist.

On the left, receding from the entrance, is a sketch of what would have been Akhenaten in his Window of Appearances rewarding Mahu. Mahu bows before a stele. Next comes a scene of rows of worshipers; Mahu is first in the lower row.

This scene continues on the rear wall with a plan of the Temple of Aten.

TOMB #1: HUYA: Huya combined two duties. He supervised the royal harem and functioned as some sort of envoy to Akhenaten's mother, Queen Tiy.

After the standard doorway scene of the tomb owner chanting the Hymn to the Aten come scenes on both front walls of a feast in honor of the dowager Queen Tiy. She came to Akhetaten in the twelfth year of her son's reign because her husband, the pharaoh Amunhotep III, had just died. On the right-hand wall Akhenaten conducts his mother by the hand to a small temple he built for both his parents. On the left-hand wall a coronation scene honors Akhenaten attaining sole possession of the throne. The king in a litter, followed by his retinue, observes emissaries from the major nations of the world who offer gifts to the new sovereign. On the rear walls is a Window of Appearances scene where Huya receives rewards for his faithful service. For unknown reasons, on the right of this rear door and below it, a sculptor named Yuti is portrayed in his studio.

The second chamber is bare but has a recess at the back that holds a crumbled statue of Huya. Around the recess are funeral banquet scenes; these, common in New Kingdom tombs, are found only in this one tomb during the Amarna period.

TOMB #4: MERI-RA: He was the high priest of the god Aten. This large tomb has scenes similar to those already described. What are special are the detailed representations of the palace and the temples of the city. These representations, done in the peculiar ancient Egyptian style, combine two perspectives in one picture. The facade of the building is shown as though you were facing it. Behind the facade, the rest of the building is shown as though you were seeing it from above. Yet human figures and objects always are shown from the side and never from overhead. Thus it takes some thinking to decipher Egyptian perspective.

TOMB #6: PANEHESY: He was the vizier of northern Egypt, and his tomb is similar to Meri-ra's. In early Christian days Copts used the tomb as a chapel, their torches darkening the walls.

TUNA EL GEBEL

This site is on the same side of the river as Minya. Drive south to Mellawi, about 25 miles. Turn right into and through Mellawi, and then across a bridge over a canal that runs parallel to the Nile. Turn right on the road just across the canal, going back in the direction of Minya. In five miles, just after the town of Ashmuneim, is a right turn that leads to Hermopolis. Continue past that turn for six miles more to a left turn that leads through fields, over another canal, and then to desert. Ahead you will see what looks like a farm with a fence. This is Tuna el Gebel. About the time it comes into view you are passing one of the 14 boundary markers erected by Akhenaten to define the limits of his city. The stele is to the right, up a hill, carved in a recess in the rocks.

Tuna el Gebel is the necropolis of the city of Hermopolis. Hermopolis, the capital of a nome, worshiped Thoth, the god of science and writing whose special creature was the ibis. Ibises no longer survive in Egypt, though they led a protected life in ancient times. Protected, that is, except for sacrifices to Thoth. At Tuna el Gebel, beneath a house formerly used by an excavating team from Chicago, is a subterranean maze where you can see tens of thousands of mummified ibises in tiny coffins.

Akhenaten built a temple to his god Aten at Hermopolis. Rameses and his father tore it down, using its blocks for temples to Thoth. Much later, when the Greeks came, they identified Thoth with their god Hermes (hence the name by which the ancient town is now known) and built temples and a lovely agora. If you have time and energy you might take an excursion to Hermopolis. Though none of the Egyptian buildings remain, the setting is lush and the agora has been reconstructed.

The gem of Hermopolis, however, is at Tuna el Gebel. Here

a Greek priest named Petosiris erected a delicate tomb in about 300 B.C. It cannot be missed, for it is not underground but rises as a tiny temple. Art historians are very interested in the carvings inside because while these depict standard Egyptian themes, they are drawn in accordance with Greek canon. Art degrees are not necessary to appreciate the gently carved forms, all in togas, painted in delicate pastels.

On the outside wall, Petosiris worships the gods of Hermopolis. In the vestibule, opposite offering scenes, craftsmen work at various trades. In between come pastoral country vignettes. Inside the chapel is the sycamore tree goddess offering life; Petosiris worships his deceased father; Petosiris sits with a brother before offering tables. Homage is given to various denizens of the underworld, including Osiris, then to various gods from above. The funeral is depicted. A pit in the center of the chapel descends to the tomb itself, now closed.

Farther up the grade after Petosiris' tomb stand several two-story buildings. The first is worth a stop. Up the stairs, you enter a small room housing the mummy of a young woman in a glass case. She is Isadora, who drowned in 120 B.C., deeply mourned by her father.

BENI HASSAN

Driving south from Minya, in 12 miles you reach Abu Gurkas. At the town center turn left toward the Nile; after crossing a canal you arrive at the shore. A small launch will ferry you across for 25 pt. On the far bank donkey drivers will fight for the chance to sell you a ride. You'll ride about a mile on top of dykes through the cultivation, then up a steep incline to a rest house. From here you must proceed on foot up an even steeper hill to the tombs near the top.

Here are the burial places for the nomarchs of the important nome of the oryx. During the First Intermediate Period and through two-thirds or more of the Middle Kingdom, a nomarch had freedom to run his state as he chose, hence grew powerful and rich. The tombs at Beni Hassan cover the last part of this era. They are large tombs, decorated with scenes that show the nomarch as a minor potentate. Tombs were carved entirely from the living rock, which here is easily worked limestone. Except for pillars, architraves, and some ceiling work, the decoration is simply painted (on a stucco base), not carved in low relief as in temples. Regrettably, much of the surface has darkened in recent decades— whether from some fungus or from preparations applied by early archaeologists is not clear. Restoration is underway but proceeds slowly.

Restoration is in order, for these paintings are treasures. Their age alone, about 2000 B.C., would make them precious, invaluable as records. They model mansions of their era, show scenes of occupations, depict processes of manufacture, and portray foreigners (including some of the oldest repre- sentations of Semites) to show life in other countries. While you'll appreciate the historical significance, what you'll adore are other scenes unique in Egypt. Here are scenes of action— dancing, wrestling, gymnastics—accurately drawn with bod- ies contorted as they would be in reality. These drawings consist of hundreds of groups in series to show the sequence of actions. What pleasant surprises these lively contortionists are after stiff Egyptian figures.

A steep path leads to a walkway below the crest of the cliffs. Stretching in both directions are entrances cut into the rock of the cliff leading to large tombs for the nobility. Farther down are smaller, more numerous holes, the entrances to shafts for less important people. Along the way you'll have splendid views over the cultivation to the distant Nile.

Four tombs are worth seeing. All lie on the left walkway and appear in the approximate order of their age, from newer to older.

TOMB #17: KHETY: In the first part of the Middle King- dom, Dynasty XI, Khety ascended to the position of nomarch which he inherited from his father whose tomb is two doors farther on. The painting in Khety's tomb is not as fine as that in three others described below. In fact, entire scenes are copies from his father's tomb. In size and architecture the tomb is also similar, though smaller.

Through a plain facade and doorway (doors, probably of wood, once closed all these tombs—stone socket holes for the door-pivots survive) you enter a large rectangular room. Beyond, two rows of columns form two back rooms. Only two of six original columns survive and are of an unusual style for ancient Egypt. Each represents four lotus stems surmounted by flower buds, tied in a bunch near the top. (Rope and knot are carved in the stone.) The remaining color shows that these represent blue lotuses. The ceiling forms a gentle arch, not flat as in New Kingdom tombs, suggesting that the tomb replicates a mansion of the period.

The top border all around the room is called a *kheker* frieze. There is some question as to what the decorative "rabbit-ear" elements reproduce. One theory claims that they derive from mats hung on the adobe walls of houses to add color and design; the *kheker* frieze would reproduce, in a stylized way, the line of ties that allowed the mat to hang from wall pegs.

The front wall is poorly done and has little of interest. The wall left of the entrance was copied in large part from the corresponding wall of Khety's father's tomb. These parts may be readily skipped for concentration on the rear wall. All along the top, in five rows, over 100 pairs of wrestlers show their holds in a cartoon strip. Below, left, is a battle scene where a fortress—possibly one in Nubia—is attacked. Across the bottom is a battle in the desert.

TOMB #15: BAKET: The nomarch Baket was Khety's father. This is the oldest of the four fine tombs and perhaps the most charming. Nowhere are the contorting figures drawn with more spirit.

The wall left of the entrance (north) has, on the top row, a desert scene where animals are driven toward a net shown above and far right. Note the fourth, fifth, sixth, and seventh animals from the left. Depictions of mythical beasts are rare in tombs, though common on magic instruments. Might it be that such beasts were believed to exist in the desert? The next row shows from the left: a barber shaving; a chiropodist, followed by scenes of the various steps in the manufacture of linen; then painters. Below, the largest figure is Baket, with his daughter behind him, watching these scenes. The third row contains female occupations—spinning and weaving, then female acrobats and jugglers, and a pig-a-back game. Below, herdsmen lead cattle and antelope (domesticated in ancient Egypt); four men clap; scribes hear a case; a flint-maker grinds a knife; men make sandals. In row five are more cattle, musicians, goldsmiths, painters, and a sculptor. At the bottom in a marsh scene, two boat crews quarrel while another hauls in the net. All around are carefully drawn representations of 30 different species of Egyptian birds with their names in hieroglyphs.

The rear wall at the back of the tomb seems alive with moving wrestlers. More than 200 pairs, each composed of a lighter and a darker figure to help distinguish the two, go through all the varieties of holds. One wonders why so much space and care would be devoted to this sport in a tomb. Was the owner a devoted fan of the sport, or a wrestler himself, or was wrestling simply a part of military training? Three lower rows contain a battle scene with all sorts of soldiers.

The rear right-hand wall has a recess, a shrine with an altar. Above it is a man beside an accurately drawn bird trap (shown from above). Beside this, various sorts of food are prepared. The rest of this wall depicts a number of pastoral occupations separated by a large figure of Baket.

TOMB #3: KHNUMHOTEP: We move forward a century to a nomarch of Dynasty XII with a tomb smaller but more sophisticated than the previous ones.

In front of this door is an outer court with two interesting columns carved with 16 slightly fluted ribs, which, along with their base and abacus, strongly suggest the Greek Doric order of column. Greeks had much commerce with Egypt before inventing their Doric temples.

Inside, the large room has the remains of four columns and ends in a rear sanctuary whose doorway once held double doors. The vaulted ceiling in the main room is nicely patterned and colored.

The wall surrounding the entrance has on the left side (facing the doorway) a top row of carpenters, followed by a row depicting boat building, then a larger row of Khnumhotep's wives and children on a pilgrimage to Abydos. Below are bakers and weavers, then sculptors. On the right side of the doorway the top three rows illustrate harvesting, then a larger row shows the pilgrimage of Khnumhotep's mummy to Abydos. Below are gardening scenes, then oxen and fishing.

The wall left of the entrance includes famous pictures of Semites. The top three rows depict the standard desert hunt with all manner of beasts. Below is a procession of light-skinned Semites. Two Egyptians with red skin lead the procession (right), then bowing in homage is Ibsha, the chief of the Yarmmu. Behind are Semite soldiers, women, and two lightly laden donkeys. Behind the second donkey a man plays on a lyre. The inscription says simply: "Coming bearing kohl which 37 Yarmmu bring to him." Note the beards and the multicolored clothes.

Farther left, antelope are butchered and birds are caught by nets. Below, bulls fight above a long procession of cattle and donkeys are brought to tax collectors—the scribes far right. Also far right is a large figure of Khnumhotep overlooking these efforts in his behalf. A small servant bearing sandals is behind him and a son is above. Three dogs surround their master. The lower two, a male and female, are of some strange dachshundlike species.

On the rear wall, Khnumhotep engages in water sports. On the left he rides a papyrus skiff, accompanied by a wife and son. He holds a throwing stick, ready to hurl at the birds in the marshes ahead. Below, men haul a net filled with fish. Over the doorway Khnumhotep hunts birds at his ease, seated in a comfortable chair behind a blind while he closes the net. On the right side he goes spear fishing. Water drips from two fish pierced with one thrust. Boatmen cavort below.

The remaining wall in the hall is one enormous banquet scene. On the top left, a wife and children prepare to eat. Khnumhotep sits at the other side before vast quantities of food, all itemized in hieroglyphs above. Servants scurry all around with more food.

The purpose of all such scenes is the magical thought that

what is pictured or named would become real in the hereafter. Khnumhotep had his favorite things painted for his eternal enjoyment.

Inside the small shrine at the rear of the hall was a seated statue of Khnumhotep on his throne; only the chair now remains. The shrine walls are painted in pedestrian funerary scenes: a banquet table with offerings, wife and children offering homage.

TOMB #2: AMUNEMHAT: He also was a nomarch, just before Khnumhotep, in Dynasty XII. All the motifs and their locations are similar to those in tombs already described, tomb #15 in particular. The right-hand wall as you enter is, however, drawn very well, and the ceiling is splendid. Two rows of columns divide the hall into three sections, each covered by a barrel vault. The brightly colored patterns represent a ceiling in a house. Down the center of each section runs a painted simulation of a wooden beam complete with grain. In the middle is painted an intricate complex of patterns. Presumably the represented ceiling had an opening there, covered by multicolored and multitextured matting.

Returning down the steep track from the tombs, you will see a split in the hills to the left. A quarter of a mile into this wadi is a rock chapel begun by the female pharaoh Hatshepsut and completed by her ward and successor, Thothmoses III (who then obliterated her name). Beside this chapel is another grotto outside of which is the name of the only child of Alexander the Great.

AMENITIES

HOTELS

Well, if not amenities, at least Minya offers shelter. Hotels are few and spartan, lacking central heat or air conditioning. We know of no restaurants, outside of hotel dining rooms. The food in hotels is hearty, however, and the service is as willing as inexperienced service can be. Minya does have one second-class hotel, but that one has been requisitioned by the army for the past decade.

Lotus Hotel. *Third Class.* (Port Said Street.) We trust that you can appreciate quaintness and maintain your good humor. Both will find exercise in the Lotus Hotel. The elevator will test your courage. And this is probably the best hotel available in Minya. Rooms are cluttered and dark, but of reasonable size. The dining room on top of the hotel is its best feature. A single room costs about LE 3; a double room goes for LE 4.

Ibn el Khasib Hotel. *Fourth Class.* (One block to the right of the train station.) About the same in accommodations and price as the Lotus Hotel.

Savoy Hotel. *Fourth Class.* (In the square of the train station.) Also about the same in accommodations and price as the Lotus Hotel.

LEAVING MINYA

If you managed to get to Minya, undoubtedly you are in command of your departure. Should a problem arise, talk with the agent at the Tourist Office. One suggestion, assuming that you are about to go south to Luxor, is to arrange an early start so you will have time to visit the temples of Denderah and Abydos on the way. This will free a day in Luxor. These sites are discussed at the end of the Luxor chapter as excursions. From Minya to Luxor is a trip of about 250 miles.

8.

Background for Luxor

Before Stonehenge was completed on England's Salisbury Plain and before civilization came to China, Egypt had already fallen from greatness into decline. In 1674 B.C. foreigners captured Memphis. The splendid times in Egypt, the periods of the Old Kingdom and of the Middle Kingdom, evidently were gone.

Unexpectedly, Egypt resurrected herself one century later, expelled the foreigners, and began her third and last great period. This New Kingdom opened violently as Egypt passed through her most militaristic era, paused for one of history's most dynamic women, then relaxed in luxury. A moment of religious fanaticism followed before Egypt slid into a final decline. Initially this decline was eclipsed by Rameses the Great, the greatest spectacle on earth; then, as weaknesses surfaced and jealous neighbors threatened, vigorous pharaohs appeared in time to avert the end. Delay was all that Egypt could hope for by the close of the New Kingdom: riches had fatally infected the nation.

Still, the end of the New Kingdom could not erase the glory

of its beginning. The Old Kingdom had been splendid, but Egypt had had no genuine competitors; the Middle Kingdom was simply a renaissance. To reach such heights a third time, Egypt had to rise from her knees. In many ways the start of the New Kingdom was Egypt's finest hour.

THE NEW KINGDOM

The world hardly noticed any change when the Middle Kingdom faded away under a series of weak rulers, because the eyes of the world were riveted on a chilling phenomenon. Hordes of strange people had flooded into Turkey and were threatening to drown the civilized world. These people spoke a new language and rode behind an animal that would revolutionize life. Their language was Indo-European, the root of Sanscrit, Persian, Greek, and Latin, hence of all modern European languages (except Finnish, Basque, and Hungarian, whose origins are mysteries). They came in carts pulled by horses, which did not then exist in the Middle East, and routed all the armies in their way.

A few decades later, a mysterious people called the Hyksos conquered Memphis. It was once believed that the Hyksos formed a branch of the Indo-European invasion, and that coming to Egypt in chariots enabled them to defeat the Egyptian forces. After a century of rule, when Egypt expelled them, they seemed to vanish as if they had never been. Now we know that the Hyksos simply were Semitic tribes (perhaps including the Hebrews as a minor element) impelled into Egypt on waves of trouble. When the influx of Indo-Europeans caused consternation in Turkey, people fled. This migration led to chaos in adjoining lands, whose people in turn fled farther west. These waves reached Palestine, and tribes there moved to the next land—the eastern part of Egypt's Delta. They arrived and settled peacefully for almost 50 years before attacking Memphis. It was hardly a military coup.

At the time Egypt was weak. An intrusion of foreigners, even a peaceful migration, would not otherwise have been tolerated. In those days Egypt, split by rival pharaohs, held separate courts in Memphis and in the Delta. The new arrivals called little attention to themselves, taking on Egyptian ways and adopting the gods of their new country. Gradually they learned that an Egypt divided was not the feared power of earlier times and that, with chariots and bronze swords, they could defeat the Egyptians who disdained all new weapons. Egypt needed a kick to waken it from the slumbers of tradition. The Hyksos seized Memphis and proceeded to give Egypt the century-long boot it needed.

Most of these new Hyksos kings bore Egyptian names, but some had names like Yakeb-hor, thinly disguising the Semitic Jacob Hur. Unused to ruling, they employed the existing bureaucratic system and its native governors—which led to their undoing. As years passed, Egyptian governors far from Memphis in the province of Thebes marshaled their strength, annexing the nomes around them as far south as Aswan. Egypt had meanwhile lost the lands below Aswan, which now had Sudanese kings, so that Thebes stood alone as an island of Egyptian power in a sea of foreign rulers. The people of Thebes hated the pharaohs living in the Delta. "Vile Asiatics," they called them, or, more simply, "foreign rulers"—*Hikau Khoswet*, which historians later shortened to *Hyksos*.

The Theban governor Kamose, who began an inevitable war for independence, said, "I wonder what is the point of my strength, when there is one chief in Avaris [in the Delta] and another in Kush? I sit joined with an Asiatic and a Nubian, each man holding his portion of Egypt."

Not for long. The next governor, Ahmose, drove the Hyksos out of the Delta and pursued them east into Palestine. (The Bible later would call these Hyksos the Canaanites.) Ahmose then drove south to reclaim Nubia so that all of Egypt was once again ruled by an Egyptian. Egypt regained sovereignty in 1567 B.C.; this was the start of the New Kingdom.

Several things were new about this era. Egypt, invigorated and impressed with her own power, having driven out an enemy so successfully, had an army at her service, an army now with bronze swords and chariot divisions. The lands east of Egypt—Palestine, Syria, and Lebanon—had drawn Egypt's attention and would become her special sphere of influence. Egypt discovered that plundered gold gleamed as brightly as mined gold and was more exciting to collect. One other new phenomenon began with the New Kingdom: while royal husbands were away at war, their wives managed the home—queens held the state together and protected the borders against sneak attacks. Women proved their mettle and earned increased respect.

The New Kingdom comprised three dynasties: XVIII, XIX, and XX. The new influences—militarism and the higher position of women—were greatest in the beginning, tapering off in time. Dynasty XVIII was a kind of golden age, filled with great events and fascinating people. This was the dynasty of Egypt's greatest pharaoh, Thothmoses III, and of the exciting women—Pharaoh Hatshepsut and Nefertiti, whose beauty became immortal. It was a time that turned to splendid luxury leading to fanaticism and to the end of the dynasty. The next dynasty, XIX, is summed up in the name of one pharaoh—Rameses the Great. Dynasty XX paid the price of years of luxury; Egypt was barely able to defend herself against new threats. Then the New Kingdom passed quietly away.

HER MAJESTY, HATSHEPSUT

Ahmose, who chased the Hyksos from Egypt, founded Dynasty XVIII. Blood still ran hot in his son who continued the military tradition. The son's name was Amunhotep, "Amun is Pleased," for this dynasty had a new favorite god—Amun of Thebes. As fortune smiled on the dynasty, its pharaohs donated riches to their god, each pharaoh adding conquests to those of his predecessors and adding buildings to Karnak Temple—which grew into a temple of temples, larger than any edifice that ever would be built for a god.

After Amunhotep, the throne passed to a remarkable man, the first of many Thothmoses and the father of Hatshepsut. Thothmoses I, with no royal blood, became a general in the pharaoh's army and rose high enough to marry one of

Amunhotep's sisters. He earned the throne through his exploits (also, suitable princes were not available); he was crowned in middle age. Still, he fathered one of the most dynamic women in history along with one weak son, and his death was important for two very different reasons.

Thothmoses prepared a new sort of tomb. The pyramids were over a thousand years old by this time and it was evident that they did not fulfill their purpose—to protect a king's body. Like beacons, the pyramids announced a wealth inside that thieves dream of. Thieves rose to the challenge, eventually succeeding in every case. All that wealth was a problem. If no "vault" was strong enough, perhaps the opposite approach might work, thought Thothmoses. In utter secrecy, the pharaoh commissioned an underground chamber in the most desolate of places, in a desert valley nestled between barren mountains away from Thebes. No sign would mark the place. To be sure, a pharaoh still needed a temple where offerings could feed his immortal soul, but Thothmoses built his funerary temple a mile from the tomb so as not to reveal the secret location. His trick would probably have succeeded except that the next pharaoh followed exactly the same plan, and the next, and the next, and on and on— Egyptians were such creatures of tradition. The secret could not be kept when 20 pharaohs, one after the other, all were buried in the same six-acre place. Eventually thieves found and robbed the tombs (even Tutankhamun's, partially). Still, Thothmoses receives credit for starting the practice of under-ground tombs in what became known as the Valley of the Kings.

Thothmoses' daughter assumed a high position at his death—a second important change. Hatshepsut was the eldest daughter of Thothmoses I through his chief wife. The royal couple had no sons, though Thothmoses had other wives and bred sons with them. The rule for succession stated that the throne came with marriage to the most royal eligible woman. It was preferable that the husband have royal blood, so Hatshepsut, now the most royal eligible woman, proceeded to marry a half-brother to make him Thothmoses II. She became his "Great Royal Wife," the queen of Egypt.

Try as she would, however, she was unable to bear the next king, producing only daughters. If her husband should die, one of his sons conceived through another wife would be the next pharaoh and Hatshepsut would lose her position of power. That prospect greatly concerned Hatshepsut. Her husband must have been aware of Hatshepsut's ambitions, for he publicly designated a successor so that she could not interfere. Then, all too soon, Hatshepsut's fears came true: her husband died suddenly after a short reign of eight years. The pharaoh designee immediately married the proper royal princess (Hatshepsut's daughter) and was coronated as Thothmoses III. Now Hatshepsut faced the imminent prospect of replacement and political oblivion though she was only 30 years old.

She had a little time to maneuver, however. Thothmoses III, not yet in his teens, was too young to actually manage the government. Hatshepsut, on the other hand, was a mature former queen and the mother of the new queen, important enough to "help" the child pharaoh. She became the regent. The pharaoh would be her ward until he reached maturity.

At first, temple carvings presented the young king as the dominant figure while Hatshepsut hovered behind him. Then they stood side by side. Within one year, Thothmoses III no longer got into pictures at all. Hatshepsut invented a story claiming her birth had been divine. Great Amun was her real father, she said, and Thothmoses I had promised her the throne. She sent the young Thothmoses III away, ostensibly for military training, actually to get him out of the country so she could deck the walls of hundreds of temples throughout Egypt with pictures and statues proclaiming that she was the true pharaoh.

Artists encountered all kinds of problems. Hieroglyphs, a language in which nouns have genders, only had masculine words referring to a king. Since a pronoun had to agree with the noun it referred to, "the pharaoh, she . . ." violated grammar. In addition, one traditional insignia of a pharaoh was a beard. Based on her statues, Hatshepsut's appearance was anything but masculine, yet her attractive face had to be surrounded by an incongruous false beard on statues.

Whether she actually wore such a thing on ceremonial occasions is not known, but it is entirely possible. As pharaoh, Hatshepsut quickly turned the bountiful energy of the country from war to civil matters. She built; she sent expeditions to distant lands. Throughout all these projects, one man stood by the widow's side. He was a commoner named Senmut, on whose shoulders offices and titles were showered until he referred to himself, boastfully but with truth, as "the greatest of the great in the entire land." Naturally, people today speculate that he was the pharaoh's lover, but with no real evidence. Ability may have earned him the responsibilities and honors—Senmut designed what art historians agree is among the most beautiful of all the buildings ever created, the temple of Dier el Bahri, an incomparable blend of structure and setting. Cliffs behind the temple form a natural pyramid, then spread on either side. Senmut nestled three spreading terraces of columns, each terrace rising farther back into the precipitous cliffs so that natural and man-made formations dramatize each other. Nothing like this temple had existed before, or since.

To finish the temple, Hatshepsut and Senmut sent an expedition to the fabled land of Punt (probably located at the "horn" of Africa, modern Somalia). The expedition returned with exotic plants, animals, birds, and most precious, the perfumed tree sap called myrrh. She also ordered enormous obelisks hewn and transported on a barge 300 feet long, towed by 27 boats, from Aswan to Karnak Temple where they were covered in electrum, an alloy of gold and silver. Her temple walls displayed these scenes proudly in the place where other pharaohs would have carved military victories.

It seemed a glorious, a renaissance, time. Hatshepsut said:

> My command stands as firm as the mountains and the sun shines its rays over the name of the august person. My falcon rises high above the kingly banner for all eternity.

Nineteen years after Hatshepsut became pharaoh, Senmut fell from grace. We do not know why. Then Egypt's territories rose in revolt. Twenty-two years after she had stolen a throne, Hatshepsut died. Her ward, who was her son-in-law as well, proceeded to erase her memory. He had her statues destroyed, her pictures chiseled out, her name smoothed over, her obelisks covered by walls. No body was ever found in her tomb. Lists of kings all omitted her name.

EGYPT'S NAPOLEON

This spiteful act was the only thing Thothmoses III ever did that was less than exemplary. The outburst is understandable enough—Hatshepsut had taken his throne and consigned him to virtual exile. After venting his anger, Thothmoses entered 32 years of unexcelled, vigorous kingship.

A comparison with Napoleon is apt (except that Napoleon should be called the Thothmoses III of France). Both were short, even for their time, and prominent noses were not their best feature. Each was a great general. Thothmoses III took his army farther than any Egyptian force had ever gone, or would again—he crossed the Euphrates River into Iran. He fought at least 17 campaigns, always successfully. He and Napoleon combined military excellence with exceptional abilities as administrators. Each was a sportsman. Thothmoses III claims the incredible bag of 120 elephants from one hunt (in Syria, of all places). Both men were patrons of the arts. Thothmoses III built constantly, and much of Karnak is due to him and his gratitude to his god Amun for all his victories. Like his mother-in-law, he erected obelisks, but larger and more numerous than hers. (One stands today in New York's Central Park—a "small" one.)

Never had Egypt been richer than during the reign of Thothmoses III. Booty from his campaigns came back to Egypt in caravan streams, and mines in Nubia were producing 10,000 grams of gold every year. The image that Egypt presented in those days is revealed in what a foreign king said to a later pharaoh (when it was no longer as true): "Send me much gold, for in Egypt gold is like the sand." Now Egypt was feared and safe. Even the Indo-Europeans stopped and retreated across the Euphrates. Thothmoses III could rest for the last decade of his life. The gold continued to flow from the mines, and would continue from Palestine and Syria in the form of tribute without the need of constant war. In the long run, this was a danger. Egypt had no desire for territory; she did not conquer countries and govern them. She relaxed, caring only for the gold which now poured in.

Slowly, but inevitably, Egypt changed. Although an aura of glory remained about soldiering, actual campaigns became fewer and fewer. For a while, athletes trained princes to ride in chariots, shoot bows, fight with swords, and navigate boats. The son of Thothmoses III, the ultimate product of such training, did not fight as his father had done, but Amunhotep II was tall, strong, and expert. No one except he could pull his bow. He shot arrows through a three-inch copper target so that the heads came out the other side. Yet he waged only two campaigns, then retired for his last 17 years. The following pharaoh, Thothmoses IV, fought even less. He is known principally for the stele he placed between the paws of the Sphinx at Giza which proclaimed that the Sphinx gave Thothmoses IV the throne in gratitude for clearing away the sand that buried it.

Times had certainly changed. The Napoleon of Egypt would not have bothered to commemorate a mere sand-cleaning operation.

TUYA AND YUYA, NEFERTITI AND TUT

The fortunes, as well as the misfortunes, of the remaining rulers of Dynasty XVIII were interwoven with a remarkable family of commoners, who appeared in higher and higher places, helping each other climb, until one of them at last became pharaoh. He reigned for a moment as the dynasty died.

We hear of the family first when the pharaoh, Amunhotep III, married. Nothing was unusual in a king marrying, even in marrying a commoner, as his 20 or so wives were royal and nonroyal women alike. What was unusual was that, when Amunhotep married a commoner named Tiy, he proclaimed the event throughout the land. Making this much of a commoner woman had never happened. The proclamation identified the new wife's parents—Tuya and Yuya. Tuya was a simple cavalry commander from the middle of Egypt; Yuya was his wife, nothing more. Though Amunhotep III had married a princess before his coronation, he shoved this royal wife aside, and the daughter of middle-class parents appeared on monuments as though she were a proper queen. Something strange was going on, and what it was is not clearly understood today.

The mummies of Tuya and Yuya (found buried in the Valley of the Kings!) are now in the Museum of Antiquities. Yuya is notable for her blonde hair, which was probably just bleached by chemicals used to prepare the mummy; however, both mummies are unusual in having narrow, almost pointed skulls, forming a bump on the backs of their heads. All the remaining pharaohs of Dynasty XVIII are unusual as well in having narrow skulls forming bumps on the backs of their heads.

Perhaps Amunhotep III was a relative of Tuya and Yuya. Although his father was the pharaoh Thothmoses IV, his mother too was a commoner who might have been Tuya's sister. If so, the sister's influence might have brought about this marriage to her niece, Tiy. Her influence must have been very great to raise her niece up to the place of a queen; but once this family got its clutches on a piece of the throne, they held tight and grabbed for more.

After the marriage, the new pharaoh acted for a time like his predecessors. For ten years he conducted minor military campaigns and engaged in sports—at least that is what his "press releases" claimed. He periodically distributed scarabs through the country with notices of his recent accomplishments carved on their bases. One scarab tells how he captured 96 wild bulls in a single hunt. Another scarab records that in ten years Amunhotep III killed 102 lions. After this start, however, Amunhotep III settled deep in the lap of luxury for 30 years, becoming an Oriental potentate, a self-aggrandizing aesthete. Dressing in flowing, diaphanous gowns, he gave splendid parties and decorated his palace with floral scenes.

We inject a few words here about ancient Egyptian palaces,

for they were not what you might expect, being neither as large nor as solid as a temple. Lacking a state palace into which each new king moved, every new pharaoh built a palace for himself. It would have been impossible to build so many in stone, nor was there any point in doing so if the structure were intended for just one lifetime. Palaces were constructed of adobe, designed with a number of individual buildings inside a walled compound. The main building was for the pharaoh and included a large courtroom. Separate buildings erected nearby housed each important wife, and if children were old enough they too might have small individual homes. Because of smells, the kitchen was a building unto itself. Separate barracks housed the palace guard. All around, flowers and trees lined artificial pools, for Egyptians loved nature. Indeed, in many cases, the palace compound contained a zoo. Amunhotep III built a palace larger than any of his predecessors' and decorated it profusely. Though the walls have crumbled, the floor plan can still be made out downstream from the Colossi of Memnon at Malkata opposite Luxor. He named his palace "House of Rejoicing," which accurately expressed his main occupation.

Amunhotep III also built a temple, not as large as Karnak, but then 20 or more pharaohs contributed to the final size of Karnak. His temple at Luxor is the largest temple ever built by a single person; the columned hall is a marvel of architectural harmony. He also constructed a funerary temple, dedicated to himself, which must have been immense. Unfortunately, it was erected too close to cultivatable land and has disappeared except for two seated statues of Amunhotep III that formed the front elements. These statues tower 65 feet high. The Greeks called them the Colossi of Memnon, and tourists came for centuries to hear these statues "sing" when the morning sun warmed the stone, causing minute cracks to make a noise like soft whistling. Last century an earthquake ended their song.

In addition to buildings, Amunhotep produced countless children, some through incestuous couplings that later became a pharaonic pattern. For example, charming Sitamun was his favorite daughter, so Amunhotep married her.

Together they had a child who became the favorite daughter of his twilight years. Amunhotep died after a reign of some 38 years, a five-feet-two-inch balding, fat man with teeth so rotted that his final years must have been spent in constant pain.

The sons of Tiy and Amunhotep III earned their own places in history. Amunhotep IV succeeded his father, then changed his name to Akhenaten and created monotheism. His story is told in Chapter 6. Akhenaten married Nefertiti of the immortal beauty, but who was she?

A hint of her origins is found in her liking for wearing a tall hat. She is, of course, sculpted with such a hat in the famous bust (now in a West Berlin museum, reproduced in countless picture books). Only occasionally do you see pictures or statues of her without a hat, and then the reason becomes clear. She had a narrow skull, forming a bump on the back of her head. For Tuya and Yuya had several other children in addition to their daughter Tiy who married Amunhotep III. One was a male named Ay who hovered in the palace background until the end of this dynasty. Ay, it seems, had a daughter named Nefertiti.

Thus, Tuya and Yuya produced, directly or indirectly, two queens and, perhaps, one pharaoh, Amunhotep III. Scholars debate over Tutankhamun's parentage; Tuya and Yuya certainly were involved in this case too. Tutankhamun reigned after Akhenaten, with an intervening reign by a man named Smenkara. Based on statues, Tutankhamun and Smenkara were so much alike they must have been brothers. Indeed, much of the material in Tutankhamun's tomb was originally made for Smenkara. Tutankhamun's name was written over his. Who were the parents of these brothers? No statues or carvings from Akhenaten's time show any sons of his, only daughters, yet both brothers claimed royal blood. That leaves Amunhotep III as the probable father. Tutankhamun preserved a little gold statue of him in a special box. In the same box was a lock of Queen Tiy's hair.

Tutankhamun came suddenly to the throne when Akhenaten and Smenkara died at about the same time. He was then a child of about seven who married one of Akhenaten's daughters to gain the final rights to the throne. At the age of seven, no one can run a country; Uncle Ay stepped in to help as the new vizier. The country regained normalcy, returning to the worship of the god Amun. Then, after 12 years on the throne—at 19—Tut died suddenly from a blow on the head. Uncle Ay took over the funeral arrangements and got his picture painted prominently in the tomb as the officiating priest.

Tutankhamun left a very young widow behind. Ankhesamun, the daughter of Akhenaten and Nefertiti, at 19, stood alone at the top of the most powerful nation in the world. She wrote to the king of the Hittites in Turkey begging him to send a prince whom she could marry quickly because she was afraid. She was wise to worry, for she was a treasure. The only royal children were two fetuses buried with Tutankhamun, so Ankhesamun was the last unmarried royal woman. Whoever married her would be the next pharaoh. The murder of a Hittite prince (on his way to marry her) confirmed her fears. Uncle Ay, her mother's father, then married the widow. No one knows if blood stained his hands.

And so the family from Middle Egypt, after promoting three of their members into queens and breeding perhaps three pharaohs, had finally seized the throne themselves. It was, however, an old Ay who donned a pharaoh's regalia. He lasted just four years more. Dynasty XVIII that began with such glory had literally run out of blood. The final pharaoh was no relation at all; he was an army general named Horemheb. (See Appendix, Dynasty XVIII, for a detailed list of pharaohs.)

RAMESES THE GREAT

Horemheb died without children. His vizier and army friend became the next pharaoh. Rameses I, the first of many of that name, fathered Dynasty XIX. Already elderly when he took the throne, he made his son co-regent to retain the throne within the family if he should die. Royal blood operates on the assumption that if you can hold a throne for some generations, your blood turns royal blue (if not already). After two years, the son, Seti I, was sole ruler.

Rameses II, "the Great," gets all the press, but in actuality, Seti did the sorts of things Rameses II only claimed to do. With all the dynastic and religious confusion at the end of Dynasty XVIII, the empire had fallen apart. The Hittites, whose power increased with the discovery of iron manufacture, encouraged rebellion in countries that formerly had paid tribute to Egypt. Seti I, the son of a general, swept through Palestine into Syria to the fortress town of Kadesh (near latter-day Damascus). He captured the fortress and established Egypt's dominance over the area. Seti I also erected the giant hypostyle hall in the temple at Karnak and a beautiful New Kingdom temple at Abydos. The Abydos temple is awesome; the carving and colors, most of which remain, are among the most delicate word pictures in ancient Egypt. His tomb, in the Valley of the Kings, is acknowledged to be the most impressive.

The son of Seti I finished these building projects interrupted by his father's death, though he did what he could to make everyone think that he, Rameses the Great, had built them. This second Rameses had a trick that gained him the nickname "the Great." The idea probably came from earlier acts—Thothmoses III had erased Hatshepsut's name; Akhenaten had scratched out all other gods except for his favorite; and Horemheb had in turn scratched out Akhenaten's name. None of this erasing brought the one who did it any credit; it was all done to spite someone else. Though Rameses did not hate anyone, he loved Rameses, so he turned this erasing device to his own advantage by inventing the instant building.

Rameses commanded stone carvers to roam over Egypt changing the name of the pharaoh who built each temple to "Rameses." Soon hundreds of temples proclaimed Rameses as their builder—no wonder later generations thought that he was great. Today almost every guide in Egypt tells the same joke—they call Rameses "the great chiseler." Funny or not so funny, it is true enough. Rameses, who knew better than anyone that a carved name might become fair game for some future eraser, had his name carved inches deep to discourage others from changing it. The device worked so well on buildings that he also used it to make instant statues. Whatever they looked like, whatever period of history they came from, whatever the original name of the owner might be, soon every available statue in Egypt said "Rameses."

We should admire the energy, if not the scruples, of this monomaniacal glory-seeker. He did construct many buildings on his own, though often by dismantling older structures to get prefabricated materials. Two projects in particular, one a building, the other a battle, deserve notice. Each was the result of the slow decline in Egypt's power.

The Hittites, pushed away by Rameses' father, returned at their peak while the son ruled, threatening the Egyptian empire. The Egyptian capital, still at Thebes, was far from the source of tribute and from the area of these political problems. Rameses decided to move closer to his concerns, establishing a new residence on the eastern side of the Delta, which grew to a city that became the capital of Egypt in later years. The Bible called it Raameses in the land called Goshen, and describes how Jews were enslaved to build this new city. But because the governing locus of Egypt had moved north, the southern border now was less well protected. To deal with this problem, Rameses undertook a project that even his greatest detractors must admire, building Abu Simbel 200 miles below the border. A wonderful temple, it is cut from living rock, with enormous front figures of Rameses that exemplify stability and power. Abu Simbel substituted for whole armies of Egyptians, which is why it overlooks the Nile, the route the Nubians would follow if they were to attack Egypt. The frightening promise of Egyptian might represented by Abu Simbel held the Nubians off for centuries.

Statues would not work on the Hittites, however. In the fifth year of his reign, Rameses took four armies on a campaign against them. His troops comprised the flower of Egypt's fighting forces, and were to be joined by the armies of allies on the march through friendly Middle East lands. Rameses hoped for a brilliant victory and was disappointed when Hittite armies didn't appear as he roamed farther and farther from home and into Palestine. Then began a series of blunders. Rameses split his forces, sending two armies to the Palestinian coast while he ran ahead inland with one army, outdistancing the one remaining. Rameses was rushing to take Kadesh where his father had gained fame.

Near Kadesh, two captured Hittite soldiers told Rameses that their forces had abandoned the fort. A more thoughtful commander would have evaluated such information carefully, given that only a quarter of the Egyptian forces were in the vicinity of Kadesh and that the Hittites were a proud people not given to running away. Indeed, the information offered by the captives proved to be one of the oldest military tricks. Rameses fell for it. He ran even farther ahead of his remaining troops in order to be the first man to enter the fort. The Hittites waited until the proper moment, then charged from hiding to surround Rameses and his army.

To hear Rameses tell it, and he told it on 20 temple walls, he alone held off the Hittite forces until the second army could join him. Then he had enough Egyptians to hold until nightfall; by dawn the Hittites had left. As Rameses tells it, the enemy fled because he had so frightened them with his personal bravery. The Hittites were defeated, if not crushed, according to his side of the story. They sued for peace.

Unfortunately for Rameses' credibility, two copies of the peace treaty exist, one Egyptian and one Hittite. From the terms of the treaty it is clear that there was no defeat; the engagement was a draw. Though Rameses mentions it only incidentally, he was probably saved, in his darkest moment, by the chance arrival of an allied army. The Hittites probably retreated because they consisted only of the troops of this one fort—not the whole might of the Hittite nation—knowing that the two remaining Egyptian armies were on the way. Rameses quit the area too after the engagement, though he does not call his own departure a retreat. Hardly a coincidence, this campaign was Rameses' last in the Middle East.

The engagement occurred in the fifth year of his reign. He spent 62 years more telling the story and otherwise propagandizing. One boast that does appear to be true relates that he fathered over 100 children. His reign was so long, however, that his eldest children were dying by the end of it. Merenptah, his thirteenth eldest son, succeeded him.

One of the Bible's great stories describes the Exodus of Jews from Egypt. Unfortunately, the king of Egypt is not named, only called *pharaoh*. As told by the departing Jews' descendants, these events were momentous. To the Egyptians, however, the Jews were an insignificant group; there is no mention of Jews at all in Egypt's records—with a single, confusing exception.

In the absence of direct confirmation, the Exodus story seems consistent with what is known about Egypt and the times. Jews probably arrived in Goshen with the Hyksos. It is not implausible that Joseph could have been the vizier of a Semitic (Hyksos) pharaoh. The city of Raameses certainly was built during the first part of Dynasty XIX, and foreign people were often enslaved within Egypt.

Rameses usually appears as candidate for the pharaoh of the Exodus since he did so much of the building at Raameses. However, his successor, Merenptah, recorded a campaign in Palestine and claimed, in a list of conquered people, that "Israel is destroyed; her seed is no more." The Bible mentions no such defeat around the time of the Exodus. To harmonize Merenptah's claim with the Bible would mean postulating a group called Israel living in Palestine at the same time that various Jewish tribes were in Egypt. The group that remained in Palestine might have been defeated by Merenptah while other tribes were wandering with Moses in the wilderness of Sinai. Merenptah's victory over Israel in Palestine, in fact, might help explain how the wanderers with Moses were able to conquer large parts of Palestine when they arrived. If there were two groups, the Bible would have focused on the wandering tribes whose story it tells.

THE END OF THE NEW KINGDOM

Merenptah was the last powerful pharaoh of Dynasty XIX. He was able to defeat a group called the Sea Peoples who retreated, licked their wounds, and returned later as the scourge of the Mediterranean. After Merenptah, Dynasty XIX faded away in a series of weak rulers and short reigns, while conditions in Egypt grew increasingly chaotic. Finally a man, of whom almost nothing is known, seized the throne and bred a new dynasty, the twentieth.

As usurpers, the pharaohs of Dynasty XX did what they could to appear legitimate. Every one of those who came after the shadowy founder of this dynasty called himself "Rameses," but only one of those eight Rameses left any mark on history. Rameses III built the great edifice of Medinet Habu on the western bank at Thebes. A strange complex, it includes both a temple and a palace of stone, all within walls almost 60 feet high and 25 feet thick. This fortress-palace-temple stood as a symbol of new and dangerous times. In the past, Egypt placed forts in conquered territories. In Dynasty XIX, Egypt began forts on her own land—in the Delta near her border with the Middle East. In Dynasty XX, a fort was built in the very heart of Egypt in the ancient capital.

Never before had Egypt needed to defend herself, to repel an invader on her own territory. The attackers, the Sea Peoples, were a migrating horde of tribes, traveling by land as well as by sea. Probably these people were related to the Indo-European migration of an earlier time, for the names of the Sea Peoples' tribes indicate they comprised ancestors of the Greeks, the Etruscans, the people of Sicily, and a tribe called Peleset who gave their name to Palestine. When this horde stormed the Delta, Rameses III met them in a combined land and sea battle. The Sea Peoples were ferocious fighters. Earlier in their journey, they had confronted the Hittites and defeated them so severely that Hittites ceased to be a Middle Eastern power thereafter. Rameses III repelled them in Egypt's last great victory. Even so, Rameses III had to wage several more campaigns in the Delta area later.

For all his powers, Rameses III could not maintain control of Egypt. The walls of his temple at Medinet Habu include pictures of his various wives and children, with spaces for names that were never filled in because, between the time of carving the pictures and the writing of the names, a palace conspiracy had erupted. A document describing the conspiracy survives in which Rameses III tells how his wives knew of and helped high-placed courtiers who plotted to kill him. So important were the courtiers that they were given fictitious names in the document. It would have been an embarrassment to reveal the depth of the plot. Rameses III tells how the guilty were tried, convicted, and punished—killed by forced suicides in most instances. There was a second and a third trial. Five of the original judges were themselves convicted of seduction by accused wives of the king while hearing their cases. Corruption infected the court and the country. A strike (the first in recorded history) ensued; workmen in the royal necropolis had not been paid for months. When payment finally was made, it was one half of what was due.

Continued decline marks the story of the remaining pharaohs of Dynasty XX, of the end of the New Kingdom. One Rameses followed another in quick succession, without distinction. As the pharaohs grew weaker, the priests' power increased correspondingly. By this time the church controlled wealth greater than what a pharaoh could command. At the end of the dynasty, the high priest of Amun, portrayed in a crown, had appropriated the titles of a pharaoh. The last of the 11 Rameses still reigned in the Delta, but a new priest ruled the south, dividing Egypt. From this time forth, Egypt's strategy was to defend and delay, leaving conquest to others—to Assyria, then Persia, followed by Greece and then Rome.

EGYPTIAN TEMPLES

With one outstanding exception (Abu Simbel), most of the great temples of ancient Egypt survive in and around Luxor. Not all the temples are here—there are Old Kingdom examples at Sakkara (Zoser's complex) and Giza (Khaefra's mortuary temple); later examples in Middle Egypt (Tuna el Gebel) and temples at Aswan—but those in the vicinity of Luxor give the proper sense of a fully developed Egyptian temple. These temples date from the last Egyptian eras, from the New Kingdom down through Ptolemaic times.

Egyptian temples become understandable once you realize that the elements are all symbolic. The later Ptolemaic temples are simplest—so much so that the symbolism is hard to discern—but the basic plan is evident in New Kingdom temples, of which Luxor Temple is a fine example.

The avenue to a temple was lined by statues, most often in the forms of sphinxes or rams. The temple proper began with two pylons, side by side. Pylons, with space for a gate between them, represented mountains through the center of which the sun would shine as it rose each day. In front of the pylons enormous wood masts held banners (the slots for such flagpoles can still be seen rising from pylon bases), symbols of divinity that derived from predynastic times when the "house" of a god was distinguished from the homes of humans not by size and material, but by a flag. Past the pylons the temple proper began, shaped in a rectangle—the entry and rear with the longest dimensions. The first part of the temple was a courtyard open to the sky and sun, the largest of three distinct areas. Here common people could worship; purification was not required. Ambulatories formed the sides composed of columns, usually in the shape of Osiris or of a pharaoh portrayed as Osiris. To impress the common people, this court contained the least sacred of the scenes in temples—pictures of pharaohs engaged in the secular exploits of which they were proudest.

After the courtyard, farther into the temple, the floors rose and the ceilings dipped (for the final two parts were roofed) to produce a darker, more sacred atmosphere. In fact, the temple proceeded not just to holier areas, but (symbolically) back to the origin of things. The rising floors represented the emergence of the primeval mound, the first act of creation.

The second temple area, up a step or a ramp, is called the hall of columns, "hypostyle hall." This area had a roof supported by massive stone pillars whose tops represented either lotus or papyrus plants. The roof was highest over the center and lower along the sides; small windows of stone carved into bars were arranged where the two heights met. Enough light filtered in to see by, but it was dim enough to create a somber mood. Reaching to its primeval beginnings, this was a marsh of the gods. Only nobility were allowed in this part of the temple. Along the walls ran pictures of the rites that pharaohs performed in the last, the most holy, place where no one but priests could go. In theory, the pharaoh (who was also a priest) was the only one who could perform religious ceremonies; in practice, priests substituted for him.

The last section, raised higher still, had a lower roof without windows. The feeling here exuded close mystery. This was the inner sanctum, the "Holy-of-Holies," where the idol resided in a separate room. Usually the Holy-of-Holies held several rooms, for a main god, his mate, and his child or some similar combination. Beyond the gods' rooms were other chambers for storing sacred utensils.

Each dawn the seal was taken from the door of the shrine in the god's room, where the idol had been locked the night before. Priests daily stripped the idol of its miniature clothes, and then fed, anointed, and dressed it in fresh clothing, all the while chanting hymns. On special holy days the idol would travel outside the temple. It was placed in a model boat (stored on a pedestal in the god's room) which was then carried on the shoulders of priests through the town. At the river the model boat and its passenger might be placed in an actual boat for a trip to visit another god in some nearby temple, but on other occasions the expedition would just circle through the town and return to the temple. Wherever this procession traveled the route was lined by the devout bowing at the waist or prostrating themselves, depending on their status. People could ask favors and questions of the idol as it passed. A sign, such as the pausing of the idol or the dipping of its litter, was the response. These signs, treated very seriously, could serve as evidence in a court of law. The petitioner was expected to make a hefty donation to the temple in return for the god's answer.

Temples, with rare exceptions for special purposes, all have the same three increasingly holy parts. However, a temple like Karnak that was constructed over the course of centuries by 20 or more pharaohs was so embellished that its fundamental plan is less evident. In some cases, too, such as with Seti's temple at Abydos, the initial courtyard is so open that you hardly notice it, making this temple seem to have only two parts. Later temples, from the times of the Ptolemies and after, in general simplified the separation of parts.

9.

Luxor

Luxor charms everyone. It still looks and feels the way it did in 1922 when Lord Carnarvon and Howard Carter discovered Tutankhamun's tomb, drawing the attention of the world to this peaceful village. Cars still are rare; taxis are horse-drawn carriages. A wide promenade beside the Nile lined with turn-of-the-century houses and an ancient temple invites evening strolls. Falcons soar overhead without a sound, sailboats glide on the river, palms wave in the gentle breezes, and across the Nile mountains are painted by the clarity of sunlight in a thousand pastel hues. The mountains seem to murmur about mysteries and about a thousand ancient tombs. "Biban el Muluk," they say—the Valley of the Kings.

The peaceful town is growing as tourists collect in ever larger numbers to see the hundred sights nearby. Almost 50,000 people now live in Luxor. They dwell back, away from the Nile and its border of hotels for visitors, presenting no pressures of city bustle. Luxor's one defect is hotel space. Although existing hotels provide comfortable accommodations, there are far too few beds. Today Luxor is the tourist bottleneck of Egypt. Rooms must be reserved early, but even exemplary promptness sometimes is not enough. Unending streams of tourists press to see the remains of the greatest city of ancient, ancient times.

Then it was called Thebes, the "city of a thousand gates" and the largest city in the world. Here resided powerful kings who ruled the greatest of earthly nations. Almost one million people crowded in rows of three-story buildings along the Nile as far as Karnak, two miles downstream. Temples proclaimed the city's position in the world, temples larger than any religious buildings ever made, large enough to survive and still amaze. Across the Nile in hills where no eyes could see, mighty kings lay in secret tombs after their days of power. Nearby they hid their queens, and not far away the wealthy men and women of the court copied their lords as best they could. Thebes was the center of the world because it was the center of holiness in Egypt. Upstream and down were other sanctified sites and temples—at Abydos, Denderah, Edfu, Esna, and Kom Ombu.

The only complaint about Luxor, after you secure a room, is that there is just too much to see. The sights can be squeezed into six days, though twice that time would be a pleasure. Even five days might do, if you visited the temples south of Luxor along the way to Aswan. Here is a five-day schedule (the sixth day's temples, between Luxor and Aswan, are discussed in Chapter 11).

Day One: See the Valley of the Kings in the morning. Wander through Luxor Temple at your leisure in the afternoon or evening.

Day Two: Travel out of town to see Denderah Temple and Abydos. In the late afternoon or early evening visit the Luxor Museum.

Day Three: Cross the Nile for most of the day to visit tombs in the Valley of the Nobles and the Valley of the Queens. Rest, then see the evening Sound and Light Show as an introduction to Karnak Temple. (If, that is, this is a night when the show is in English. Check at your hotel desk.)

Day Four: Make a serious visit to the Karnak Temple. Use

the afternoon as you wish—to walk, to sail leisurely to Banana Island, to buy kaftans.

Day Five: Cross the Nile to see the temples of the Ramesseum, Dier el Bahri, and Medinet Habu. Relax in the afternoon or return to see more nobles' tombs.

Beware of sunburn and salt loss when scurrying from tomb to tomb. The sun shines every day in Luxor and the limestone hills bounce all the heat back to your face. Sun without humidity dehydrates and burns the skin more than moist heat, all without familiar perspiration signals from your body. Covering up is a better defense than exposing the skin. In the summer, when temperatures can pass 120°, it is best to go out only until 10 a.m. and after 5 p.m.

Climbing hills and slippery passages requires shoes that are comfortable and that grip the terrain firmly. Dust inside tombs and outdoors may cause respiratory irritations—some people cover their nose and mouth with a bandanna. A flashlight is very desirable since few tombs are electrically lighted. Binoculars prove useful for carvings on the high walls and ceilings of temples.

The Nile separates the sights into two groups—those across the river on the west bank and others on the east, the Luxor side. On the east bank are the temples of Luxor and Karnak, the Luxor Museum, and various excursion sights. The west bank is dusty, bleak, and crammed with temples and tombs. Variety, as well as muscles tired from climbs in and out of tombs, calls for alternating trips west with visits along the east bank. However, for convenience of reference, each bank is treated separately.

THE SIGHTS ON THE WEST BANK

Barren hills in the distance shelter the last resting places of the royal and the rich. Between the river and the hills the land, stretching as flat as water, is lush with green crops. The green forms a line so sharp that you can place one foot in fertile fields and the other on desert sterility. Just over this

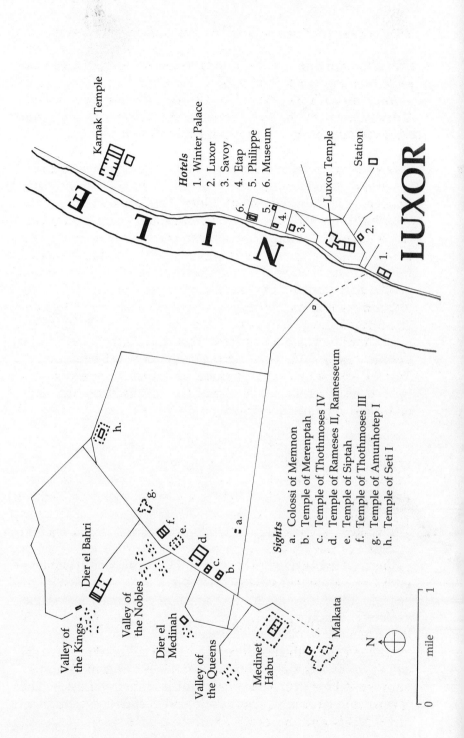

LUXOR

NILE

Karnak Temple

Hotels
1. Winter Palace
2. Luxor
3. Savoy
4. Etap
5. Philippe
6. Museum

Luxor Temple

Station

Sights
a. Colossi of Memnon
b. Temple of Merenptah
c. Temple of Thothmoses IV
d. Temple of Rameses II, Ramesseum
e. Temple of Siptah
f. Temple of Thothmoses III
g. Temple of Amunhotep I
h. Temple of Seti I

Valley of
the Kings

Dier el Bahri

Valley of
the Nobles

Dier el
Medinah

Valley of
the Queens

Medinet
Habu

Malkata

N

0   mile   1

line, all parallel to the river, are a string of temples raised by the various pharaohs of the New Kingdom to proclaim their hidden tombs.

The west bank is appropriately quiet. There are only two small villages—one for the farmers who tend the land, and Gurnah where many tomb robbers live. Gurnah, a village built over the tombs of ancient nobles, has hidden tunnels that run to places only the robbers know. Although their profession is only the second oldest, these people can trace their work through continuous generations back to the time of the New Kingdom. On this bank cars are almost entirely for tourist hire; camels and donkeys serve the local people. Here, where so many tourists come, for some reason the people are more traditional in their Islamic faith. You may often see veiled women.

To cross the Nile take the ferry that departs from the pier in front of the Winter Palace Hotel. On the west bank, stairs lead to a booth where tickets for all the sights are on sale. Here you must decide the day's program, for each area requires a separate ticket, valid only for that day.

Valley of the Kings	LE 2
Valley of the Nobles	LE 1
Dier el Bahri	LE 1
Ramesseum	LE 1
Medinet Habu	LE 1
Temple of Seti I	50 pt
Valley of the Queens	50 pt

Taxis wait beside the ticket booth. If you don't want to travel by donkey or by bicycle (see Luxor transportation, below), these antique cars and vans are your only reasonable choice: The sights are up to six miles away (for the Valley of the Kings). Despite appearances and the sound of their engines, these vehicles do run and will take you to a half-day's worth of sights for about LE 5, after bargaining. However, whenever he leaves you the driver will ask when you wish to be picked up for your next destination. This is so he can do other trips in the meantime. Drivers are quite reliable in meeting their appointments.

To test your patience, swarms of eager vendors will assault you with their outrageously overpriced wares during these arrangements. To ease your way through arrangements, a guide is recommended, especially for your first trip, and he will fend off the avid hawkers. Your hotel can find a licensed guide for about LE 5 the half-day. He will be especially worthwhile for visits to tombs, getting keys for some that ordinarily are closed and handling tips for the guards.

The layout of sights is quite simple. A road runs straight away from the Nile over the cultivated land, passing the two lonely Colossi of Memnon on the right. A quarter of a mile farther on, a road crosses, parallel to the Nile. Left on this second road in a quarter of a mile is *Medinet Habu*—the palace-temple-fortress of Rameses III. Just past Medinet Habu is the "Malkata Palace" (where you need special permission to enter), the ruins of the palace of Amunhotep III. Before Medinet Habu a road leads away from the Nile toward the *Valley of the Queens.*

But if instead of turning left onto the crossing road you turn right, you will pass temple after temple of the pharaohs of the New Kingdom. Most of these temples are so ruined, you can pass right by. First is that of Merenptah (who "destroyed Israel"), then Thothmoses IV (of the Sphinx stele), followed by Rameses the Great, Amunhotep II, and Thothmoses III. From this road of temples running parallel to the Nile a series of roads lead away from the river, to the left as you ride.

The temple of Rameses, the *Ramesseum,* is worth stopping at; then a road goes off to *Dier el Medinah*—where you can see the village of those who worked on all the tombs along with interesting tombs of the lower classes. Second on the left is the road to the Tombs of the Nobles. The third road going left leads past more nobles' tombs toward the magnificent temple of Hatshepsut at *Dier el Bahri.* If you continue all the way to the end of the temple road, you arrive at a "T." A right turn will take you to the *Temple of Seti I*. A left turn will take you over a winding two-mile drive through desolate hills along exactly the route that ancient funeral processions followed to Biban el Muluk, the *Valley of the Kings*.

THE VALLEY OF THE KINGS

After leaving the parking lot and passing through narrow entrance gates, two things strike almost every visitor. How desolate and poor is this land beneath which treasures beyond imagination once were buried. And how confined it is, barely six acres in area.

Not a thing grows. Insects and birds pass through as quickly as they can. Rain almost never falls on this tiny valley, even when it wets the hills nearby. The area is confined because it was first chosen for the tomb of just one pharaoh, Thothmoses I. Like lemmings, succeeding pharaohs followed him and made their tombs close by. The 57 known tombs in this valley (four more are in a valley over the hill) are numbered pretty much in the order of their discovery. Tombs of 23 pharaohs, one prince, one queen, and 6 nobles are known. Outside of these, tombs mainly are unadorned (probably because they were never completed). All date from one dynasty or another of the New Kingdom.

In the beginning of a pharaoh's reign a site was selected and plans drawn for his tomb. Two teams of between 25 and 50 men each worked for ten-day shifts during which time they lived in stone huts in this valley; after the first team returned to their village (Dier el Medinah), the second team took over the work. They dug through the soft limestone with bronze tools and used oil lamps to light their way. Craftsmen followed, smoothing the walls, repairing with plaster when necessary. Then an artist sketched scenes that painters finished (often adjusting the original sketches). A modest tomb for a king would take about five years to complete. After the pharaoh with his gold jewelry, perfumes, furniture, and food—all the things he might need in the next world—was buried inside, the entrance was plastered shut and stamped with the seal of the dog-god Anubis, god of the necropolis. Then the descending stairs would be filled in with rubble and covered with smooth earth to hide any sign of the tomb.

Both the plan of a tomb and the nature of its painted decoration differed greatly, depending on whether it was intended for a pharaoh or for a noble. Pharaohs' tombs begin with long, relatively narrow corridors, toward the end of which larger rooms (as few as one or as many as 20) branch off from the corridor. In general, the corridors of Dynasty XVIII tombs bend several times and run more deeply underground, while later dynasties have straight corridors lying closer to the surface. The decoration of a pharaoh's tomb is always religious in character, while scenes from life decorate nobles' tombs. The major pharaonic theme is the journey of the gods through the netherworld, for the pharaoh aspired to be a god and to travel with his divine peers. The walls depict the journey of the sun after it sets. The sun sails by boat past mythical denizens of the netherworld—those who threaten and those who protect. The pharaoh is shown in the company of gods: with Khepher—the beetle who represents existence; with Anubis—the dog-headed god who preserved the body; with Maat—the goddess of truth and order wearing a single feather; with Osiris—the green-skinned, mummylike king of the netherworld; and with his wife Isis—wearing a step-shaped throne. Other gods and goddesses, too numerous to describe, also appear. The principle behind these paintings was that of sympathetic magic: paint the pharaoh whole and safe in scenes of all the stages of the journey, and the journey would happen in just that way.

What follows is a priority list of tombs. If your time is short, you will see a varied sample by visiting #62 (Tutankhamun), #17 (Seti I), #9 (Rameses VI), and either #34 (Thothmoses III) or #35 (Amunhotep II). Recent changes in humidity have caused the closing of tombs formerly open. Check with guards to find which tombs remain accessible. A minimal visit to four tombs will take almost two hours. It is best to plan a leisurely half-day here rather than overpacking your schedule. There is a rest house for snacks and beverages.

#62 TOMB OF TUTANKHAMUN: Late Dynasty XVIII. *(Directly opposite the front of the rest house.)* The tomb was robbed once, shortly after Tutankhamun's burial, by thieves who took mainly precious oils. Something made them hurry and they managed to remove only a small percentage of the valuables. The robbery was discovered and the tomb was resealed until 1922 when Howard Carter rediscovered it. What saved the tomb was that Rameses VI, two dynasties later, had built his tomb on the rise just above. Because the location of Tutankhamun's tomb had been forgotten, the workmen for Rameses VI's tomb placed their huts directly over Tutankhamun. Everyone, both ancient robbers and modern archaeologists, knew that houses for the living would never be placed upon hallowed ground, so the site was never investigated. However, Howard Carter was so methodical that he followed routine rather than reason and dug every inch of ground in the valley, including this place. His first clue was a sudden quiet that came over his diggers. He ran to the site and found the top of a step showing through limestone chips.

The tomb is unbelievably small. One cannot help but think that Tutankhamun's early death meant that his tomb was far from completed. Either his partial tomb was put in some order, or another tomb for a lesser personage was appropriated for Tutankhamun, probably the latter. The quantity of goods found inside—objects piled as high as a man—further confirms the inappropriateness of this space for a pharaoh.

Through the door you enter a vestibule, 30 feet by ten, the largest part of the tomb. To the right is a tiny room (now sealed); to the left is the burial room on a lower level. You can look down on the pink-granite sarcophagus, protected by Isis and her sisters at the corners, containing one of the three original nestled coffins. This one is the outermost, of gilded wood. Though it cannot be seen, Tutankhamun's mummy still reposes in his coffin. It was decided that since his rest had lasted for 3300 years, he should not be disturbed in 1922.

The only decoration in the tomb is painted, not carved, on the walls of the burial chamber. On the right Tut's coffin is shown being transported to the tomb. Then Ay, the vizier and next pharaoh, is portrayed as a priest (in leopard skin) performing the last rites on Tutankhamun's mummy. With an adzelike instrument, Ay is performing symbolically the "Opening of the Mouth" ceremony, making Tutankhamun relive. Farther left, Tutankhamun makes an obeisance to Nut, goddess of the sky. Then Tutankhamun, along with his double (his soul), stands before Osiris, the king of the next world. On the left wall a solar boat carries the sun, shown in the guise of the beetle of existence; below this baboons (thought to be the elect of the sun, for they do sometimes raise their heads to the sky) pray.

#9 TOMB OF RAMESES VI: Dynasty XX. *(Directly above Tutankhamun's tomb.)* Carved scenes cover both sides of the long entrance corridor. The left wall describes the journey of the sun at night; the right wall shows the places and the beings of the next world. In the next-to-last room are texts from the Book of the Dead (spells like the Pyramid Texts of an earlier time). The final and largest room is pillared and has remains of an enormous sarcophagus in the center. Covering the ceiling is a dramatic scene of the sky goddess Nut shown twice as a naked woman touching the earth with her hands and feet while her body arches above. Along one of her bodies, red suns symbolize the 12 hours of the day and along the other body are the hours of the night. (Egyptians invented the division of a day into 24 parts.)

#17 TOMB OF SETI I: Early Dynasty XIX. *(Walk back toward the rest house, then along its side. This is the second tomb after passing the rest house.)* Of all the tombs in the valley this is the largest (over 350 feet long) and the most beautifully carved and painted.

The king greets you on the left, while protective vultures hover on the ceiling. The walls proclaim all the attributes of the sun in pictures. Just before the first pillared hall Seti is welcomed by various gods. On the pillars of the following room, Seti stands with different gods while the wall scenes portray the stages of the mysterious night journey made by the sun. When the corridor continues, it shows the resurrection ritual of "Opening the Mouth." At its end the corridor lets into a large pillared room in which Seti's sarcophagus once rested. One ceiling is covered by a spectacular scene of the zodiac sky.

Off to the right is a small room telling the story of the destruction of mankind. Our species had forgotten its god, the sun, who became so angered that he unleashed the lion goddess Sekhmet to destroy humanity. Ra's anger soon passed, but to stop Sekhmet he had to pour wine on the ground which she drank thinking it was blood. The wine made her sleep and thus mankind was saved. In this room is a lovely picture of the sky as a cow supported by the god Shu (air).

This tomb is the aesthetic culmination of the finely decorated kind. You may feel that similar tombs will pale after this one and may wish to skip to the tomb of Amunhotep II.

#11 TOMB OF RAMESES III: Early Dynasty XX. *(Return to the rest house, left past the tomb of Rameses VI—#9 described above. This is the second tomb, up the start of the hill.)* The tomb is almost as large as Seti's, but the last half is ruined and closed. What is special are the scenes in the small chambers off the main corridor. They are more lively than those of any other pharaoh. Especially charming are the harpers singing hymns to various gods in the fifth room on the left side.

#35 TOMB OF AMUNHOTEP II: Middle Dynasty XVIII. *(Continue up the path for ten yards or so, taking the right path when you come to the fork. The tomb is at the end of this path.)* A long, steep corridor comes to a shaft that is covered by a modern footbridge. A large unfinished chamber leads into an even larger room with pillars; just before the pillared room, on the right, is an ancient plan of the tomb left by an architect. In the burial chamber the walls are yellow to suggest the color of papyrus, for the whole room replicates a papyrus roll on which outline scenes of the sun's night journey are painted. It is all so simple and clean that it seems brilliant after the multicolored, complex compositions of later pharaohs.

#34 TOMB OF THOTHMOSES III: Middle Dynasty XVIII. *(Return to the main path which you follow up the hill, going left at the next fork. You are aiming for a narrow ravine in the cliffs. Climb the iron stairs. This tomb is on the right at the top. Sometimes closed; it is wise to check at the ticket booth before making the trek.)* This tomb is even simpler than the preceding tomb for Amunhotep II; it belonged to his father. Egypt's Napoleon needed no grand tomb when his deeds already had earned him a god's place. This tomb, shaped like a sarcophagus, still has the sarcophagus in it. The journey of the sun is depicted by stick figures. Somehow it is enchanting.

#6 TOMB OF RAMESES IX: Late Dynasty XX. *(All the way back to the rest house. This tomb is the second past the rest house, just before the parking lot.)* The first tomb past the rest house (#55) belonged to queen Tiy, wife of Amunhotep III and probable mother of Tut. This tomb (#6) belonged to the last pharaoh of the New Kingdom. It is similar in theme and style to the tomb of Rameses VI.

#16 TOMB OF RAMESES I: Early Dynasty XIX. *(Just before the tomb of Seti I—#17 described above.)* The colors are remarkably well preserved in this tomb of the founder of Dynasty XIX.

#57 TOMB OF HOREMHEB: Late Dynasty XVIII. *(At tomb #11, described above, take the right fork instead of the left which led to Thothmoses III.)* Special because so much of the decoration was unfinished and clearly shows the stages of decorating a tomb.

DIER EL BAHRI

Nestled into an amphitheater of precipitous cliffs, Hatshepsut's temple looks at once modern in its simplicity and at the same time eternal in its harmony with the site. It is now in the process of reconstruction, so its stones are clean and bright. It ranks with the most beautiful buildings in the world.

This funerary temple for the departed Hatshepsut was a place for offerings and prayers. Every pharaoh who lived long enough during the New Kingdom had such a temple. This one is unique in form, probably because the site was special. Funerary temples usually are far from royal tombs, but this one is just a hill away. The hill above the temple looks down on the Valley of the Kings. Hatshepsut planned to connect her tomb in the valley to the back of this temple, although the tunnel never was finished. Proximity to her tomb, rather than distance so as not to reveal the tomb's location, seemed to have influenced the placement and perhaps the design. Usually funerary temples were rectangular like other temples. This one hugs the cliffs in a line. When it was designed, there was another temple beside it belonging to Montuhotep, founder of the Middle Kingdom. That temple is so ruined now that its plan can hardly be deciphered, but originally it consisted of a pyramid surrounded by pillared open walkways. The pillar design may have inspired the architect Senmut; the mountain peak behind Hatshepsut's temple may have been seen as her pyramid. Of course this is all speculation. The fact remains that this terrace and ramp design is unique, as is the decoration.

Although you can appreciate the harmony of the plan from a distance, close viewing is necessary for the exquisite carving on the walls of the colonnades. These pictures, the culmination of the New Kingdom style, should be leisurely appreciated. It may take about an hour.

Originally an avenue of sphinxes bearing Hatshepsut's face led to the temple. One lion remains. The two broad lower terraces were planted as gardens with exotic trees, some brought from the fabled land of Punt. Two stumps, still visible in wire "baskets" by the entrance, were persea trees, sacred to the ancient Egyptians. Near the end of each of the three terraces stood giant statues of Osiris, appropriate for a funerary temple, some of which have been reerected.

The walls of the right colonnade on this first terrace are carved with sporting scenes, which harken to similar ones in the Old Kingdom mastabas. At each end of the colonnade is a representation of Hatshepsut in the guise of Osiris. The figures are still recognizable, though her ward Thothmoses III ordered every representation of Hatshepsut and occurrence of her name chiseled out after he came to power. The colonnade shows two obelisks towed on a barge by a flotilla of 27 boats from Aswan. Later the obelisks were erected in Karnak Temple.

A ramp leads to a second terrace and two more colonnades with chapels at either end. The walls of the right colonnade show the story of Hatshepsut's divine birth. Amun visits Hatshepsut's mother (in a vulture headdress). Seti I restored this carving in ancient times after Akhenaten had erased a representation of a god he considered false. The queen (Ahmose) is led to a birth chamber, waited upon by various divinities. The creator god Khnum (with ram's horns) molds the child Hatshepsut (shown as a male!), and her double, or soul. On the square pillars scenes of Hatshepsut (erased) and Thothmoses III blessed by Amun alternate. On the right end of this colonnade is the sanctuary of Anubis—dog-headed god of mummification. The columns here are lovely fluted ones of a type that influenced the later Greek Doric columns.

The colonnade on the left side houses charming scenes of the expedition Hatshepsut sent to the land of Punt. You can see the flora, fauna, people, and the stilt houses of this fabled place (probably modern Somalia). At the end, when the expedition returned, offerings were made by Hatshepsut and by Thothmoses III (whose face is exquisite). At the extreme left is a chapel for the cow goddess Hat-hor. The pillars are justly famous. They reproduce a rattle, called a *sistrum*, used in rites for Hat-hor. The bottom of the pillars correspond to the handle; near the top are lovely faces of Hat-hor, above which is a representation of the part housing the rattles. In the sanctuary itself a door opens on the left into another room. Senmut wrote his name where it would be covered by this door when anyone opened it to enter. Those who came to erase his memory never found it.

The third terrace, unfortunately, is being reconstructed and may not be visited. It contains the most holy chapel, dedicated to Amun, cut into the mountainside. This was a holy place long after Hatshepsut's disgrace. On the right is a chapel dedicated to Ra; on the left is one dedicated to the woman who built this wonderful temple.

THE RAMESSEUM

This, the funerary temple for Rameses the Great, is quite ruined. Worth seeing, though are the grandiose statues and the decoration for effect that developed in Dynasty XIX out of Dynasty XVIII delicacy.

Originally the Ramesseum was a large complex whose main element was a grand mortuary temple. A small "palace" (more a place where Rameses could stay when he visited than his permanent residence) was off the first courtyard. Surrounding these buildings are hundreds of adobe rooms, called storerooms, for some unclear purpose. The plan of so much ruin is difficult to discern, so we will discuss only the notable features.

After entering, go left into what was the first of two courtyards. There, at the far end, are two pylons of the intended entrance to the complex. Covering the faces of these pylons are scenes of Rameses on his campaign to Kadesh. The left pylon (as you face them) lists and pictures the fortresses in Syria that he captured. Scenes of his army camp contain fascinating details of military arrangements in the 13th century B.C. Above, on the right side of this pylon, is a scene of Hittite spies being interrogated (perhaps these are the spies who gave false information that led Rameses on his rash march). The right pylon contains the dramatic scene of the Kadesh battle. In his chariot Rameses looks every inch the fearless warrior amid the confusion of his foes.

Continuing along the courtyard, you pass a double aisle of pillars that led to the "palace." Toward the back lies a colossal statue of Rameses that fell in an earthquake. When whole, the statue would have been 60 feet high—one finger is more than three feet long—and would have weighed over two million pounds.

Up steps, you enter a second courtyard through smaller pylons. The pylon to your right has more scenes of the battle of Kadesh. This courtyard was lined by columns (four of which remain) in the form of Osiris. A large, granite head of Rameses lies on the ground. Up steps again is a vestibule (with some nice reliefs), and beyond is the hypostyle hall with more than half of its tall columns in place.

MEDINET HABU

Rameses III, the great pharaoh of Dynasty XX, built most of this complex. It appears to be a fortress, though it was more a temple and a palace. Comparatively well preserved, it has several unique features.

You enter through a great gate, like that of a fortress in ancient Syria, flanked by two tall towers with high windows. Below the windows, heads of enemies protrude so the pharaoh would seem, when he appeared at the window, to be standing on his foes. You can visit the apartments in these towers by climbing the stairs outside around the back. The view gives you a clear idea of the temple complex. Two nice granite statues of Sekhmet, the lioness who almost ate mankind, are on either side of the entrance.

Through the gate you enter a large open courtyard; straight ahead is the temple. To the left in the courtyard is a small later temple from Dynasty XXIII; on the right is an elegant Dynasty XVIII temple around which Rameses III built his complex. This temple was begun by Hatshepsut and finished by Thothmoses III. Unfortunately, later kings made numerous alterations.

The main temple, that of Rameses III, begins with two pylons. They commemorate this pharaoh's battles in Nubia and Syria. At some point in your visit you should circle around the outer walls of the temple. Besides being imposing, with lion rainspouts and carvings all over, some of the scenes are special enough to deserve a pause. On the right-hand wall (near a small door) is a scene of the great naval battle in which Rameses III fought the Sea People. Gashes in the walls were made by the fingernails of people who wanted stone dust for good luck from this sacred place. Where the pylon meets this wall a staircase leads to the top of the pylon and a fine view. On the left wall, against the temple, is

Rameses III's "palace." The dias of a throne and a nearby latrine can still be made out.

Through the pylons is the first courtyard of the temple. On the left-hand wall is a scene where soldiers show trophies to Rameses III. The soldiers won awards based on the number of enemies they had slain. To avoid fraud, proof in the form of severed hands was required. Because enterprising soldiers sometimes took the hands of women to increase their scores, this wall depicts heaped penises, the ultimate proof of males killed.

The second courtyard is reached through pylons again. The right wall has nice scenes of the festival of the fertility god Min. Continuing through the temple, you pass through a doorway into the hypostyle hall. To the left are a series of treasure rooms still with roofs. Of course the treasures are long gone, but are still depicted on the walls. To the right lie various sanctuaries. Numerous chambers ring the rear of the temple.

TEMPLE OF SETI I

Though ruined, this temple still has lovely reliefs in places. The walls and chapels along the sides of the hypostyle hall are especially well carved.

TOMBS OF THE NOBLES

Although some were made for princes and queens, the vast majority of these tombs were commissioned by court officials. You may visit most of the more than 400 known tombs. These tombs for the nonroyal contain paintings that rank with the finest art in all of ancient Egypt. You will probably find them more exciting than pharaohs' tombs.

As Egypt grew rich during the New Kingdom, nonroyal people increasingly were able to provide for their own afterlife. They too could construct a tomb and decorate the walls, have an offering chapel and a sarcophagus, modeling their preparations on those of a pharaoh. These tombs naturally were smaller, and the decorative themes appropriate for a pharaoh, a future god, were not suited to commoners. Instead, commoners painted scenes of what they loved or were proud of, what they wanted to remember for eternity. The scenes are charming as well as interesting for the abundant information they convey. They are "snapshots" of life as it was more than 3000 years ago.

The basic plan of these tombs is a T-shape, upside down. You enter a long room, the length of which spreads on either side of the door rather than to the back. Painted scenes from life activities run along the walls. Straight back you follow a narrow corridor that ends, usually, in a niche for a statue of the tomb owner, often with his wife. Scenes in this room are more religious, stereotyped, and less interesting (prayers, offerings, mere lists of offices.) Together these two chambers form the chapel. The burial chamber, a room at the bottom of a shaft, usually has magic texts, is seldom of interest, and most often has been sealed over by the authorities to prevent accidental falls. Thus, you usually see only the T-shaped chapel. Richer people had larger chapels that later grew more complex, adding rooms and even pillars by leaving some unexcavated rock.

The rooms were cut through limestone rock which in this part of Egypt is rather friable. Thus painting replaced carved reliefs. The walls therefore needed a smooth surface, usually achieved with a coat of plaster. Where the rock was especially weak, a mud and straw coating was laid down before a final thin plaster cover. The style of painting, and to some extent the subject matter, changed with the dynasties (though every tomb commonly visited, except one, dates from the New Kingdom). In Dynasty XVIII, early tomb paintings were dignified and strong; the latter part of this dynasty developed a delicate "classical" style. Dynasty XIX tended to refinement and more hasty execution that evolved into a heavy style in Dynasty XX. The backgrounds changed over time—first gray, then white at the end of Dynasty XVIII until the yellow backgrounds that begin in Dynasty XIX. As time passed, the painted scenes grew more religious in their themes.

The paintings themselves, especially earlier ones, depict the tomb owner in activities that proclaim his position and show what he loved. Usually a large scene of the owner is accompanied by strips of smaller vignettes, like comic books, detailing a sequence of events. These can run in either direction—right to left or left to right. The sequences go from the top of the wall to the bottom (although there are exceptions); and the direction of events starts from the side toward which most of the figures face and ends at their backs. The figures are formal because the purpose (like that of hieroglyphs) is to tell a story rather than to replicate a living event. The colors are few and basic; they could be diluted for lightening or painted in several coats for darker tones. Shadowing and shading are rare but do exist. The miracle is that so much bright color survives all the years. Because many of the tombs were left unfinished, you can see the stages of production. They were not finished because to do so before the owner died would have been bad luck; people seldom died on schedule.

For some viewers the interest of these tombs is educational, for others it is a graceful line forming a beautiful face, a charming cat peering from under a chair, or a flowing composition of musicians and dancers. The miracle of the greatest of these tombs is that they are both informative and of surpassing beauty. With so many tombs available, selection is imperative. The tombs spread in no compact order—this visit is one for which a hired guide is extremely helpful. He can lead you and you can get keys when necessary for the tombs you wish to see. You will need a flashlight (even though the doorkeepers reflect light inside with tinfoil mirrors).

Here is a selection of the best tombs from Sheikh el Gurnah, where most tombs are situated. Anyone who can visit all 14 tombs described below will have a day of pure pleasure. Our condolences if a full day is not possible, but do everything you can to arrange your schedule for at least a half-day and at least five wonderful experiences: #52 Nakht, #69 Menna, #55 Ramose, #100 Rekhmire, and #96 Sennefer. If you can, add #60 Antefeker (Middle Kingdom) and #51 Userhat (Dynasty XIX), for the five tombs above all fall within Dynasty XVIII. If you love Ramose's tomb, #57 Khaemhat next door is similar in style and some consider it comparable. Although #93, Kenamun's tomb, might have the finest art of all, it is somewhat damaged. Other tombs might especially interest you for qualities described below. It is far better to savor these paintings slowly, to inspect and appreciate, rather than to gulp them down in the pursuit of quantity. The descriptions below are arranged by the order in which the tombs are traversed, from the plain up the steep hill.

#52 TOMB OF NAKHT: Middle of Dynasty XVIII. *(By the road from the Ramesseum to Dier el Bahri.)* Small; only the first chamber is decorated, but the paint is preserved brilliantly and the scenes are charming. Nakht was a priest and astronomer, and his wife was a "singer of Amun." The walls, however, show nothing of their professions, just banquets and country life. Evidently, pleasures took precedence over business.

The left side as you enter is most famous. On the wall by the entrance, large figures of Nakht and his wife (Nakht in a diaphanous outer kilt) pour oil over a heap of offerings. Below a cow is butchered and farther below is a map of their estate, with workmen repairing canals. Nakht watches from the porch of his house at the end of the wall (twice). Then come harvesting scenes. At the top is the winnowing of grain, then gathering, then the grain is poured into a basket—a man leaps to use his weight to pack down the overflow. The end wall has a false door through which Nakht's soul could fly. His picture is repeated all around offering prayers. The next wall is damaged on top but shows festive banquet scenes below. At the end, beside the false door, is one of the most often reproduced pictures from ancient Egypt. At the top remaining register is a blind harper, his age and affliction well conveyed with just the turn of a line or two. His hands are graceful. (The blind often were harpist-singers in ancient times.) Beside and below, trailing after the large banquet picture, are three women musicians. The turn of the middle (practically naked) lutist, her foot raised, makes the scene live. Most of those at the banquet have cones on their heads. Such cones were common.

Perfumed animal fat melted as a guest grew hotter, masking the odor of perspiration with perfume. Notice the cat hiding with his stolen fish under the chair of Nakht's wife.

The right wing is unfinished, but the far wall has some charming pictures of animals and birds. See the girl with a bird in her hand. Nakht and his wife watch from under an arbor.

#69 TOMB OF MENNA: Middle of Dynasty XVIII. *(By the bottom of the enclosure wall.)* "Charming" is the only word for these paintings. This unknown artist could not paint a merely standard scene. He added details, elements never used in the standard Egyptian repertoire, to bring his scenes to life. His paintings need study to reveal wonderful details.

Along the entrance passage, Menna and his family make devotions to the sun. Left, inside along the left-hand wall, Menna sits beside offerings where he can watch the agricultural scenes around him. Menna had enemies it seems, for his eyes have been scratched out to blind him for eternity. How sad, for Menna was a steward of the king's farms who obviously took delight in his duties, so charmingly reproduced. At the top left, revenue officers measure and collect their due. A man offers a "corn doll" in a peasant custom. On the top right, cheaters are beaten. Below, two girls fight over stray heads of grain while another helps a friend remove a thorn from her foot. A man naps under a tree while his friend plays a flute. Below, men spread the wheat for threshing watched by their boss, leaning so casually on his staff.

In the right wing, only the wall alongside the entrance is special. In particular the women are beautiful (especially the daughters), watching over offerings and bringing bouquets to their deceased parents. Offering bearers are below. Note the one carrying an antelope over his shoulders.

In this tomb the narrow chapel is worth seeing, especially the right side. A magnificent hunting and fishing scene occupies the center. Menna harpoons fish, a naked girl smells a lotus, birds land on the water, and a baby crocodile tries to eat a fish much too large for it. Back toward the beginning of this wall is a scene of the ritual pilgrimage of the mummy. Again, the artist includes his touches from life—the man bending down from the boat to scoop some water, the man at the very bottom who badly needs a shave (many sets of razors have been found in excavations, by the way), and so on.

#51 TOMB OF USERHAT: Early Dynasty XIX. *(Continue along this path.)* Userhat was a priest of the cult for the first Thothmoses, who was still revered a dynasty later. His artist worked on the white background commonly used early in Dynasty XIX. You can see pieces of the straw compound which prepared the wall under the plaster. His artist loved the fluid line, the spare form.

In the right wing Userhat, two wives, his son, and probably his mother offer sacrifices. The clothes and jewelry are admirably done. Farther along mourners and priests offer incense to the dead couple. The priests are delicately drawn with elongated heads—the legacy of the Amarna style. Across the rear wall is a charming scene of a sycamore tree, the tree of life, personified in the shape of a woman offering water to the deceased, his wife, and probably his mother as the trio sits elegantly beneath the tree. Human-headed birds (symbols of souls) drink from the pond.

#55 TOMB OF RAMOSE: Toward the end of Dynasty XVIII. *(Downstream on the plain.)* Sublime classical art at its peak was produced for this mayor of Thebes. The style changed as time passed in constructing this tomb, until at the far, unfinished wall the revolutionary Amarna style of Akhenaten begins. Much of this large tomb is carved in the most elegant of reliefs, some is merely painted. Only one large room was decorated, for the owner left Thebes to follow Akhenaten to his new capital in Middle Egypt.

The right-hand wall starts at a high pitch, with delicate portraits of Ramose and his beautiful wife. The offering bearers and young girls holding sacred rattles are equally exquisite.

The wall to the left of the entrance is outstanding with

more bearers, singers, and scribes. The next wall, the side, is not carved, but painted in funeral scenes. The group of mourning women with tears and bared breasts is among the most famous of all Egyptian artworks. The back wall contains a scene in which Ramose offers flowers to Akhenaten (at this time still called Amunhotep). Then come unfinished scenes in the more extreme Amarna style where Akhenaten has grown grotesque. The wall is a record of the development of the Amarna style.

This tomb is one for which description would be wasted; it is intended for tender appreciation.

#57 TOMB OF KHAEMHAT: End of Dynasty XVIII. *(Next to Ramose.)* Similar in style to the preceding, for it was made during the reign of Akhenaten's father, Amunhotep III. This tomb is as lovely as Ramoses' tomb in detail, but has busier, more complex scenes. Note the graceful cattle to the left side on the right-hand wall. On the right side, Amunhotep III (his face is a cast from the original, now in Berlin) rewards Khaemhat. The faces are lovely. A second chamber with processions and a pilgrimage leads into a chapel with graceful but darkened statues.

#56 TOMB OF USERHAT: Middle of Dynasty XVIII. *(In line with Khaemhat.)* He was raised in the royal nursery and became a palace scribe in the reign of Amunhotep II, the son of Thothmoses III. In the left wing is the usual offering scene with surrounding views from country life. Notice the cow licking its calf. Then comes the false-door wall and the banquet wall. Children offer flowers to their parents; monkeys play under the chairs. The right wing displays standard offering scenes, an homage to Osiris. The rear wall of this wing shows Userhat bringing bouquets to Amunhotep II, troops being recruited, and a rare barbering scene.

Userhat loved the hunt and had his best scenes painted in the receding corridor on the left-hand wall. Note the panicked rabbit under the charging horses of his chariot. Just to the right is a dying fox with faint indications of blood spurting from his mouth and eye. Farther right is a charming grape harvest, across from a funeral procession where the mourners truly express passion.

#100 TOMB OF REKHMIRE: Middle of Dynasty XVIII. *(Up the start of the hill, toward the downstream end.)* Although it is accurate, the drawing is not so fine as in other tombs, yet there is more information about life in ancient Egypt than in volumes of books.

Rekhmire was the vizier of Thothmoses III and, for a while, of Amunhotep II. The left side of the first chamber shows him performing his duties—assessing taxes and, on the end wall, receiving foreign tributaries. You can see well-observed representations of the dress and faces of people from Punt, Crete, Nubia, and Syria (top to bottom), with the produce of their countries.

Rekhmire placed a premium on accuracy and left us a record of almost all the professions of ancient Egypt on the walls of the long receding corridor with steeply rising ceiling. You see vase makers, goldsmiths, leatherworkers, rope makers, carpenters, cabinetmakers, blacksmiths, brickmakers and bricklayers, sculptors, and on, and on. On the middle of the right-hand wall, the third register, is a rare back view of a lovely servant girl pouring drinks during a banquet.

#93 TOMB OF KENAMUN: Middle of Dynasty XVIII. *(Nearby Rekhmire.)* If this tomb were not so damaged, people would be lined up to see it. The subtle rendering of texture, the inclusion of the smallest details, are remarkable.

In the first room, the right wing is best. In particular the back wall with scenes of Amunhotep II and prisoners kneeling would, if cleaned, be a gem. The second chamber, on the right-hand wall, shows a wonderful desert hunt, then fowling and fishing in the marshes. Everything is wonderful, the animals and the people.

#96 TOMB OF SENNEFER: Middle of Dynasty XVIII. *(Nearby Rekhmire.)* The chapel is closed, in need of repair. The burial chamber, which in other tombs is hardly worth a visit, is the star of this tomb. Down steep stairs you arrive in a small room with nicely colored paintings of the deceased and his daughter awaiting the equipment for the tomb. You have come to this place for the second room, the burial chamber. The painting is bright but sketchy, with religious scenes and texts from the Book of the Dead. Overhead is a spectacular device—the ceiling was left uneven and painted all over with grapes. You are in a grape arbor, 3000 years old, and you can practically smell the sweet nectar.

#60 TOMB OF ANTEFEKER: Middle Kingdom, Dynasty XII. (*Moving farther up the hill.*) Here you are back to the Middle Kingdom. The paint is remarkable, given its age; the style is rigid but strong (reminiscent of very early art of Dynasty XVIII). It is interesting to see scenes you have already viewed in this very different style. This is Bach to the Beethoven opuses already seen.

#74 TOMB OF THUNANY: Middle of Dynasty XVIII. (*Up toward the top of the hill.*) Thunany was a scribe in the army during the time of Thothmoses III. His artist forswore delicacy for broad strokes and strong colors. His eye was no less accurate for being quicker. Not surprisingly, army affairs are much in evidence in this tomb. Burly soldiers were perfect subjects for this painter's style. So study the left-hand wall in the right wing. Note the pot-bellied "bully" of a standard bearer and the costumes of the troops. In the right-hand wing, powerful steeds and strong bulls show this style at its best.

#71 TOMB OF SENMUT: Middle of Dynasty XVIII. (*Nearby Thunany.*) This colleague of Hatshepsut was hated by Thothmoses III whose agents destroyed most of his tomb (and another he built beside the lower terrace of Hatshepsut's temple). Only fragments remain to hint at its majesty. A historical imagination working on the scene of tribute bearers from Crete under a frieze of Hat-hor heads may be able to fill in its former glory.

#78 TOMB OF HOREMHEB: Middle of Dynasty XVIII. (*Same area as Senmut.*) Like Thanuny, Horemheb was an army scribe; similar, too, are the broad strokes of this artist. The right wing of the first room shows wonderful horses and a procession of red Syrians and black Nubians. Opposite, in the familiar banquet scene, is a charming picture of Horemheb with a royal princess on his lap. The female musicians, the dancing girl, and the blind harpist are caught perfectly. In the second chamber, the left-hand wall funeral scene shows true passion. Precious details fill the right-hand wall hunting and fishing scenes.

#82 TOMB OF AMUNEMHAT: Middle of Dynasty XVIII. *(Same area as Senmut.)* Unfortunately the first chamber is damaged; what remains tells us what we have lost. Below, the banquet scene in the left wing portrays a fight between bulls and a magnificent bull in command of his herd. The right wing still has wonderful scenes of a hunt for birds. The passageway to the chapel, on the right-hand wall, holds a charming group of three musicians. The left-hand wall of the back room displays the festival of the cow goddess Hat-hor with animated scenes of dancing and singing.

VALLEY OF THE QUEENS

The site is reminiscent of the desolateness of the Valley of the Kings. Almost eighty tombs are here for princes, princesses, and queens, most from the last two dynasties of the New Kingdom. These are small tombs, like those of the nobles. The tomb of Queen Nefertari—wife of Rameses the Great—ranks far above the others. However, the plaster on which the paint was laid is turning to dust. No longer may you enter, for even the air moved by walking brings down the paint. Without Nefertari's, however, two other tombs are lovely enough to justify the trip. Both these tombs lie along the central path.

#55 TOMB OF PRINCE AMUNHORKEPSHEF: Dynasty XX. *(At the end of the central path.)* He was a son of Rameses III, shown with his proud father in this tomb. The son is shown with a sidelock (the hair style worn by children) as his father introduces him to various gods. The colors are pastel hues.

You'll be moved by the pathos of the death of so lovely a child and understand the care expended on the tomb. You can empathize with a father who would want his son to live in the next world, if not in this one.

#52 TOMB OF QUEEN TITI: Dynasty XX. *(Halfway along the central path.)* Ruined in parts, elsewhere the colors are lovely. The queen is shown communing more with goddeses than would be pictured in a male's tomb. See Maat, the goddess of order and justice with one feather on her head; Neith, goddess of the hunt; and Serket with a scorpion on her head. The final chamber has a scene of the queen praying to a group of gods while they enjoy a banquet.

DIER EL MEDINAH

The workers who excavated and decorated all the tombs for the royalty and nobility lived here. Small ordered houses, a sort of housing project, were surrounded by a wall to lock the workers inside at night. Nearby some of the workers made their own tombs, incredibly placing small pyramids above (hitherto reserved for royalty). Dug deeply below are the vaulted burial chambers that bring visitors here. One tomb has colors as fresh as the day the paintings were finished, another has scenes done nowhere else. All these tombs are interesting for the way lower classes mimicked the royal and the rich. All are located at the south (upstream) end of the village's ruins.

#1 TOMB OF SENNEDJEM: Early Dynasty XX. The yellow background adds richness to the dark reds, greens, and blacks. All is vibrant and fresh. Ra sails overhead while Sennedjem enters the next world and greets various gods (as a pharaoh would do!). But first, the dog-headed Anubis prepares the mummy of Sennedjem in a strong scene, and the green-skinned Osiris judges his soul. One entire wall describes the Garden of Ialu, the next world, an island of flowers floating in the sea. Nearby, the family offers food to Sennedjem and his wife.

#3 TOMB OF PASHEDU: Dynasty XX. The paint has flaked away but not in the lovely scene of Pashedu drinking from a stream beneath a dom palm tree. On the left wall are pictures of his charming children.

#359 TOMB OF INHERKHAU: Dynasty XX. The owner was himself an overseer of artists, which explains the careful work in his tomb. The left wall shows Inherkhau smelling a lotus; a cat killing a snake. The harpist in the offering scene below is alive. On the opposite wall children (grandchildren?) are so charmingly depicted that we understand why the man who rested in this tomb wanted to remember them for eternity.

THE SIGHTS ON THE EAST BANK

Here are three collections of special antiquities. Luxor Temple takes only an hour to wander through. The Luxor Museum is open late. Karnak Temple is so large that half a day would not exhaust its details. The best approach to Karnak is to spend an hour for orientation one evening at the Sound and Light show, then wander leisurely one morning (when the crowds are smaller) or one afternoon (when the sun makes dramatic shadows).

LUXOR TEMPLE

This temple gleams like a fairy palace from across the river. Lights have been installed to make a night display. The festive look of sharp shadows and bright light in the evening is more suggestive of its original impression—all brightly painted and busy with priests and pilgrims—than the naked ruin whose every defect is harshly shown by the sun. Visit at night if you can (for twice the day price of LE 1).

Aesthetically, Luxor Temple is finer than Karnak. Almost all of it was the work of one man with a single plan. This was Amunhotep III's offering to Amun—possibly with a contrite heart for the heresy of Atenism that was born in Akhenaten, his son.

The site was sacred before Amunhotep III raised his large

temple. Every year the god Amun came here to procreate during a festival called *Opet*—"Beginnings." On New Year's Day Amun left his house, the temple of Karnak, and sailed in a sacred boat two miles up the river to Luxor, leading his wife (the goddess Mut) and his son (Khonsu). In Luxor Temple Amun was cloistered for ten days before returning "home." During those days of privacy he symbolically impregnated his wife, which insured that the earth would be fertile for another year. Thus the Southern Harem, as ancient Egyptians called Luxor Temple, was more than a place where Amun visited; it represented the power of creation and fertility.

Rameses the Great later added two pylons in front and a courtyard skewed to face the direction of Karnak Temple. Alexander the Great added rooms in the rear. In Roman times a large number of brick buildings surrounded the temple, perhaps forming an army encampment. An avenue of hundreds of sphinxes originally stretched two miles to Karnak; some have been found and replaced.

Large statues of Rameses sit in front of the pylons along with one obelisk (the other obelisk was removed to the Place de la Concorde in Paris). The pylons which depict Rameses' battle at Kadesh each show two vertical slots for flagpoles. The courtyard beyond the pylons was added by Rameses, who placed statues of himself between rows of columns. To the left, as high as the temple roof, a small mosque perches incongruously. The mosque was built on the silt of ages which had risen so high by our era. In the left near corner of the courtyard is an original small temple by Thothmoses III with reliefs recarved by Rameses. In the far left corner of the courtyard is an unusual relief showing this very temple as it looked when festive and new. A procession of 17 sons of Rameses precedes this scene behind which troop sacrificial oxen, strangely bedecked.

Two large seated statues of Rameses lead into a colonnade hall—the first of the structures of Amunhotep III. This narrow entry is an unusual feature for an Egyptian temple, preceding the expected courtyard. The walls contain scenes of the *Opet* procession and festival. After the hall, the temple proper commences with a grand court and then a hypostyle hall of lovely harmony. Near the end, on the left, is a Roman altar dedicated to Constantine. The final part, the Holy-of-Holies, begins with a columned room later remodeled to make a chapel for the worship of Roman emperors. Fragments of Roman painting can be picked out here and there. Flanking either side are small sanctuaries dedicated to Mut (the mother) on the left and to Khonsu (the son) on the right. Farther back in the darkness a small offering chapel precedes a room for the sacred boat that transported the statue of Amun. Inside the room Alexander the Great left a tiny shrine. To the left of the chapel a small room shows Amunhotep III's coronation and behind this is another room with pictures of his divine birth. On the walls are the two gods of childbirth: the dwarf Bes, with hanging tongue, and Thouris, an erect fat hippopotamus with four breasts.

KARNAK TEMPLE

(Karnak, two miles downstream from Luxor, takes time to explore. It is open from 7 a.m. to 5 p.m. Admission is LE 2.)

The precincts cover about 40 acres—enough ruins in this one area to match those of almost any other whole country. It was the supreme manifestation of ancient Egypt's power and riches, as impressive in its way as the pyramids. Unfortunately, imagination is required to appreciate such scale and ruin. Karnak shows best in the dramatic lighting of a Sound and Light show, where the parts are picked out for study, or in the quiet of an early morning visit before the tourists arrive. Wander as if you had all the time in the world. Make your own discoveries; watch excavating teams at work; browse.

Before the time of the New Kingdom, there were temples here for Montu, the war god of the Middle Kingdom. (One Middle Kingdom chapel, more harmonious, more "perfect" than the massive later buildings, has in fact been reconstructed, from its blocks that had been reused as fill in a pylon.) What survives today is the structure established by New Kingdom pharaohs for their patron god Amun. Once begun, it became the most holy temple in Egypt, a focus of religious devotion. Later pharaohs added their homage both to Amun and to bygone times of greatness. It became a temple of temples, a history in stone, so many pharaohs left their mark. Every element of the three basic temple parts was added to, embellished, and made multiple, which is why the plan is so confusing now. There is not just one front pylon as with most temples, but ten pylons spread all around. Even with the embellishments, however, some parts were so perfect that they still stand out.

The site consists of one main temple to Amun running back from the river. Another axis, crossing this one, leads upstream to the precinct of Montu, god of war, and downstream to the precinct of Mut, wife of Amun.

Ram-headed sphinxes, each with a tiny pharaoh between their paws, lead to the first pylon where Karnak temple proper begins. This pylon is both the largest and the most recent (Ptolemaic or later), undecorated and uneven (the left side is lower). You can climb the stairs on the left for a view of Karnak, though a better view waits at the next pylons. Through the entrance is the great courtyard. You can see the brick scaffolding left by the builders of the first pylons. Left in the court is a temple of Seti II with three chapels: for Amun, Mut, and Khonsu. Sphinxes by Rameses the Great line either side of the court, for this was the original avenue to the temple before the later pylons and columns were added. To the right, toward the second pylon, is a temple built by Rameses III. It is itself an entire temple, complete with pylons, where the sacred barques of Amun, Mut, and Khonsu rested before their journey. In the center as you passs through the courtyard is a group of late columns preceded by an alabaster sphinx with Tutankhamun's face.

At the extreme right end of the second pair of pylons (which show signs of a fire) is a scene carved by the pharaoh Sheshonk (*Shishak* in the Bible) to commemorate his victory over Rehoboam, Solomon's son. Stairs at the extreme end of the left pylon lead to the top and to the best view of the Karnak complex. (In the open space next to these stairs are rows of blocks belonging to earlier temples excavated from

KARNAK
Temple of Amun-Ra

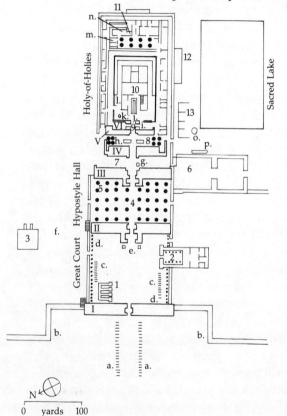

I. Pylon: Ptolemaic
II. Pylon: Horemheb, Sheshonk
III. Pylon: Amunhotep III
IV. Pylon: Amunhotep I
V. Pylon: Thothmoses I
VI. Pylon: Thothmoses III
1. Temple of Seti II
2. Temple of Rameses III
3. Temple of Senusert I
4. Columns of Amunhotep III
5. Columns of Seti I
6. Court of Cachette
7. Court of Amunhotep I
8. Court of Thothmoses I
9. Court of Thothmoses III
10. Site of Original Temple
11. Temple of Thothmoses III
12. Snacks and Souvenirs
13. Temple of Taharka
a. Ram-sphinxes of Rameses II
b. Enclosure Wall
c. Ram-sphinxes of Older Avenue
d. Arcade
e. Statues of Rameses II
f. Blocks of Hatshepsut
g. Obelisk of Thothmoses I
h. Obelisk of Hatshepsut
i. Pillars of Thothmoses III
j. Sanctuary of Sacred Boats
k. Statues of Tutankhamun
l. Wall by Hatshepsut
m. "Observatory"
n. "Botanical Garden" Room
o. Scarab of Amunhotep III
p. Broken Obelisk of Hatshepsut

within pylons. The carvings from Hatshepsut's temple are lovely, especially those of dancers, but a guard soon will chase you. Here, too, is the small but perfect Middle Kingdom chapel of Senusert I to which *baksheesh* may gain you entry.)

Through the gate of the second pylons you pass statues of Rameses the Great and then enter the fabled hypostyle hall of Karnak. It is a football field wide and half as long; the central avenue of six pairs of mammoth columns was a wonder of the ancient world. Herodotus, the Greek historian, claimed that 100 men could stand on the spreading papyrus capitals of one of these columns, which tower 70 feet high and are formed of a pile of stone drums. A few of the original stone grill windows are still in place, above left. Amunhotep III raised these columns, but Seti I, from the next dynasty, added over 100 more with closed papyrus bud capitals, and his son Rameses put his name on them all. The intended effect of such dense rows of massive columns makes a human feel that he walks through a papyrus marsh of the gods. Man becomes insignificant.

Across the hall is a third pair of pylons by Amunhotep III separated by a small court from yet another pair, possibly by Thothmoses I. In this court, four bases remain but only one obelisk (by Thothmoses I) has lasted. Through these pylons is another open place. Here the one intact obelisk of Hatshepsut survives (out of four she erected in Karnak). Once this court carried a roof; Thothmoses III, in his campaign against Hatshepsut, walled off her obelisk so it could not be seen. Through yet another pair of pylons and then through the ruined sixth pair stands the most sacred part of the temple.

First come two elegant pink-granite pillars, one with stylized papyrus on top (for the north of Egypt), the other with the sedge plant (of the south). To the left stands a pair of statues to Amun and to Amunet (one of the names of his wife) carved during the reign of Tut and bearing his likeness. Farther back in the center a sanctuary houses the sacred boats that carried the idols. The present structure is a late rebuilding by a brother of Alexander the Great. On the downstream wall outside (right), scenes of transporting the gods still bear traces of paint. You can view the reliefs by climbing the stairs beside them. Rooms built by Hatshepsut and by Thothmoses III surround this sanctuary. Left is a wall (now within a room) by Hatshepsut that was concealed by her ward; for this reason its colors are preserved better than any others in Karnak.

After a large open space farther back (the site of the original Middle Kingdom temple) comes a Festival Hall built by Thothmoses III. Two rows of unusual columns in the center still carry an intact roof. The columns are models of wooden tent poles, growing in diameter as they rise. Narrow rooms on the left enclose a stairway that leads to a platform with an altar on top—nothing like this "altar" has been found elsewhere. For want of another theory, some call it an observatory. Slightly right and behind the columns of the Festival Hall are four lovely papyrus-bundle columns leading to a room depicting the plants and animals that Thothmoses III found on his Syrian campaigns.

Outside the main temple and around to the right are the stagnant waters of the sacred lake of the temple. (A snack booth with souvenirs is beside it.) On its pedestal a giant stone scarab at the near end of the lake is dedicated to Amunhotep III. Nearby, you can comfortably inspect the tip from Hatshepsut's second obelisk, since it now lies on the ground, to see the clear and simple carving. Notice the areas chiseled out and recarved by later pharaohs. Upstream a series of buildings and pylons lead to the precinct of Mut, which consists of an entire complex of additional temples (closed because of excavations in progress.)

THE LUXOR MUSEUM

(On the Corniche Road half a mile downstream from Luxor Temple. Open from 8 a.m. to 1 p.m. and again from 4 p.m. to 10 p.m. Admission is LE 1.)

This is a lovely museum; it is everything that the great Museum of Antiquities in Cairo is not. It is brand-new, spacious, well-lit, and displays only a few pieces, though each artifact is choice indeed. Spend a tranquil hour or two.

Immediately inside is a treasure from Tutankhamun's tomb. This wooden head of a cow goddess has a gilded face and horns made of copper but covered by black pitch to produce a contrast that enlivens the gold. The pitch dripped from the horns onto the ears. If a more sensitive sculpture of a cow exists anywhere, we do not know it. The museum owns a few other things from Tutankhamun's tomb: some arrows, two model boats, and two pairs of sandals.

Luxor Museum is an educational opportunity where you can watch the change in art styles beginning with the Middle Kingdom; pieces are arranged chronologically. Especially fine from the Middle Kingdom are the heads of Senusert (Sesostris) I and Senusert III. Compare these with faces of Hatshepsut and Thothmoses III. The former show more character (note the sensitive mouths and expressive eyelids), the latter are as fine but more formal with their secret smiles. The striding statue (now, however, without legs) in smooth gray stone of Thothmoses III is a New Kingdom classic. Then comes Amunhotep III with more realistic features: his face is round, his body is squat with hardly a neck, his upper lip protrudes. (See, too, the great statue of his vizier, Amunhotep, son of Hapu, seated as a scribe, with age wrinkles.) A break comes with his son Akhenaten, who started a new style. A long case in the center of the second floor holds blocks from a temple of his at Karnak. Faces become shapes— pointed chins, thick lips, sloping brows, pointed skulls. The climax of this exaggeration shows in the giant statue faces of Akhenaten. Then in the sphinx of Tut, a face is rendered again in the main Egyptian style, though with thick lips. Tutankhamun's statues may be closer to the actual appearance of Akhenaten than his own, extremely stylized, statues. For the ensuing dynasties (note Rameses the Great portrayed as Osiris), the art grows formal again, more a copying from earlier art than from the subject.

THE SIGHTS NEAR LUXOR

The upstream sights in the direction of Aswan are described in Chapter 11. If you do not plan to travel by land or by boat to Aswan, a day trip upstream to Esna, Edfu, and Kom Ombu may be easily arranged in Luxor. (See "Leaving Luxor," below.)

The two downstream sights are Abydos and Denderah, each special in different ways. At Abydos, the oldest cemetery in Egypt, the first pharaohs are buried, and it boasts the best preserved New Kingdom temple—that of Seti I. Denderah is much later, Ptolemaic in fact, but every visitor loves it for its manageable proportions and its forest of columns with Hat-hor heads. Both may be seen in one easy day. (Abydos, the farther of the two, is 100 miles from Luxor.)

Going by rail is a problem because despite a stop at Abydos (the Balyanah stop) and at Denderah (the Kena stop) the trains are so infrequent that you cannot schedule both places in the same day. Better sign up for one of the regularly offered tours and go on the bus. Or rent a taxi for a day (about LE 15). Or hire a car and driver (costing about LE 14) either through your hotel or through a travel agency.

ABYDOS

Karnak is larger, for it was endowed by all the mighty pharaohs of the New Kingdom, but Abydos has an unrivaled tradition of sanctity. The first pharaohs came from the town of This which was nearby (though its precise location is not certain) and were buried at Abydos. Traditional Egyptians worshiped the place where their forefathers lay. Toward the end of the Old Kingdom the religion of Osiris grew into the great cult of Egypt. Osiris was cut into pieces, according to the myth, and spread over Egypt, but Abydos, already a revered place at the time this myth began, was singled out as the place where Osiris' head was buried (some sources claim it was his phallus). Abydos grew into the center for Osiris worship and for the presentation of "mysteries"—passion plays reenacting the myth with actors, a chorus, and participation by the audience who lit lamps to represent the search by Isis for the pieces of her husband.

Osiris, the first who ever resurrected, was king of the next world. His permission must be secured to gain an afterlife. So

Abydos became a place of pilgrimage, both real and symbolic. Osiris also represented a broader concept of regeneration, the fertility of the land. In pictures Osiris' skin is painted green, and he stands with arms crossed over his chest in the form of a mummy. Although many pharaohs had temples and tombs at Abydos, these were often dummy tombs so they could be near Osiris by magic, and the pharaoh's body actually lay closer to his home. The greatest surviving temple is that built by Seti I (with finishing touches by Rameses, his son). Also here are a mysterious structure, half underwater, called the Osireion, and the remains of a temple by Rameses the Great.

No Egyptian temples can match the carvings and the colors in the temple by Seti I from the beginning of Dynasty XIX. The temple is amazingly well preserved. It is unusual, too, in being dedicated to seven different gods (one of which was Seti himself). Since the preservation is so perfect, you can study ancient religious ceremonies, for they are pictured on the walls of the seven chapels.

The pylons now are gone so that you can hardly tell that the way to the temple was originally a courtyard. The area from the stairs to the temple facade covers a second courtyard. The temple was designed in the form of seven aisles, each leading to one of seven sanctuaries spread across the back. Now there is only a single entrance to the temple, up a small ramp, because six of the original entrances were closed by Rameses. You enter a portico that leads to the first hypostyle hall with carvings mainly by Rameses. Seven entrances lead to a second hypostyle hall, this one with painted limestone reliefs by Seti I. Few finer reliefs survive anywhere in Egypt. Seti offers incense to a series of gods and goddesses (especially nice on the right-hand wall).

Next come the seven chapels. Before entering each chapel, look at the scenes between the doorways, as each shows Seti (beautifully carved) with the god of whichever chapel is behind. After inspecting a chapel, circle around out the entrance again to go to the next in line. (The chapel of Osiris, third from the right, has a rear passage leading back to more rooms.) The rightmost chapel, dedicated to Horus, we will describe in detail. These themes are repeated for each different god in his or her respective room.

Scenes around the wall depict in order the daily ritual of worship. Seti is shown as the officiating high priest; Horus has the head of a falcon. Starting to the right of the entrance, priests purify Seti with holy oil (the liquid streams are made up of the hieroglyphs for life (the *ankh)* and for prosperity (the jackal-headed *was* scepter). Seti approaches the sanctuary in a simple kilt; he carries a pipe for incense and an oil lamp to see by in the sacred darkness of the sanctuary. He opens the door of the idol's shrine and bows (twice), then anoints the idol. He embraces the idol, then presents an Eye of Horus, a symbol of regeneration, to bring the idol to life. Every scene is repeated, harkening back to the duality of two countries from the first days of Egypt, united by the pharaoh. The second time the idol is offered, instead of an Eye of Horus, a figurine of the goddess Maat who represented proper order and was associated with the sun. Seti takes the idol and places it on a mound while he consecrates four boxes of clothes and ointments. Four times he circles the idol, then washes and dresses it with materials from these boxes. With a final purification, he returns the idol, now attired for the new day, to its shrine. Then the king withdraws, bowing, and sweeps away his footsteps.

Each chapel repeats these scenes for (from right to left after the chapel of Horus): Isis (Horus' mother, Osiris' wife, with a throne on her head), Osiris (shown with green skin as a mummy), Amun-Ra (the New Kingdom form of the sun god Ra), Ra-Horakhty ("Horus of the Horizon"), Ptah (the creator god with a blue skullcap, holding a *was* scepter), and finally, Seti I (where Seti performs these ceremonies on an idol of himself).

Left of Seti's own chapel a doorway leads farther left. This opens to a gallery with (on the right side) one of the few ancient lists of the pharaohs of Egypt. This list is an expurgated one—it omits the names of Hatshepsut and Akhenaten, for example. The first name (upper left) is that of Menes, the first pharaoh. Seti stands behind a child (with hair drawn into a sidelock) who offers incense to this list which both father and son would like to suggest were their ancestors. Seti, however, was the son of a royal father who was not in direct line to the throne; his child is the future Rameses the Great. A number of unfinished rooms for the storage of temple equipment lead off from the gallery.

The gallery is also an exit that leads to the unusual structure, called the Osireion, where pillars rise from a pool of water. Perhaps the structure—now underwater—had to do with creation, which in Egyptian theories began with a hill rising from primordial waters. Then again, the scenes (underwater) carved inside this building describe the underworld and are those carved in pharaohs' tombs. So this may have been a tomb for Seti, a dummy tomb, because his real one is the famous one in the Valley of the Kings.

To the right of Seti's complex is a temple built by Rameses the Great. Only the foundation and walls remain, but the carvings retain some color. Scenes of animals are especially good.

TEMPLE OF DENDERAH

This temple was truly mystical, covered with astral and zodiac scenes, yet the columns with cows' heads at the top and the relatively small scale of the building make it somehow cute. By Egyptian standards it is a very late temple. The last Ptolemies started it, Cleopatra did some work, then it was finished by Roman emperors. Egyptian religious ideas translated by Greek and Roman minds grew complex and strange. You will see more animal-headed gods in such temples than in any built by native Egyptian rulers.

Hat-hor was a genuine enough Egyptian goddess with roots as old as any, going back to the times of the first pharaohs. She was represented as a cow with a face that looked human. Her name, Hat-hor, meant "temple of Horus." To the Egyptians she was the one who watched over Horus (each pharaoh was reincarnated as Horus), a sort of mother goddess. And she came to symbolize love, not only of the maternal sort. On the other hand, one myth claimed that she, not Sekhmet, would have destroyed humanity if she had not drunk wine, thinking that it was blood, and fallen into an intoxicated sleep. A goddess of love and of drunken orgies appealed to the Romans.

A *sistrum* (a special rattle) was used to drive away evil spirits in ceremonies for Hat-hor. It had a straight round handle with Hat-hor's cow head at the top surmounted by a cap in the form of a shrine that held the rattling pellets. The columns in Hat-hor's temple are giant representations of these *sistrums*.

The temple never had a pylon entrance, only a stone doorway in a wall. Without its walls, the giant doorway now stands dramatically alone. Ahead is the temple of Hat-hor; to the right are a series of other buildings. The nearest of these buildings is a *mammisi*, a birth temple, in which were celebrated the births of new pharaohs. Since this one was Roman-built, it was used for prayers in behalf of the new sons of emperors. Next to it is a badly preserved Coptic church built from the stone of earlier temples. Beyond are two more, earlier, *mammisis*.

The Hat-hor temple presents a grand impression with its clean soaring columns and charming cow heads on top. In this temple where the wall carvings are not artful, the best work is on the ceiling. Vultures alternate with the winged disc of the sun and with stars; there are signs of the zodiac and of the planets. Unfortunately, much of the color was blackened by Copts who lived inside at a time when the silt of the ages had reached close to the ceiling, so their torches did much damage.

Beyond the hypostyle hall is a maze of smaller rooms that forms the inner sanctuary. At the back, in a room just left of center, is a trapdoor in the floor leading to crypts under the sanctuary. As the carvings illustrate, valuable equipment was hidden inside. If you are inclined to bat-filled corridors, the gatekeeper may allow you to climb down.

Beyond the second, small hypostyle hall on the left-hand side of the temple, a stairway leads to the roof. This is the only temple with preserved buildings on its roof, although such elements were common on late temples. At the rear left of the roof is a kiosk with 12 columns where the idols were brought once a year to enjoy the warming rays of the sun. Also on the roof are two other structures for Osiris. The view from the roof is lovely. Behind the temple you can see the ruins of a small temple for Isis; beside it is the sacred lake of the temple.

AMENITIES

LUXOR TRANSPORTATION

Apart from taxis (available on either bank) and horse-drawn carriages in Luxor, you can ride a bike (even on the west bank to the temples and tombs), ride donkeys (only on the west bank), or sail to nowhere special.

Bikes are offered for rent next to the New Winter Palace hotel and near the Horus Hotel. Cost will be about LE 2 for a day.

To hire a donkey, do not take the tourist ferry over to the west bank. Instead take the ferry that locals use, leaving from near the restaurant Chez Farouk. This ferry lets you off by the donkey stables and costs only 10 pt. When you dock, scramble up the bank where you will be besieged by donkey vendors. You will need to hire a donkey for yourself as well as one for an assistant—a child who will lead you and take care of any problems. Sit as though you had all the time in the world, and negotiate to a price that should be about LE 2 per donkey. Do not be concerned when you lift your American bulk on such small animals, they easily carry greater loads. Donkeys are slow but their natures are gentle and their footing is sure. There is no better way to experience the environment of the west bank.

Small sailboats wait by the tourist ferry dock. A boat, along with a captain and a young assistant, should cost LE 2 by the hour. One relaxing trip takes you to Banana Island a mile or so upstream. At this plantation you sit after your sail to have a soft drink or tea and all the tiny sweet bananas you can eat.

HOTELS

Beds in Luxor are more prized than diamonds. The reservation process ought to begin one year in advance of a visit.

Here are the few choices. In a town so small, all hotels are located conveniently.

Winter Palace and **New Winter Palace.** *Deluxe.* (The Nile Corniche, south.) The grand dowager of Luxor hotels, where Lord Carnarvon stayed, now is joined by a new, less charming, wing to yield more than 500 beds. Though they share facilities, for Egyptian reasons the older part is classed deluxe while the newer wing is only first class, but prices are the same. The original hotel is elegant and spacious, both its public areas and rooms; the new wing we rate as just a decent hotel. All rooms have views either over the Nile or on the magnificent gardens behind the hotel. Food is adequate but, in our opinion, standard hotel fare. Open all year, air-conditioned. Compulsory half-board. Single rooms LE 21 in winter months, LE 19 in summer; double rooms cost LE 23, but LE 21 in the summer. Egyptian Hotels Company.

Etap International. *First Class.* (The Nile Corniche, one block south of Luxor Museum.) This is the newest hotel in town and sparkling with marble in the rich, open lobby. Rooms, however, are ordinary, though all 128 rooms have a terrace and a view of the Nile. We found meals sometimes a subtle notch above those at the Winter Palace. Three nights per week a local band and belly dancer play in the dining room. Open all year, air-conditioned. Compulsory half-board. Single rooms rent at LE 23.60, LE 21 in summer; double rooms cost LE 26, LE 23 off season. Etap Hotels International.

Savoy Hotel. *First Class.* (The Nile Corniche and El Nil Street, two blocks south of Luxor Museum.) We think this hotel has been living too long off its reputation and could be rated second class for seediness. Rooms contain inadvertent antiques. Some of the 240 rooms are in the main building, others are in two-story cabins around a spacious garden. Food is ample. Open all year, partly air-conditioned. Compulsory half-board. Singles cost from LE 7 in the main building, LE 16.50 in the cabins, LE 1 less off season; doubles cost LE 8.50 without private bath, LE 10 with bath and LE 19 in the cabins, decreasing by off season. Egyptian Hotels Company.

Luxor Hotel. *First Class.* (Karnak Temple Street, opposite Luxor Temple.) Comparable in age and accommodation to the Savoy, but with more charm and nice views of Luxor Temple. Recent renovations improved the plumbing, raised prices, and perhaps threatened the former comfortable feeling. With the relative intimacy of less than 100 rooms, it should retain its admirers, however, even after remodeling. Hearty food. Open all year, mostly air-conditioned. Compulsory half-board. Price for a single is LE 17, LE 16 off season; doubles go for LE 18 and LE 17 in summer. Egyptian Hotel Company.

Hotel Philippe. *Not Classified.* (The street alongside the Etap Hotel.) Now privately owned, nothing grand, but the 40 rooms are adequate if spare. A roof garden is pleasant for drinks. Food can be tastier than at the larger hotels. Open all year, partly air-conditioned (LE 1.50 surcharge). Compulsory half-board. The most expensive single costs LE 10, the corresponding double goes for LE 12.

In desperation you can try the **Nile Belladonna**—room trailers south of Luxor, the **Horus Hotel** by the north end of Luxor Temple, or **Hotel Dina** behind Karnak Street.

RESTAURANTS

Luxor is no place for gourmets. Outside of hotels, two places are worth a try, mainly for their atmosphere.

Chez Farouk perches on the bank of the Nile across from Luxor Temple. Food is plain, in the LE 3 range. At night loud music is provided. But for a simple lunch so close to the river that you feel a part of the curious riverine traffic, we recommend this place.

Marhaba Restaurant occupies the roof of the Tourist Bazaar Building north of the New Winter Palace Hotel. Sit on the broad terrace watching the Theban hills across the Nile and you will not care if the food is unsophisticated. At least, with this change from your hotel, you can order Egyptian dishes, and the view does surpass what the best restaurant in New York can offer.

SHOPPING

Luxor is as good a place as any to buy *gallabiyahs* (kaftans). The **souk** is manageable, less pressuring than in larger cities. The souk runs for two blocks parallel to the Nile, beginning one block back from the northern end of Luxor Temple. Wander past spice shops, vegetable and meat marts, and a score of fabric stores. Inspect the patterns as you pass the fabrics and ask for prices. Competition is stiff in this little bazaar; you should be able to buy *gallabiyahs* for LE 5 or 6, made to order, ready the next day.

Tourist trinkets, alabaster, and jade antiques are sold in the shops of the **Tourist Bazaar,** touching the north end of the New Winter Palace Hotel. Hawkers also sell such products on the street and near tourist sights. They ask for more than store prices, but with energetic bargaining can be driven down to less.

Gaddis is a well-known store in the south arcade of the Winter Palace Hotel that has a bit of everything at prices we find high, but it is convenient.

LEAVING LUXOR

TO ASWAN: The best bus transport to Aswan are the new, usually air-conditioned, buses engaged by travel agents in Luxor. The advantage of these buses is that they stop at Esna, Edfu, and Kom Ombu temples along the way (descriptions in Chapter 11). Costs are reasonable, in the LE 25 range, and include a picnic lunch. The trip with these stops begins early in the morning in Luxor and arrives in Aswan after dark. The arcade south of the Winter Palace Hotel contains an American Express, Cook's, Misr Travel, and a local travel agent, Muhammad Hassani. A private car and driver can be hired for about the cost of the tour bus seat.

By train it is impossible to coordinate stops at the temples en route to Aswan in any single day. You might as well take the express train, then, instead of a local. Express trains leave Luxor three times a day for Aswan: 6:05 a.m., 8:25 a.m., and 6:30 p.m. They arrive at Aswan respectively at 10:00 a.m.,

12:58 p.m., and 11:20 p.m. First class, air-conditioned rooms cost LE 5.50; second class costs LE 4. The train station in Luxor is at the end of Shari el Mahatta, the main street perpendicular to the pylons of Luxor Temple.

TO ABU SIMBEL: The only practical way to Abu Simbel is to fly. A flight from Luxor will land in Aswan—but only to take on passengers—then fly to Abu Simbel. The fare is LE 29, and the 30-minute flights are frequent. For times and reservations, stop by the Egyptair office in the south arcade by the Winter Palace Hotel.

TO CAIRO: Planes fly almost every hour to Cairo. The airfare is LE 29. Reservations may be made at the Egyptair office in the south arcade by the Winter Palace Hotel.

Trains leave for Cairo at 9:19 p.m., 5:05 a.m., and 10:14 a.m. The first-class sleeper is LE 14.25, second-class sleeper is LE 8.50. Although both are air-conditioned compartments, first class is less crowded. The train station is at the end of Shari el Mahatta. Reservations should be made several days in advance—either at the train station, or through a travel agent, who may be able to get tickets when none are available at the train station.

TO HURGHADAH: See Chapter 14 for transportation and a discussion of this unusual resort.

10.

Background for Aswan

The drowsy heat of Aswan is as good a place as any to think about the decline and end of ancient Egypt. By the border of ancient Nubia, we can recall a time when Nubia, the vassal, ruled Egypt for a while.

When we left the history of ancient Egypt in Chapter 8, the capital had been moved to Raameses in the Delta and a priest ruled the south. The last dynasty of the New Kingdom had trailed away with indistinguishable Rameses after Rameses. Now corruption found opportunities to grasp the center of the stage at Thebes. Thebes was divided: one mayor governed the city, another mayor controlled the temples and tombs on the western side of the Nile. A recently discovered document from this time shows us how far affairs had declined.

Paser, the mayor of the city of Thebes, learned that various tombs across the river had been robbed. He filed charges, stating that ten pharaohs', four queens', and various nobles' tombs had been plundered. The vizier of Egypt appointed a committee to investigate the accusations. Incredibly, to head the investigation, the vizier named Paweraa, the mayor of the west bank, the person to whom the safety of the tombs had been entrusted. Even so, the committee found in its report that the charges were correct about the nobles' tombs, though only one pharaoh and two queens had been robbed. The report then went on to castigate Paser, who had raised the alarm, for his errors. Because his numbers were a little off, Paser was vilified and finally hounded from office; meanwhile, Paweraa, who had failed in his responsibilities, remained mayor for 17 years more.

Affairs only deteriorated further in the next dynasty, Dynasty XXI. Pharaohs ceased to maintain an interest in the south, even digging their tombs near the Delta capital. There, in the 1950s, an intact royal burial of this era was found. Not at all like Tutankhamun's in the richness of the furnishings, it was a profound illustration of the change in Egypt's position and power. Tutankhamun's coffin had been pure gold, exquisitely made; the pharaoh Psusenns's coffin was crudely worked in silver.

Conditions had grown so chaotic in this dynasty that the priests who still governed the south were forced to a drastic decision. Tombs, extremely personal and important, bore the owner's name and image throughout; owners expended great care in the choice of text and pictures. The magic of names, pictures, and texts was truth for the Egyptians, but in this era tombs no longer were secure. So in the darkest hour of night, a delegation of priests, sworn by the strongest oaths to secrecy, went through all the royal tombs that still contained bodies, wrenching the mummies from their "houses." They placed all the bodies in makeshift wood coffins, each with an identifying label, then hid them in a natural cleft in the cliffs behind Dier el Bahri.

The secret was a very well-kept one—until A.D. 1881. At that time objects with famous pharaohs' names suddenly began to appear in quantity on antique markets. The finger of suspicion pointed to the Rasals family who lived in the village of Gurnah, famous for its tomb robbers. Even under questioning punctuated by torture, no one confessed to anything, until the family had a falling out when the one who had been most tortured demanded a larger share for his suffering. Angered by his family's refusal, he led authorities to the cleft in the cliffs where such pharaohs as Thothmoses III and Seti I had rested since 1000 B.C. The royal mummies were carefully hoisted by ropes out of the cavern and transported to the Nile where ships waited to carry them to Cairo. As they passed through Egypt, people, as if by a sixth sense, lined the banks wailing and beating their breasts exactly as they had during funeral processions in the times of the pharaohs. These mummies are now the stars of the Mummy Room in the Museum of Antiquities.

The last pharaoh of Dynasty XXI was succeeded by a Libyan, an instance of a recurring historical phenomenon. Immigrant Libyans had lived for two centuries in Egypt, originally as slaves captured in battles with the Sea Peoples whose side Libya had unwisely joined. Often immigrants adopt their new country with greater fervor than do the native-born, and they try harder. One such Libyan achieved so much success and wealth in business that the last pharaoh of Dynasty XXI married the Libyan's daughter—the dowry may have contributed to her attractiveness. The merchant's son, in turn, married the pharaoh's daughter and received the throne when the king died. He began Dynasty XXII—the Libyans.

The new pharaohs, more dynamic than their predecessors, reestablished Egypt as a potent force in the Middle East. These are the first pharaohs mentioned by name in the Bible—in particular Sheshonk (with the spelling *Shishak*). When the Libyan line ran out, Dynasty XXIII followed, which left so faint a mark on history that almost nothing is known about it.

In the meantime, Nubians watched these events with concern and anger. Nubia had been Egypt's vassal for close to 2000 years and was thoroughly Egyptianized. Egypt had not been a harsh master, interested only in gold and other materials, and treated Nubia with the respect of its economic importance.

A special governor with the high title "the King's Son of Kush" lived in and governed Nubia and Kush. He had his entourage of Egyptians; Egyptian troops were garrisoned in Nubia; and Egyptian traders flooded the area. With so much long contact, it was no wonder that Nubians adopted the worship of Amun and Horus. Nubian kings even constructed pyramids, and continued the practice for 1500 years after Egypt no longer bothered.

By the time of the next dynasty, the shadowy twenty-fourth, Nubians became convinced that Egypt was hopelessly decadent. They were probably correct. After 2000 years of struggles and of contact with foreign people and ideas, the culture and religion of Egypt could not remain pure. Nubian kings, more isolated from other foreign influences, now were more conservative than their parent culture. They viewed Egypt's loss of prestige as a religious insult. Whatever affected the prestige of a nation reflected on its gods, gods that the Nubians worshiped.

The Nubian king planned a holy crusade to save Egypt from herself and to punish those who permitted decline and corruption. He marched north to cleanse Egypt with his sword—which easily sliced through Egypt. He thereby became the first pharaoh of Dynasty XXV, a Nubian dynasty.

There is no telling what benefits this infusion of vigorous southern blood might have offered Egypt, because the Nubian kings had the misfortune of attaining power at the time that a Middle Eastern war machine gathered its momentum. Assyria harassed Egypt's allies in Syria and Palestine until the Nubians were forced to fight. The Nubians lost the first encounter and won the second; the third marked a disaster for Egypt.

Assyrians routed the Egyptian armies, swept into Egypt, raided Thebes, and pushed the Nubian pharaoh with his army and court south again into Nubia. The Assyrians plundered and left. Nubians then returned to Egypt prepared to fight once more. Again they were defeated by an army that had been bred for nothing but war, and which possessed the first mounted cavalry. This time the Nubians went home crushed, never again attempting to exercise control over Egypt.

Egypt was then wholly in the grasp of Assyrians who could

do whatever they wished. Assyrian leaders, however, occupied with rebellions in the far parts of their new empire,
appointed a native Egyptian to govern in their place. The
predictable happened. Seeing that Assyria was too troubled
to interfere, the Egyptian governor declared Egypt independent and himself the pharaoh.

Events had made Egypt an actor in a larger play involving
the entire Middle East. Immigrants and troops now poured
into Egypt from countries at war with Assyria. In particular,
Egypt began a long alliance with Greece, a country known
not for her cultural achievements but for the growing prow-
ess of her soldiers. Egypt turned into an international
garrison strong enough to make Assyria hesitate, especially
with problems closer to home. Babylon was rising for its
second ascendancy (led by Nebuchadnessar); peoples known
as the Scyths and the Medes were frightening everyone.

For a while the Medes and the Scyths acted as the dogs that
harried the Assyrian lion so it could not turn on Egypt. Egypt
enjoyed a period of quiet from 665 to 525 B.C., and with
sovereignty regained, began a kind of renaissance—at least in
art and building. It was not a time for advance but for
remembering—a century-long celebration by Egypt of her
bimillennial. Arts returned to the Old Kingdom models,
sometimes copying earlier pieces so exactly as to fool modern
Egyptologists. Pharaohs of this dynasty, known as the Saitic
pharaohs, came from a Delta town called Sais.

While Egypt dreamed of her past, the future was being
born. Assyria, which loved war but never learned the art of
governing, turned this way and that to face various foes,
leaving Persia free to organize. In 525 B.C., Cambysus led the
largest army in the world through Assyria, then through the
Middle East and into Egypt. It seemed that nothing could
stop the Persians. Darius, son of Cambysus, then set out to
surpass his father and conquer what remained of the world,
marching confidently into backward Greece. Through valor,
luck, and surprise, the Greeks held their lines at Marathon
and turned Darius away. Shaken by the obdurate Greeks and
past her peak, Persia now had to struggle to preserve the
empire already won. Again and again Egypt emerged with

periods of autonomy quickly followed by Persian recon-
quests, until Egypt was like a boxer knocked dizzy and Persia
was tired from all the punches she had thrown. Greece,
meanwhile, nurtured new confidence and power until, in 334
B.C., Alexander the Great came out of northern Greece and
conquered the world.

Once the greatest power in the world, Egypt had been
elbowed back and would begin falling further and further
behind. Today almost everyone who sees the relics from the
great eras of Egypt in the context of her present condition is
struck by the disparity. Yet every great civilization lasts for
only a while; a leader is always pursued by others who watch
for evidence of weakness. Eventually every nation stumbles.
Once a country suffers actual conquest, it seems held in
place, marking time while the rest of the world moves ahead.
Seldom do such countries regain their former strength.
History gives evidence that leadership is fleeting, a fall is
inevitable, and after a fall it is almost impossible to rise again
to the front rank. In Egypt's case, Persian conquest was
followed by Greek, Roman, Arab, French, and English
victories. From 525 B.C. until A.D. 1952, when Abdul Gamel
Nasser revolted against King Farouk, Egypt was ruled by
foreigners.

The surprise is not that Egypt fell, but that she survived
and flourished for so long. People refer with awe to the great
Roman Empire, dominant for 450 years—compared to a century for ancient Greece and perhaps 150 years for Babylon.
Measured against Egypt, however, Rome fades to a distant
second place. Egypt first became the world's great power in
3000 B.C. and with minor setbacks maintained dominance
until 525 B.C. Egypt outlasted more than five Roman Empires;
Egypt was preeminent through all of the first half of recorded
history.

Egypt's success was due in the first place to nature. Egypt,
the most fertile area in the ancient world, had a dependable
fertility based on the ecology of a seasonal river inundation,
rather than on the unpredictability of weather. Egyptians
could work less each year to gain larger crops. Because of the

great fertility of the land, Egypt supported a relatively large population, one that could afford time away from farms in pursuit of greater glories. On this natural foundation, the people of Egypt added an element of equal importance: most of the time they were as united as any country could ever be. They developed the peculiar pharonic form of government in which one man's voice spoke for every citizen. This unity, central to the form of government, was not dependent on the happenstance of particular, special leaders. Religion and cosmology joined in telling the ancient Egyptians that chaos rife with all manner of injustice could be avoided only by respect for the authority of the pharaoh.

Though they were conquerors, individually the Egyptians were not especially good fighters. The idea that Egyptians gained advantage through powerful secrets is exciting to think about, but the truth is more mundane. Egyptians worked hard, there were many of them, they were blessed by nature, and they were more unified for longer periods than other countries. Proper credit is due them not for dark secrets, but for industry and cooperation. That is admirable enough.

11.
Aswan and Abu Simbel

The wealthy, who have known about Aswan since before the turn of the century, come for winter vacations. Aswan is quiet. Things to do are few, and none are so compelling that you would have great regrets if you skipped them. Aswan is beautiful. Here the Nile runs into granite rocks that form a cataract, breaking the river into streams running around islands, forcing it to flow more quickly and deeply to make up for the loss of space. For a tourist, the main function of Aswan is rest and recuperation, complete with pleasant diversions.

Many people use Aswan as a jumping-off place for Abu Simbel, to rest—after visiting three more temples en route— eyes and muscles already tired from Luxor. We will treat Aswan in this way. It is not essential to go to Aswan. You can fly to Abu Simbel from Luxor too. The temples en route can be visited from Luxor and they are not as important as those discussed in the Luxor chapter.

THE SIGHTS FROM LUXOR TO ASWAN

By boat, bus, or car (arrangements are discussed at the end of Chapter 9) you first come to Esna after 35 miles; Edfu is 30 miles more, and the Nile valley narrows as hills march down to the river. Then comes Kom Ombu, 105 miles from Luxor, and finally Aswan. The trip is 135 miles, one full day with the three stops.

TEMPLE OF ESNA: *(Open during daylight hours. Admission is 50 pt.)* Once in an antique store in Luxor that sold fakes as well as ancient objects we asked the owner if a certain object was old. He said, "No. It is Roman." In Egypt you naturally get caught up in such ancient civilization that you forget that other wonderful things are old enough, even if not as ancient as Egypt. At Esna a hypostyle hall was built between 170 B.C. and A.D. 250—that is roughly as old as the Colosseum in Rome. If viewed as a Roman building, it would be one of the finest in the world.

The site is interesting, for a town surrounds it entirely. Before excavation the town spread over the temple roof. Only the hypostyle hall has been cleared so far; houses still sit above the rest. The temple seems to be in a valley because the silt deposited by 2000 years of Nile overflow (and by winds) has added about 20 feet to the land. A hall of lovely proportion formed by 24 columns with almost as many different styles of capital above them remains visible. The carvings on the walls, not wonderful to begin with, have suffered from salts and smoke. Much of the building was erected by the emperor Claudius, and the temple is dedicated to Khnum, the creator god.

TEMPLE OF EDFU: *(Open during the day. Admission is LE 1.)* Twelve miles before reaching Edfu, you pass by the site of ancient Hieraconpolis, across the river. This was the greatest southern city of predynastic times. The town acquired the god Horus from nearby Edfu and then passed Horus on to Narmer, who unified Egypt and adopted this hawk-god as his protector and symbol. As the special god of pharaohs,

Horus stood among the most important Egyptian deities. Here, where the cult of Horus began, stands his most important temple. It is a "late" temple, completed just before the birth of Jesus. In its innermost recesses, however, the original shrine from 3100 B.C. has been remodeled. In front of the temple is a single giant hawk with the crown of a king, simple and dignified.

The completeness of this temple, even to the original roof and grill windows, gives you an accurate feeling of an ancient religious environment. You experience the change in darkness and quiet while passing through the parts. Beyond the usual hypostyle hall comes the inner shrine copying in stone the earliest form of reed temple. Resting on a pedestal inside is a reconstruction of the boat in which the sacred idol was carried in processions. The mood is appropriately dark and solemn.

TEMPLE OF KOM OMBU: *(Open until dusk. Admission is 50 pt.)* Not as well preserved as the two preceding temples, Kom Ombu has the advantage of its site—on a bluff overlooking miles of Nile. The temple is a composite in which two halves were separated for two distinct gods, not forming a group as in other temples. Half of the temple, with a separate door and aisle, was for Hor-wer, Horus the Elder. The other half was dedicated to Sobek, the crocodile. A gruesome sight greets visitors. In a chamber, fronted by bars, a heap of mummified crocodiles seem to peer at you as you pass. They do not look friendly.

Because the temple lacks a roof, the carvings are lit by the sun, providing clear examples of Ptolemaic art. In the times after the Egyptian pharaohs, figures grew bellies, belly buttons were proudly displayed, and shapes became rounded. These are traditional Egyptian scenes, done for Greek eyes.

THE SIGHTS OF ASWAN

Originally Aswan was a border town, defending Egypt against Nubia and serving as a depot to receive trade from as far south as the center of Africa. Today the town still mixes Egyptian and African culture. In the beginning Aswan centered on a fortress island in the Nile—called Elephantine because of the mammoth granite boulders that look fat like pachyderms. Some ruins remain on the island, including a nilometer (to gauge the height of the yearly flood before it reached the heart of Egypt), but the most striking feature now is a soaring modern hotel. Surrounding Aswan were quarries for the pink granite—the favorite material for statues and decorations of ancient temples.

Although building the High Dam brought prosperity to Aswan during the 1960s, it also brought Nubians displaced by Lake Nasser trailing 300 miles behind the dam. Since the completion of the dam, some industry has come to use the electric power. The population now is said to reach a half million, but you would never guess it from the drowsy center of town where the hotels sit along the Nile. The first street back from the Nile is the old market area.

Because Aswan sits on the Tropic of Cancer (only the equator is hotter) 130° in the summer is not uncommon. During the winter it is warmer than any Egyptian town, sometimes warm enough for a dip in the hotel pool. In summer, nothing moves from noon until late afternoon— except for an occasional unwary tourist. Almost a curfew, a law bans tourist visits during these hours, for their own protection.

Sights in and around Aswan include some tombs from the First Intermediate Period; Philae, a small gem of a Ptolemaic temple floating in the water behind the High Dam; the temple of Kalabsha; the beautiful hilltop mosque where the Aga Khan is buried. A Nubian village outside of Aswan introduces a charming folk culture and lovely handcrafts. The major sight at this end of Egypt, however, is 200 miles south—Abu Simbel (see below).

All the sights on the river or on the west bank are most pleasantly and easily reached by a *falucca* sail. Depending on competition and your bargaining ability, for an hour the cost will run between LE 1 and 2 (per boat, not per person). Land travel is either by tour company buses or by taxi. Taxis usually are cheaper here than in Cairo—LE 1 to 2 per hour. None of the visits need be long. This is a place where a fast half-day group tour is almost as good as arranging things yourself.

ELEPHANTINE ISLAND: The southern tip (upstream) of the largest island in Aswan (almost one mile long) contains a variety of Egyptian ruins. This island was the original town, for it was eminently defensible. New temples continued to dot the island even after the Egyptians had little to fear from Nubia, when the town spread along the east bank, because this ancient island had special significance. The special god of Aswan in pharaonic times was the ram Khnum who created humans as a potter makes pots, from clay on his wheel.

From the town on the east bank, you land at a quay whose newest paving is Roman, covering much older stones below. Just a few yards to the left is the well-preserved nilometer, a square well with stairs going down. Marks on the walls indicate how high the river had risen compared to prior years. From this the ancient Egyptians could calculate how high the flood would be down the river, how much land would be irrigated, and thus how large the crop yields would be. This calculation determined the taxes for all of Egypt. The nilometer here is dank, dirty, and eerie. Inscriptions on the walls are Greek and French (for this was as far as Napoleon's men got in their attempt to conquer Egypt) as well as Arabic.

Just inland is the small Aswan Museum. Spend a half hour looking at objects from prehistoric to Ptolemaic and Roman times. Farther across the island and moving north (downstream), remains of three temples lie in a tumble. The first you reach was begun in the last Egyptian dynasties, probably to honor Khnum, and was finished by the Ptolemies. The view is pleasant, and the columns and doorway probably are more majestic as ruins than the finished temple would have been. Farther north, side by side, are the other two temples. Of the left one only the foundation survives. Mummies of rams were uncovered nearby—a clue that this temple was dedicated to the ram god, Khnum. To the right of these foundations, and lower down because it is much older, is a temple to a man revered in Aswan—Heka-ib, who governed Aswan at the end of the Old Kingdom. This temple to his memory was constructed during the start of the Middle Kingdom (about 2000 B.C.) by a later governor. Because these sites are still under excavation, you'll feel an aura of discovery during your visit.

Kitchener Island, between Elephantine and the west bank, is now a botanical garden, with tropical plants. Here scientists experiment on new crops for Egypt's farms. Lord Kitchener once owned this island (such things were possible then) and stopped here on his way to Khartoum and death.

TOMBS OF THE NOBLES: Downstream from Kitchener's small island, you can see two rows of holes in the hill on the west bank. Steps run down to the river. The age of the tombs inside the holes ranges from the very end of the Old Kingdom through the First Intermediate Period (from 2325 B.C. to 2125 B.C.), with one later tomb. Modest in size, they were built by local gentry who lived far from the center of culture. The carvings are crude, for the best craftsmen and latest styles were in the capital at Memphis. It is not art so much as caricature—a provincial and rustic style that nonetheless has charm.

The first tombs from the landing stairs are late Old Kingdom and not very exciting inside, although #31 (Sirenput II) does have interesting statues and a fair painting of an offering table scene. The next tomb, of Khunes from the Old Kingdom, has good colors because his paintings were covered with plaster (since removed) by Coptic monks who once lived inside. Steps in the back lead down to another, later, tomb.

The next tomb, despite lacking dramatic colors or carvings, is special for the human touch of the hieroglyphic message inside. The owner, Harukef, had been so proud to have received a letter from his pharaoh that he had the letter carved in the stone wall on the front of the tomb. Harukef had been sent on an expedition to the "Land of the Spirits" (somewhere south) and returned with many valuable things. He sent word of his success and a list of his treasures to the court in Memphis. Among the products Harukef brought was a dwarf, one who could dance. The pharaoh, Pepi II (discussed in Chapter 4), was still a child. Pepi II wrote excitedly, "Come north to the court immediately; bring this dwarf with you . . . so the dances for the god may please and make happy the heart of the king. . . . My majesty desires to see this dwarf more than all the goods of Sinai and of Punt."

Past tomb #35 is the tomb of Heka-ib who was deified in a special temple on Elephantine Island. The entrance and the sporting reliefs inside are worth seeing. The best tomb is probably the one near the end of the row, #36 for Sirenput I (a different Sirenput from the one with a tomb earlier on). It contains decent Middle Kingdom carving.

SAINT SIMEON'S MONASTERY: This is quite a nice Coptic monastery, begun in the 6th century and modified over the years until it was abandoned in the 12th or 13th century. It lies about a half hour's walk across the desert, due west. You can climb to the top of the hill where the nobles' tombs are to begin the trek, or climb the hill (upstream) where the tomb of the Aga Khan is. The monastery is visible across the sands on top of the plateau. In all likelihood you will find yourself exploring alone; you can fantasize in utter peace.

A 20-foot wall surrounds a complex of two-level buildings. The lower story of the main building contains a large central vault with cells on each side where monks lived. On the right-hand wall is an interesting painting of Christ on his throne with six apostles and the Archangel Michael. Stairs run down below the main building to more cells cut in the rock and a chapel with painted ceiling and pictures of saints. The second floor contains a kitchen, dining hall, and more cells. The church is outside, near the wall. Parts of two fine frescoes remain on the ceiling.

THE MAUSOLEUM OF AGA KHAN: Beaming from the very top of a hill on the west bank, just opposite the end of Elephantine Island where the ancient ruins are, is a small white mosque. It was built in 1959 for the Aga Khan, the religious leader of a special Islamic sect whose members all but worship their leaders. The Aga Khan (father of the present one) so loved his winter vacations in Aswan that he wished to be buried here. Outside the structure is simple; inside it is exquisite. At the bottom of the hill is the villa of the Khan's aged widow.

THE ANCIENT QUARRIES: After leaving Aswan a kilometer behind on the road south to the High Dam, a turnoff on the left leads to the quarries. Pink granite was a favorite pharaonic stone, both for its color and durability. Granite quarries were owned by the king who might grant his stone as a favor to a high courtier.

Speculation remains about how ancient Egyptians were able to cut such hard stone at a time when the only metals in use, copper and later bronze, were not durable enough for this work. As with so many questions about the mechanics of early engineering projects, the answers have more to do with effort and simple ingenuity than with dark secrets. Quartz is harder than granite and could be used as an abrasive, rubbed with a copper saw or drill until it cut through the granite. Quartz is the major constituent of sand. With this abrasive, workmen could make a hole or a ridge along the length of any piece that they desired to free from surrounding rock. A wooden wedge could be placed in the hole and the wood dampened. The inexorable expansion of wet wood creates a tremendous force, enough to split even granite.

In the quarry is a giant unfinished obelisk that would have been the largest ever made—over 120 feet long—had it not cracked in the process of splitting it free. You can see, however, that the stone was finished and dressed—polished by rubbing with harder stones—while the freeing proceeded.

Near the obelisk are the usual vendors with wares for sale. Often, however, you'll find an unusual product here. Large (sometimes six-inch) chunks of colored transparent material look like (and may even be described by the sellers as) topaz, actually are a form of natural glass found in the near desert. Scientists are not certain what produces this glass. It might just be lightning that strikes desert sands full of silicas, the basis of glass. In any case, these are unusual souvenirs for LE 1 to LE 2.

THE HIGH DAM: So many organized tours include a stop at the dam that something should be said about it. Guides will proudly cite strings of numbers about the dam, for Egyptians are truly proud of this work. They will say it is two miles long (almost) and close to a mile thick at the base. Covered by cement, it is made of enough rubble to match 15 Great Pyramids in volume (if anyone would care to). The water backed up behind the dam has made Lake Nasser 300 miles long (it is, however, narrow). The dam produces ten million kilowatts of electricity per hour.

Worldwide discussion of the High Dam in the media has usually emphasized problems caused by the dam. Bad news is more interesting than good, as any newsperson well appreciates. Yet Egypt was desperate when the dam was approved. Population was growing at a rate that could not be fed by the arable land in the country and Egypt had little to offer in trade for foreign food. Also, Egypt has a tradition of past engineering works that smooths the way for new ones. In 2000 B.C. dams and canals were dug to irrigate tens of thousands of acres in the Faiyum. In the last ancient dynasties a canal was dug to connect the Red Sea with the Mediterranean—a forerunner of the Suez Canal of the last century.

Egypt was prepared to try anything to stave off fatal population pressures. The new dam held promise. With the tremendous increase in electrical power, Egypt would be able to expand her industry. With the control of waterflow, Egypt would be saved both from too much water flooding the land and from too little water dehydrating crops. This control and the construction of additional canals would bring water to places it never reached before. Millions of acres of new farms would be created.

The cost, however, has been dreadful. No longer does the Nile overflow its banks each year in a flood that cleans the land and deposits a new layer of nutrients. Consequently, for the first time in history, the topsoil has been depleted; now Egyptians need costly chemical fertilizers. More serious, the soil now grows increasingly salty, which kills crops. But a tragic problem difficult to calculate in monetary terms is the danger to the tombs near Luxor. A thousand years pass between rains in the Valley of the Kings. The paint in the ancient tombs still remains fresh precisely because of this absence of moisture. Now nearby is 300-mile Lake Nasser created by the High Dam, enough water in a waterless land to change the weather. Today the sky is often gray above the Valley of the Kings; people fear that it will begin to rain.

It would take a greater judge than most of us to weigh such pros and cons. It was Egypt's decision and it was Egypt who faced a desperate future. All we can do is wish her well.

TEMPLE OF KALABSHA: Eight miles south of the High Dam on a promontory on the west side of Lake Nasser now stands this reconstructed temple, carried stone by stone from its original home 30 miles south beneath Lake Nasser.

Although the emperor August commissioned the temple, the decoration was never finished. The temple was dedicated to a form of Horus. The pylon and first court are skewed compared to the orientation of the rest of the temple. Not much remains of the small hypostyle hall, but behind it are three well-preserved sanctuaries, one after the other, growing larger as they go back. Outside the hypostyle hall (the left side) is a ruined nilometer that naturally no longer reaches to the water (which in any case no longer rises and falls as it once did).

TEMPLE OF PHILAE: *(Admission is LE 2.)* Once this ranked among the great tourist attractions in Egypt. It was a gem, ornate and small, on its own island in the Nile. The main part was dedicated to Isis, the mother of Horus and the symbol of affection. The setting greatly contributed to its charm, but when the Nile began rising early in this century when the first dam was constructed, the island became submerged for much of the year. A rescue mission moved all the stones to an island nearby, blasted into the shape of the original site. Located just downstream from the High Dam, it can be reached by hired boat.

You step onto the island near a small portico built by a pharaoh from the last Egyptian dynasty, the oldest building on the island. The columns have Hat-hor head capitals. Ahead, two long rows of columns form a walkway to the Temple of Isis. The temple begins with the usual pylons, here decorated with the figures of Isis and Horus her son, with a pharaoh beside them. Two lions, not fierce at all, guard the gate. The courtyard contains a *mammisi* (birth house) on the left side with more Hat-hor columns. A second set of pylons leads to a small hypostyle hall followed by a sanctuary (some nice reliefs) behind which stairs lead to the roof.

Left of the hypostyle hall is the emperor Hadrian's gateway. Inside, on the left, a relief depicts the source of the Nile in a fantastic interpretation where the god of the river, strangled by a serpent, still pours water out of two vessels. Above, on a rock, sit a vulture and a falcon. The birds, of course, represent the pharaoh who in turn stood for all of Egypt. They sit on a rock above the source because the Egyptians believed that their river began at a spring.

On the edge of the island, past Roman ruins, is a nilometer. On the other end of the island is a temple for Hat-hor with pretty scenes, and at the island's edge stands a jewel of a building by the emperor Trajan. Long submersion has been hard on these buildings, robbing them of much of their delicacy, but the harmony of this collection of "little" buildings is unsurpassed in Egypt, if not in the world.

ABU SIMBEL

See four colossal stone Rameses carved out of a sandstone hill above quiet Lake Nasser. They overlook the watery southern road to Egypt today as they always did. Behind them is an entire temple, a cave carved from solid rock—quite a feat of ancient engineering. Now it is a trick, based on a modern engineering feat. In the 1960s the original temple was cut into blocks and reassembled higher than the rising lake created by the High Dam. What had been a sandstone hill today is a concrete dome so cleverly covered by blocks that it fools every eye except those that look closely. The original site is below your feet.

Abu Simbel cannot be called the greatest artistic achievement of Egypt, yet tourists all want to see it and few are disappointed. The temple, in a quiet place far from civilization, is completely successful in the majesty of its design. Colossal statues outside set the tone to which the cavern inside follows as a surprising counterpoint.

A hydrofoil boat once ran from Aswan to Abu Simbel. The ten-hour round trip carried no food, but the quiet lake views were pleasant. At present, however, this run has been discontinued, perhaps for good.

The plane from Aswan takes 40 minutes. It refuels before flying back (and in the afternoon goes all the way to Cairo after stops at Aswan and Luxor). From the airport a free bus runs to Abu Simbel and returns to catch the next available plane. Two hours is enough for most people to see the two temples at Abu Simbel. Take a picnic lunch (your hotel will prepare one), for there are no restaurants near the temples. Admission of LE 5, paid after leaving the bus, includes the price of the guide who takes the busload around.

Rameses the Great was all for show. After his tragic experience at Kadesh he lost his taste for battle but not for bravado. He proceeded to build several rock temples in Nubia, although Abu Simbel is far grander than the others. Like other temples, these were dedicated to a major god and offered subsidiary services for other gods, but the rock temples all had a special purpose beyond religion. By then, Egypt worried about invasion attempts on all of its borders, including the south. Rameses raised a southern temple at Abu Simbel to demonstrate Egypt's love of the colossal; it showed what Egypt was capable of accomplishing when wishing to undertake a large project. The temple presented the pharaoh of Egypt as a giant, even when seated. Rameses expected that this sight would give long pause to any Nubian thoughts about war with Egypt. Even modern visitors are impressed with a feeling of the power of Rameses. How much more would ancient people, more open to magic, be impressed by this vision. A nation, or a leader, who could create Abu Simbel radiated power equivalent to an army in deterrent effects.

Downhill from the bus parking lot, left around the hill, a

grassy knoll stretches to the edge of the lake, and opposite is the facade of the first temple. This temple has Rameses' giant statues in front and is dedicated primarily to Ra-Horakhty, secondarily to Rameses himself. A second temple farther along the knoll is dedicated to Hat-hor and decorated with statues of Rameses' great wife, Nefertari.

TEMPLE OF RA-HORAKHTY: *Ra-Horakhty* means "the sun who is Horus of the horizon." What this god represented to the Egyptians is not entirely clear to the modern mind, but Ra-Horakhty became very important in Egypt as time passed. He was an amalgam of the two earlier important gods, Ra and Horus. The "of the Horizon" part of his name suggests concepts of rising and setting, though most scholars go no further than to say that this god stood for the power of the sky. Pictured as a human with a falcon's head, the god wears a sun disk. He stands over the entrance leading to the inner temple. Alongside two carvings of Rameses kneel and offer a tiny idol of the goddess Maat to Ra-Horakhty. Egyptians often made puns. This group is a pun consisting of *was* plus *Maat* plus *Ra*, spelling the beginning of Rameses' first name. Rameses wears the "blue" crown, a New Kingdom addition to the wardrobe of a pharaoh, often worn in battle.

The facade forms the shape of a pylon such as would front a normal temple. As with any other Egyptian religious complex, the temple waits behind—it happens in this case that the edifice was hollowed from solid rock. Along the top of the facade a row of baboons lift paws in adoration of the rising sun. In nature baboons sometimes do this, and the ancient Egyptians were impressed. They thought that an animal who worshiped must be favored by the god he prayed to.

It is impossible to look at the facade of this temple without being struck by the colossal figures of Rameses. Commonly temples had large statues in front of the pharaoh who built them, but only the Colossi of Memnon that once fronted Amunhotep III's temple are larger than these. Sitting, Rameses towers more than 65 feet tall. He wears three different crowns combined in a sort of royal overkill. Highest is the cone-shaped crown of the south (in every case now almost entirely knocked off), then the crown of the north, a kind of pillbox with a projection rising in the back. Under these two is the Old Kingdom *nemes* crown—a kerchief with lappets dangling over the shoulders. The carving of these figures was intended for the perspective of a distant view. Up close most of the figures appear chunky and crude, but the faces are effective—sensitive and dignified. Signs of repair in the form of bricks surround the figures. These were added by Seti II, two pharaohs after Rameses. Why repairs would be necessary so soon after the construction is not clear.

Hugging the legs of the four Rameses are various smaller statues of his family. To appreciate the size of the colossi, note that these "tiny" family members are substantially more than life-size. The colossus farthest left is flanked by two princesses—Nebet-Tawi and Benet-Anet, with a presumed third between them, now nameless. The next colossus is hugged by Rameses' mother Tuiy (left) and his primary wife of this period, Nefertari (right). Between the legs stands prince Amunhorkopshef. Graffiti on the smooth legs in ancient Greek, Persian, and Phoenician show how old the impulse is to leave your name where you have been. The newest graffiti is 19th century.

Passing through the entrance between the colossi, you see reliefs carved on the facing sides of the center thrones. A sagging-breasted Nile god holds together the lotus plant of the south and the papyrus of the north to represent the unity of one country. In fact, the god ties these plants around a hieroglyphic sign that means "unity." Below are bound prisoners—Nubians on the left throne, Syrians on the right.

The temple extends back 180 feet back into the hill. First is the analogue of the open court (here, of course, within the rock), almost square, surrounded by a colonnade of pillars in front of which are large statues with Rameses' face. Those to the left (south) wear the southern crown, those to the right wear the northern crown. Vultures fly overhead.

On both entrance walls Amun-Ra (left) or Ra-Horakhty (right) offers a sword to Rameses who hardly seems to need it as he grasps his enemies by their hair and is about to bash them with his mace. Behind him is his own "double," or soul. Below a line of his daughters holds sacred rattles. Of the reliefs covering the walls of the court, those on the left are more interesting artistically. Here Rameses does battle with Libya below scenes of the ritual of worship. One chief is arched in death, impaled by Rameses' lance, while enemies writhe under the pharaoh's feet and another chief rushes rashly to join the fight. The composition is vigorous. The right-hand wall has yet another portrayal of the Battle of Kadesh. By this time the scenes had been repeated so often that you may sense a loss of interest even by the sculptors.

The right chambers that fan off from this court are not visually interesting, though a question remains about their function. Some experts claim that they were storerooms for temple equipment, but benches line the walls.

Going back from the court is the small hypostyle hall. Four pillars brace the ceiling. Rameses offers incense to sacred boats that carry the idols of the gods, followed by his Queen Nefertari shaking rattles. After the hall is a vestibule with three doorways; the flanking ones lead to small chambers, while the center doorway leads to the sanctuary with four statues carved from the rock. In front of the statues is a pedestal for sacred boats. The statues portray four gods: Ptah (left), Amun, Rameses himself, and Ra-Horakhty (right).

Now you have reached the extreme rear of the temple, having passed through rooms growing progressively lower and smaller on the way. From this far end the light of the open entrance seems far away and small. Yet twice each year (usually on February 15 and October 15) when the sun rises on the horizon, it reaches back to the rear to shine for a minute on the statue of Rameses. Presumably this was not an accidental effect. Could one of these dates be Rameses' birthday?

On the way to the second temple is a metal door in the rock. Go inside. It leads behind the scenes of the show. You come into an enormous open space, a dome rising hundreds of feet. This is the structure built to save the Abu Simbel temples from drowning beneath the lake's water. Now you can see that the hill is concrete. Moving these stone temples was extremely difficult, the stone being of poor quality and easily broken. Special saws were used to cut the temple into portable blocks. Water could not be used to cool the saws for fear of dissolving the stone; synthetic chemical was injected into the stones to prevent their crumbling. The original hill had to be leveled before the temple could be erected again above it. Blasting was out of the question—three million pounds of hill were removed by simply digging. Then all the blocks of stone were carefully put together again and the dome built above and faced by stone to resemble the original hill. Calculations were perfectly precise to preserve the exact orientation of the temple. The sun shines to the rear of the temple on Rameses' statue of the same days of the year it always has. Work began in 1964. It was completed in 1970.

TEMPLE OF HAT-HOR: Earlier we mentioned how a god would travel at certain times to the temple of a goddess in order to consummate their union. For example, Horus would travel from the temple at Esna to Hat-hor at the Denderah Temple. No temples or large towns were in the area of Abu Simbel nor any ancient tradition of worship, so Rameses built two temples close together to serve this function. Ra-Horakhty could then visit Hat-hor just around the hill. In the present reconstruction, they are even closer—just yards away.

It was extremely unusual for a temple to be dedicated to a queen as this one was, though Rameses gets his statues in here too. Queen Nefertari stands 33 feet high in front on either side of the entrance, flanked by Rameses. The statues do not seem even half the size of the colossi next door, probably because these are standing and thus are much less than half as massive. The temple itself is small; it would fit in the first room of the other temple. In general the carving is uninspired; appropriately, though, the exception is the carved women, Nefertari and the various goddesses.

The court has Hat-hor pillars with the cow face etched in simple lines rather than carved more deeply. Perhaps the most interesting carvings are in the next section, the vestibule. On either side wall above doors to unfinished chambers, Hat-hor is portrayed as a cow sailing in a marsh. The reeds provide a perfect frame for the composition. On the far side of the vestibule, the goddesses Isis and Hat-hor crown Nefertari. The women are slender and elegant. Nefertari smiles graciously, holding her dress in one hand and the *ankh*, symbol of life, in the other. In the tiny sanctuary a Hat-hor cow half emerges from the rock. Rameses kneels to suckle from her life-giving milk. Spaces were left free of carvings on both side walls, presumably for doors to side chambers which were never finished.

AMENITIES IN ASWAN

HOTELS

The hotel situation is tight in Aswan, and while not as strained as Luxor, still requires early reservations. All the hotels either line the Nile Corniche or are on islands in the river. Some hotels are extremely pleasant.

Cataract Hotel and **New Cataract Hotel.** *Deluxe.* (The Nile Corniche, south by the upstream end of Elephantine Island.) On a bluff to gain splendid views, the grand older hotel is wedded to a modern addition, together offering 330 rooms. Often featured in the movies set in Egypt, this is a sister in elegance to the Winter Palace in Luxor. The old part has all the charm—unfortunately partly faded—and lower prices. Only the new wing is air-conditioned. New Cataract open all year, air-conditioned, compulsory half-board; single rooms cost 21.50 in season, 20 in summer, but doubles are only LE 2 more without views, the same as singles with views. The old Cataract goes for LE 13.25 per single, LE 14.50 per double, and drops by LE 2 in the summer.

Aswan Oberoi. *Deluxe.* (On Elephantine Island. Private launch for commuting.) The most deluxe new hotel in Egypt. With roof pool, splendid views from each of the 150 rooms, and an even more splendid panorama from the tower bar and restaurant, this hotel has every amenity plus quiet. If you stick to the Indian dishes on the menu, you will have one of your best meals in Egypt. Open all year, air-conditioned.

Compulsory half-board. Singles are LE 27 to LE 25 out of season; doubles are LE 30 dropping to LE 28. Duplex suites are LE 45. Oberoi International Hotels.

Amun Hotel. *First Class.* (On its own island, opposite the Cataract Hotel.) Intimate (only 36 rooms) and as peaceful as a hotel can be. The flowered garden is a jewel, and the veranda takes you back to more gracious days; only the rooms are ordinary—though they do have views. We rate the food uninspired. Open all year, air-conditioned. Compulsory half-board. Prices for singles are LE 11; doubles are LE 12; LE 1 less in summer.

Kalabsha Hotel. *First Class.* (Behind the Cataract Hotel.) Fine views because of its elevation, but an older hotel that, even when young, never pretended elegance. Still, its 150 rooms are less expensive than the preceding choices. Open all year, air-conditioned. Compulsory half-board. Singles are LE 11, LE 10 out of season; small doubles for LE 12 go down to LE 11 when summer arrives. Egyptian Hotel Company.

Grand Hotel. *Third Class.* (The Nile Corniche, opposite Elephantine Island.) Grand it is not; old it is. We judge this shabby and dark place a solution for those turned away elsewhere or those on a very tight budget. At least the rooms are large. The nightclub with its loud music was too much for us. Open all year, not air-conditioned (nor heated in winter). Singles cost LE 4 with bath, LE 3 without; doubles are LE 6 with bath, LE 4.70 without.

After these, we list only for the homeless the **Hotel Abu Simbel**—north on the Corniche, the **Happi Hotel**—behind the Abu Simbel, and the **Hotel Philae**—on the Corniche opposite the Oberoi.

RESTAURANTS

Outside of those in hotels, we know of none.

SHOPPING

The best buys in Aswan are anything Nubian, especially baskets and jewelry. These are sold in the bazaar but the most enjoyable way to acquire Nubian crafts is in the course of a visit to one of the **Nubian villages** where you will shop for less, be invited into houses for tea, and generally receive a true taste of this separate culture. Especially recommended are the small villages on any of the large islands in the Nile.

LEAVING ASWAN

TO ABU SIMBEL: Our latest information tells us that the hydrofoil boat across Lake Nasser is out of service for the indefinite future. The only choice remaining is to fly. Six daily flights leave at 6:30 a.m., 8:20 a.m., 10:10 a.m., noon, 1:50 p.m., and 3:40 p.m., which refuel and leave 55 minutes later. Fares to Aswan are LE 17.50.

TO CAIRO: Planes leave several times each day. Inquire at your hotel desk. The fare is LE 40.50.

12.

Background for Alexandria

Alexandria was a special city for two of the most famous people in history, Alexander the Great and Cleopatra. Both are buried beneath her streets, though no one knows where. Think about grand ambitions and tragedies as you walk within the center of the city.

ALEXANDER THE GREAT

Though not the most royal male, Alexander's father, Philip II, became king of Macedonia because an assembly of nobles could consider ability in addition to blood lines when choosing a ruler. He proved to be an outstanding choice. Philip defeated the neighbors surrounding Macedonia to make his the most powerful state in Greece. Then he planned to fulfill the dream of all Greeks, to invade Turkey and reclaim the lost Greek colonies of Iona where philosophy had been born. With finances supplied by newly discovered Macedonian gold mines, Philip organized a Greek confederation and sent an army off to Turkey. Before joining his troops, Philip first had to settle an affair: he planned to marry again after divorcing his wife. Alexander sat in the wedding audience waiting for his father to marry a new wife who would displace his mother and himself. Philip was assassinated on his way to the ceremony.

There is little likelihood that Alexander plotted the murder. Athens was conspiring with Persia at the time and either could have seen the advantages of eliminating the Greek general about to invade Persia's territory. Or, Alexander's mother may have arranged the deed.

At the time, Alexander was a man of 20 torn apart by his family. His father hated his mother, who returned the feeling with passion and filled her son's head with her venom. Alexander clothed his battered emotions in his dreams of world conquest. Shorter than average and stocky, he had gray eyes and the blond complexion characteristic of the northern Greeks. He had been educated by Aristotle, the wisest man in the world. Unloved by his parents, he treated others with great affection and generated in return extraordinary devotion from friends and from his troops. His only enduring relationships were with males. Only one woman attracted him—for a month—after which she joined the baggage of his army.

Various Greek states took Philip's death as an excuse to test Alexander, soon after he received the throne. He defeated them decisively, then marched to Turkey to join the advancing army sent by his father. His opponent, the Persian king, was a six-and-one-half-foot giant in body but a dwarf as far as courage went. Ominously for the Persians, he was named Darius for the man who had retreated from Marathon. While Alexander won small engagements, Darius avoided battle until he could collect an army that outnumbered Alexander's by perhaps four times. When Darius finally took to the field, Alexander drove straight for the center of the Persian army where the king stood. Darius panicked. His flight threw the Persian army into confusion, and Alexander won a tremendous victory that opened all of the Middle East to him.

By the time Alexander reached Egypt, the Persian governor, who could count neither on his own king nor on the Egyptians to support him, gave up without a fight. Alexander was greeted as a savior and crowned pharaoh in Memphis.

Alexander was driven: everything he did was directed toward conquest or toward establishing the foundation for a stable empire—with two exceptions. While in Turkey, he detoured for several days to visit the ruins of Troy. He made offers at a Greek temple there and took away a shield—said to be from the time of the Trojan Wars—which he used in battle for the rest of his life. The second exception took place in Egypt where Alexander set out on a pilgrimage to the oasis of Siwa, near the Lybian border.

A famous temple stood in Siwa dedicated to Amun (who was portrayed as a ram). Its repute came from the powers of its oracle. Priests rushed to greet Alexander when he arrived, proclaiming him as the veritable son of Amun. Many modern history books contend that Alexander went to Siwa for this reason—to be recognized as a god and hence as the pharaoh. Yet he had been crowned previously in Memphis and thus would have been greeted as a god at any temple in Egypt. No other pharaoh had ever visited Siwa, in fact. More likely Alexander journeyed to Siwa to ask a question of the famed oracle. He did enter the Holy-of-Holies to confront the oracle, with only the high priest, while his fellow Greeks waited outside. When he returned, he told no one what his question had been, or the answer—not then, nor at any later time in his life. All that he said was that he had received the answer he wanted.

Scholars can guess at his question and its answer. When still a child, Alexander had been told by his mother that his father actually was not Philip, whom she so despised, but was a god. In the dark inner sanctum at Siwa, Alexander may well have asked who his true father was. Surely, in this temple, the answer would have been Amun. On coins produced later in his life, the head of Alexander shows faint ram's horns through his curls.

Alexander soon left Egypt, for the 24-year-old had much to do and, as it happened, little time. He bequeathed one memento to Egypt. On his way from Siwa he passed a lovely spot on the Mediterranean coast where he believed a great city could be built. He helped with the plans for the future city of Alexandria, then left the actual construction to others, hurrying out of Egypt.

Alexander's appointment was again with Darius, who had collected another army. Across the Tigris River, 250,000 Persians and mercenaries waited for Alexander's 50,000 men. Many strategists consider this the most brilliant battle in history. In many ways, however, it repeated Alexander's first engagement with Darius. Again Alexander attacked the strength of the enemy at the point Darius commanded. This time Darius sat behind 15 Indian elephants. The charge and yells of the Greek cavalry, the only arm of Alexander's army superior to the Persians, drove the elephants mad. Their stampede created confusion that spread back until it reached Darius who, as before, fled.

Alexander ruled the Middle East now without rivals, but he remained a driven man. He had to continue to the end of the world which, as far as the Greeks knew, was India. His troops followed him through high mountain passes to the plains of northern India, defeating every army on the march across the top of India. Alexander then planned to drive to the southern tip of India where, cartographers assured him, the world ended. From there he believed—for the Greeks thought that the world was round—he could again reach Greece after a short sail east. But it was the season of the monsoons. After seven straight years of fighting, his men were tired, miserably wet, and sick. Alexander never had, nor ever would, lose a battle, but his men lost their wills in northern India. They refused to move a step farther from home.

Alexander had no choice but to return. The journey from India, by a southern route, became a nightmare. Food and water were scarce, disease broke out, enemies appeared at every turn. Alexander led, as he always did, in the front rank, wearing a special helmet so his troops could see and be inspired to follow. Seven times he had been wounded, but never seriously until his luck ran out on the way home from India.

He, with three comrades, was the first on the ramparts of the hundredth town that stood in their way. Rocks and arrows fell all around them. As always, his troops rushed to join Alexander, but the ladder broke from their weight. For some minutes, until other ladders were in place, four men fought against a town. A three-foot-long arrow pierced Alexander's chest. He fought until blood and bubbles, a sign of hemorrhaged lungs, spurted from the wound, then fell unconscious.

He survived, even through the terrible 1000-mile journey that remained—one on which healthy men died from heat and disease. But never again would he be the man he had been. With weakened lungs, he lasted only three more years. On the eve of another expedition, at 33, he caught a fever and died in Babylon.

He left a son in the womb of his wife, the residue of Alexander's one romance with a woman. Ever since he had become king, he had been urged to secure the throne with an heir, but he would not or could not, until he met the fair Roxane. She was the daughter of a minor Persian chief; it was not a political union. For one month they found happiness, after which Alexander returned to his men. But when he died, Alexander left power such as had never existed, and a son too young to control it.

A worldwide struggle for pieces of the empire began. The first casualty was Alexander's child, assassinated by the man entrusted with the governorship of Macedonia. The next casualty was a dimwitted half brother of Alexander, killed by Alexander's mother. She was next. The field then was open to anyone with strength, and the strongest were the generals of Alexander's army. Each grabbed whatever parts of the world they could reach, splitting the empire into seven parts.

One of these generals was Ptolemy, a friend and possible half brother of Alexander. He raced for Egypt. He wanted his capital to be in the north of Egypt, close to the trouble expected from the other generals. For his city he chose the one begun by his dead friend—Alexandria. The world then settled into its seven pieces while Ptolemy bred a dynasty of Ptolemies, embellishing Alexandria until it became the greatest city in the world.

CLEOPATRA

Cleopatra, the Queen of the Nile, who enchanted two leaders of the world with her dark and sultry looks and who died from love when she lost Marc Antony, is a character in a tale told by Shakespeare. The dramatist knew how to bend the facts in the interest of a story. His outline is accurate enough—his audience would not accept a gross historical gaffe—but he invented enough details to change the character if not the order of the truth.

Nothing was either dark or sultry about Cleopatra; not a drop of Egyptian blood flowed in her veins. She was of the family Ptolemy, a Macedonian. Her family had lived for almost 300 years in Egypt, but they married only relatives— brothers and sisters, aunts and uncles, fathers and daughters—the only exceptions being children of other Macedonian generals who had thrones elsewhere in the Middle East. Cleopatra probably had blue eyes; her complexion would be fair, not tanned, for that would have been considered lower class; her hair would be light brown or perhaps even blond. All of Shakespeare's suggestions that her exotic looks dazzled the Romans is historically backwards. Cleopatra's appeal lay in looks that would please Roman mothers.

Unfortunately, few portraits of Cleopatra survive from her time, and those are just of her head on coins. She looks rather ordinary, and by our standards she would be much too plump. But Cleopatra was more than a woman, she was Egypt—which is not to say that Caesar and Antony did not love her. She had her youth to attract the older Julius Caesar, and position and wealth. She was probably the richest person in the world. She was intelligent. Antony, too, fell in love with the whole package, for none of us can successfully isolate physical features from what a person represents. Marc

Antony was an ambitious man; Cleopatra's wealth fit in nicely with his plans.

Cleopatra was one of a long line of women with that name, the seventh Cleopatra in the Ptolemaic line, all named after the sister of Alexander the Great. The name is even older—it meant "father's glory" in Greek and was thus popular. The most famous Cleopatra began as a normal Ptolemaic daughter born to a pharaoh. Ptolemies excelled in intrigue. Cleopatra had two older sisters and two younger brothers: one older sister grabbed the throne while her father was in Rome gathering political support. Then the sister on the throne, it appears, poisoned the other older sister. When her father returned, after securing Rome's support, the daughter tried to fight. When she lost, she killed herself. That left Cleopatra as the eldest surviving royal daughter.

Ptolemies followed the ancient Egyptian practice of marrying the heir to the most royal daughter, so Cleopatra at 17 married her 10-year-old brother, Ptolemy XIV. When their father died, Cleopatra schemed to take the throne but was discovered and expelled by her husband. Meanwhile, Julius Caesar and Pompey had warred, and the beaten Pompey fled to Egypt. (Pompey was the guardian for Cleopatra and her husband.) Caesar, pursuing Pompey, arrived in Egypt to find that the new Pharaoh Ptolemy had killed Pompey in an effort to curry Caesar's favor. Such crass opportunism impressed Caesar not a all, but the nubile Cleopatra did when she gained an audience with him. A Roman alliance was her only hope of regaining power. Cleopatra's alliance with Caesar was successful in every sense—she even became pregnant with his son. The affair lasted four years, ending when Caesar was assassinated in the Roman Senate.

Caesar's adopted son Octavian then shared rule with Marc Antony, and together they defeated the Roman faction that favored a republic over a kingship. Antony set out to conquer the Middle East, while Cleopatra set out to conquer Antony. It was an attraction of similars; the two became lovers and married. Octavian, however, was not pleased. In part it was a matter of competition for power; in part it was that Antony had offended Roman sensibilities—Antony was already married to Octavian's sister. Officially, the Romans of the time were prudish, no matter what their private activities might have included. Octavian had an excuse to make war on the man who had insulted his sister, hence his family and Rome.

Antony, a proven general, thought he would have no difficulty defeating the untried Octavian. But Antony relied on mercenaries and imprudently entered into a sea battle rather than a land engagement, where his experience lay. Off the coast of Greece near Actium, Antony was soundly beaten. He crawled back to Egypt to raise another army, pursued by Octavian. An Egyptian army was no match for Romans. Antony, aware that capture was inevitable, took his own life.

Shakespeare creates the impression that Cleopatra committed suicide because life without Antony was not worth the struggle, although he never exactly states that. In fact, Cleopatra lived some weeks longer than Antony. She tried her wiles on Octavian, but failed; he did not need her. After having defeated Egypt's army, he was already in control of the country, and Cleopatra by then was an older woman—39 to Octavian's 26.

Cleopatra committed suicide probably because she foresaw no future for herself. She knew that she would no longer be anyone's queen and that she would be humiliated by the Romans. No evidence exists to show how she took her life. An asp, as Shakespeare has it happen, is less likely than a potion of some sort brewed by her doctors. The Ptolemies and their doctors had great experience with poisons.

Cleopatra represents the second end for Egypt. The first came with the final Egyptian pharaoh; Cleopatra was the last true pharaoh of any nationality. Though under Roman rule the reigning emperor was called "pharaoh" in Egypt, the country was no more than a Roman province. Egypt was bled of her produce to supply the populace of Rome so that emperors could behave with impunity and excess. Egypt had become a Roman farm.

13.

Alexandria

You catch a hint of the mystique of Alexandria while passing through on a day's visit, though what the mystique is is as hard to name as the aroma of unfamiliar food. It disappears if you stay several days, lost in the conviction that Alexandria is all wrong—crowded and dirty yet new. Alexandria is hardly Egyptian. But in a week you may find that special feeling again and, if so, Alexandria will be your special city. Do not go to Alexandria to see a group of monuments; go for the character conveyed by instant intuition or learned by living with it. Come for a day or stay a week; anything between is wasted.

Alexandria, Egypt's alter-ego, her European face, lines the Mediterranean as though stretching against Egypt to reach toward Europe. Cairo looks inward, is Egyptian to the core; but Alexandria speaks in tongues—English, French, Greek, Italian, Hebrew, Armenian, and Turkish, as well as Arabic. It was a place where the foreignness of 20 countries came together to produce a character different from any of them. Now the babble of voices has faded, since nationalism crowded out 750,000 foreigners after the independence revolution in 1952. The realist today sees a rundown beachside city, though the romantic senses levantine and oriental mysteries. Lawrence Durrell captured this Alexandria completely—Clea, Justine, Mountolive, and Balthazar still live as they always did, only it takes a certain sensitivity now to find them.

The present city is the second Alexandria, dating from the 19th century. When Napoleon landed in 1798 in an effort to duplicate the conquests of Alexander the Great, he found only a fishing village here. After some months of military success his fleet was destroyed in a sudden raid. Napoleon saved his skin by slipping away in the night, leaving his troops behind to surrender to the English. Five thousand Frenchmen landed at Alexandria—they matched the city's population then. So ended Napoleon's dream, but Alexander's dream had faded too as the decline in the size of his city shows. Today Alexandria has a population of between three million and four million but it has nothing to do with its namesake except to house his ghost.

The first Alexandria did owe its existence to the great Alexander who came upon the site on his way to another town. He saw a small village beside a natural harbor so wonderful that he stopped. Just below the water a limestone ridge made a basin where ships could find protected anchorage. Behind a thin stretch of dry land waited a freshwater lake. The area contained everything a city would need. Tempered by the Mediterranean Sea, the climate was ideal. Deciding to erect a city, Alexander walked over the bare land with architects and pointed to where the market should be and the temple and houses. After instructing the workmen to lay out a town in the orderly Greek manner, Alexander departed to conquer the world and die. He saw not a single building, nor had he much effect on the future splendors of Alexandria, his namesake.

After Alexander's empire split into warring factions on his death, Ptolemy, his general and childhood friend, seized Egypt, crowned himself pharaoh, and made Alexandria his

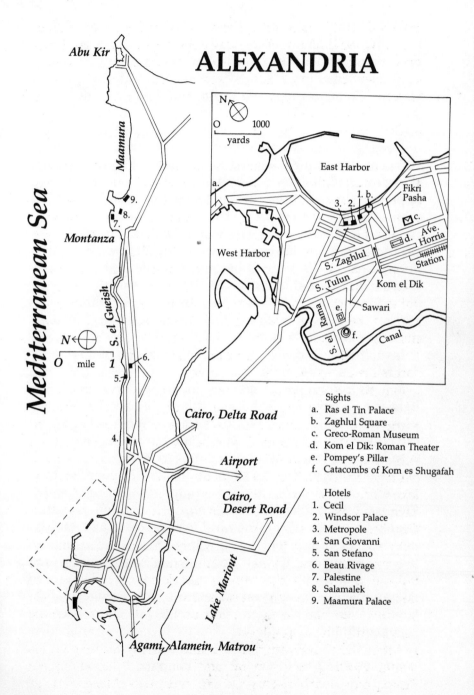

ALEXANDRIA

Mediterranean Sea

Abu Kir

Maamura

Montanza

S. el Gueish

N←

O mile 1

East Harbor

West Harbor

Fikri
Pasha

Ras el Tin Palace (a.)

S. Zaghlul

S. Tulun

Kom el Dik

Sawari

S. el Rama

Canal

Ave. Horria

Station

N

O 1000
yards

Cairo, Delta Road

Airport

Cairo,
Desert Road

Lake Mariout

Agami, Alamein, Matrou

Sights
a. Ras el Tin Palace
b. Zaghlul Square
c. Greco-Roman Museum
d. Kom el Dik: Roman Theater
e. Pompey's Pillar
f. Catacombs of Kom es Shugafah

Hotels
1. Cecil
2. Windsor Palace
3. Metropole
4. San Giovanni
5. San Stefano
6. Beau Rivage
7. Palestine
8. Salamalek
9. Maamura Palace

capital. From sentiment, and because Alexander was believed to be a god, Ptolemy brought his body here in a gold coffin borne on a golden cart pulled by 64 mules. The cart and its body all were buried somewhere in the center of the city where each succeeding heir of Ptolemy made a tomb beside Alexander. No coffins or bodies ever have been found.

This first Ptolemy, nicknamed Soter ("Savior"), commenced work on what he called the Mouseion. It was a complex of buildings devoted to the study of all the arts and sciences, all superintended by a pupil of Aristotle and named after the Greek Muses, the goddesses of knowledge. Our word *museum* comes from this. Here, the first librarian collected and edited Homer's works, which preserved them for the future. Euclid began a school of mathematics. Alexandria was on its way to becoming the largest, most cosmopolitan, most educated city in the ancient world.

Under successors, all named Ptolemy, a lighthouse was built in the harbor. So low is the alluvial coastline that some mark which could be seen from the sea was needed to guide ships to the harbor. An artificial mountain of a building, 500 feet tall, was raised in the bay on a promontory called Pharos. Scientists from the Mouseion designed a system to produce a light visible from far at the sea. It became one of the Seven Wonders of the Ancient World, but the secret of the light and the building that housed it were lost in an earthquake in our 15th century. The location now is uncertain.

Descendants of the first Ptolemy jealously guarded their power, intermarrying to keep control within the family. Ptolemy after Ptolemy ruled, almost all married to sisters named Cleopatra. Finally, it was Ptolemy XIV at age ten who married his 17-year-old sister, Cleopatra VII, who immortalized the name. By this time Romans had connived and bullied their way to power around the world. They eyed Alexandria rapaciously for its store of knowledge and its control over Egypt's grain. The city fell to them after the Cleopatra/Julius Caesar/Marc Antony love story outlined in Chapter 12.

Roman rule transformed Alexandria from a national into a

provincial capital; her greatest days were gone. Alexandria made one final mark on history when Greek descendants living there were among the first to convert to a new religion from Palestine based on the martyred Jesus Christ. They spread the word and soon Egypt was the first Christian country. The Arab invasion in A.D. 643 ended that, and Alexandria too. Arabs sought religious purity, not international trade; they had no interest in a Mediterranean port. The invaders created an Arab capital at Cairo, and Alexandria wasted to the pitiable state that Napoleon found.

Modern Alexandria is due to Pasha Muhammad Ali from Albania, in fact not far from the Macedonia of Alexander. He ruled Egypt first as an agent of Turkey, then increasingly as his own man. His ambition was to make Egypt modern, to open the country to European ideas. Alexandria became his virtual capital and grew with the notice. By the end of his line, when King Farouk was overthrown, Alexandria had blossomed into the second city of Egypt. In summer the court came to avoid the Cairo inferno. The tradition persists, for all those who can (including most government officials) still summer here and double the city's population for the season.

If you come for a day or a week to discover Alexandria, stay in the city center. Here, with abundant taxis, transportation is no problem. In winter rooms are plentiful. In warmer seasons you can find lovely beaches—not in the city where they tend to be overused and polluted, but in charming towns that stretch 50 miles east or west of the city proper. Rooms are difficult to find in summer.

Alexandria, long and thin, hugs the sea; the center is just inland from the promontory that forms the main bay, Ras el Tin. Shari 26 July, the corniche road, runs around the bay after which it changes its name to Shari el Gueish and follows the sea east. Back one street from where the corniche straightens and changes its name is the main square of the city, Midan Saad Zaghlul. Here, by a grassy park, sits the grand Cecil Hotel. Many claim that Lawrence Durell stayed here; it looks as though he should have. All the sights are within a mile or a mile-and-a-half of this hub.

THE SIGHTS IN ALEXANDRIA

Do not expect to see the famous lighthouse, the Mouseion, the famous library, or the tomb of Alexander. A few stones and pillars mark the place where the Mouseion stood, but of the others not even locations are certain. You can see the several minor sights while drinking in the atmosphere of the city. All but the Greco-Roman Museum can be seen in four or five hours. Hire a taxi which will cost LE 7–9 for half a day. Have one taxi take you to the museum; pick up a new ride from there when you are ready to tour the other sites. You can instead join a group tour which will cost less for one person than a taxi, but more for two people.

THE ROMAN REMAINS: Two blocks back from Midan Zaghlul and a turn east lies a quiet park, Kom el Dik. An old fort that once stood here was torn down in 1959 to make room for much needed modern housing. When the work began, Roman artifacts were unearthed in great quantities. The housing was not to be. Systematic excavation soon exposed an almost perfectly preserved ancient theater. Beside it a complex of Roman baths is under excavation.

Columns all around the theater suggest that this was an odeon, a covered theater. The green columns are from Asia Minor, the pink from Aswan, and the seats are European marble. About 700 people could listen to music or watch a wrestling or boxing match when the theater opened for business in the 3rd century A.D. The theater is small for a major city, so larger ones must still be buried somewhere under the earth. Though grander Roman theaters have been uncovered in other parts of the world, none are more elegant than this. Crosses on the back of some seats show that the theater was used as late as early Christian times.

West of the theater, in a depression, are other Roman buildings, of brick, including a large bathhouse and numerous dwellings. While excavation is in progress you may look from above. The Greco-Roman Museum (see below) is across the street toward the bay.

POMPEY'S PILLAR: *(Admission is 50 pt.)* The pillar and the catacombs are near the canal farther back from the sea and west of the Roman theater. The pillar, on a hill visible for quite a distance on Amud el Sawari, marks the site of a later Mouseion.

Pompey's name has a certain magic, more so than Diocletian, which is the only reason this column is called "Pompey's" rather than by the name of the man to whom it was dedicated. It was a victory memorial erected just before the 4th century A.D. by the soldiers of Diocletian to his honor and had soldiers' names affixed on a plaque (now in the Greco-Roman Museum). The column, 85 feet high, is of highly polished Aswan granite. The capital is perfect. Looking carefully at its base, you can make out faint hieroglyphs on stones appropriated by Romans from a building of Seti I. Originally the column formed part of the decoration of a great temple—the Serapeum—dedicated to both Osiris and the sacred Apis bull. It was a grand temple in Ptolemaic times, majestic on its hill like the Acropolis in Athens. Here a second library was built after the original was burned during a rebellion against Caesar. Christians, followed by Arabs, followed by moderns with needs for building supplies have all but denuded this hill where acres of buildings once stood. Near the column remain three crude sphinxes and assorted stones from the former buildings. Some catacombs (not always open), probably a part of the Serapeum, are west of the pillar. Now it is a meditative place.

CATACOMBS OF KOM ES SHUGAFAH: *(Open 7 a.m. to 5 p.m. Admission is 50 pt.)* Latter-day attempts to reproduce earlier styles seldom are exactly right. Although the founder of Woolworth's made a mausoleum for himself in a New York cemetery that reproduces an ancient Egyptian temple, Egyptian temples were not mausoleums. In Alexandria, Romans took on the ways and religion of the larger, older culture around them. Several of their mausoleums have been found and they are indeed curious. The most interesting is the Catacombs of Kom es Shugafah, one block farther from the bay and west of Pompey's Pillar.

The entrance is at the top of an open hill through a well-like structure. Down winding stairs you may visit level after level of pagan Roman burials. They date to the 2nd century, before Christianity took over, and they represent Egyptian religious beliefs as the Romans interpreted them. Likely the complex was a burial business where a person could buy space for himself and his family. The bodies were lowered by ropes down the "well."

On the first lower level is a vestibule with side benches surmounted by a ceiling in the form of a shell. Then comes a rotunda on pillars leading to the second lower level. A large room left of the rotunda served as a place for banquets. Thus, cut from the rock, are couches where food could be eaten Roman style, while reclining. Romans in Alexandria took over the ancient Egyptian belief that relatives should visit the dead yearly and share a feast in their memory.

Down through the rotunda stairs to the second level are the burial chambers (yet another level, farther down, is now underwater). First comes a vestibule that attempts to be Egyptian. Two pillars have papyrus capitals, and a winged sun and falcon soar overhead. Statues of a Roman man and woman are on opposite sides in niches—the owners of this tomb, probably. On the end wall two serpents guarding the door wear the double crown of upper and lower Egypt but hold the baton of the Roman god Hermes. Above is Medusa's face on a shield. Farther along is a tomb chamber with sarcophagi cut from the rock of three walls. The lids are unmovable because bodies were shoved inside from a passage behind these walls (although none of these sarcophagi seems to have been used). Over each sarcophagus are carvings of strange Egypto-Roman mixtures. The right side shows a prince with the Egyptian double crown offering a necklace to the Apis bull. Isis protects the bull with her spread wings. In this standard scene every component is Egyptian, but it is not right somehow. The feeling is Roman.

The same is true of the carving in the far niche where Anubis works on a mummy lying on a bed with lion heads. The extremes of bastardization line either side of the entrance. Anubis (it surely is his doglike head) wears Roman armor and carries a stout Roman sword along with a shield and lance. Opposite is the crocodile Sobek, looking even more uncomfortable in Roman attire. Around this central chamber runs a broad passage lined with niches for over 200 mummies and with holes by which the sarcophagi in the central room were hollowed out. Left is a large gallery for more bodies.

From one side of the rotunda you can enter another set of rooms. The first large hall is lined with cavities for more bodies; bones of people and horses once littered the floor. At the end and left is a smaller room covered in stucco with traces of paint. Note the Romanized sphinx above the entrance.

RAS EL TIN PALACE: *(Open 9 a.m. to 5 p.m. Admission is 25 pt.)* At the west end of the promontory in the bay is this former palace begun by Muhammad Ali and used by his heirs until the last, King Farouk, abdicated and sailed away. Salmon colored, looking very Mediterranean, it was "modernized" in 1925 to the height of grandiosity and depths of taste. The throne room does not awe at all; the Marble Hall seems to have no function except to show that the owner could afford a hall of marble. The palace is worth a look to see what bad taste money can buy.

THE GRECO-ROMAN MUSEUM: *(Open from 8 a.m. to 4 p.m. Fridays and in the summer it closes at 1 p.m. Admission is 50 pt. The museum is in a thin, block-long building, between Horriah and Sultan Hussein Kamel Streets, across from Kom el Dik.)*

Because the Museum of Antiquities in Cairo gets first pick of anything found in Egypt, the Alexandria museum makes do with the leftovers. While you will not see masterpieces, many pieces are as interesting, if not more so, than the more aesthetic works in Cairo. The specialty is Greek and Roman, but there are earlier and later objects as well.

Although the museum sells a nice guidebook (LE 1) of the objects in the museum and of ancient sights in Alexandria, the book is not of much help for touring the museum because the exhibits were redone after the book was printed.

RESORTS IN ALEXANDRIA

From Alexandria, at the western side of the Delta, the Delta stretches all the way to the Sinai—to Port Said, the mouth of the Suez Canal. Although beaches are better on the western side of Alexandria, the east boasts finer accomodations.

Between Alexandria and the Libyan border on the west are some of the finest beaches anywhere on the Mediterranean. Someday this area will be developed. As of this writing accommodations and transportation are rather minimal, but for quiet and natural beauty this area wins.

EAST OF ALEXANDRIA

MONTANZA PARK: Six miles east from central Alexandria is an estate King Farouk once owned. It consists of 350 acres of park and garden on its own promontory overlooking the sea. Two pleasant hotels sit in the park, including the only deluxe hotel near Alexandria.

The beaches here usually are less crowded than those closer to the city. The sea is calmed by a jetty. Living, even for just a few days, on such spacious private grounds promotes a feeling of richness.

Palestine Hotel. *Deluxe.* In such a setting a hotel that offers all services would naturally be ranked Deluxe. Unfortunately, the Palestine is neither old enough for charm nor new enough for sparkle. It has 243 rooms, all comfortable if not spotless, each with a balcony overlooking either the grounds or the sea. The best features are terraces directly above the bay where guests can relax with a view. Surprisingly the beach is poor, but two others are on the park grounds not far away. The kitchen produces ordinary hotel food, best for the Egyptian dishes. Open all year, air-conditioned. Compulsory half-board in summer. In summer a double room costs LE 18.75, a single LE 17.50; each is LE 1.50 less in other seasons. Egyptian Hotels Company.

Salamalek Hotel. *First Class.* Enjoy the same park for less than the Palestine guests by staying in this converted outbuilding of Farouk's palace where his visitors were put up.

Small, with only 30 rooms, it is friendly and comfortable rather than fancy. We rate the food adequate. Open all year, air-conditioned. Compulsory half-board in summer. Singles are LE 8; doubles cost LE 11. Sphinx Tours.

MAAMURA BEACH: Half a mile farther east is a better beach, but without the private park. Less protected, the bathers get some waves. As a bonus, the town of Abu Kir with the best fresh seafood restaurants in the Alexandria area is only two miles away. **Zephyrion** restaurant has the best reputation.

Maamura Palace Hotel. *First Class.* The hotel caters mainly to Egyptians, is not new, and in our view could be cleaner and better repaired. Guests come for the beaches, not the hotel. All the 80 rooms are doubles at LE 10 up.

WEST OF ALEXANDRIA

AGAMI BEACH: The best beaches near Alexandria are those at Agami and Hanoville, about 12 miles west. Hanoville, the farther west of the two, is least crowded. Either is better for beaches and swimming than places to the east of Alexandria, though the town areas and the hotels around them are more rustic.

Agami Palace Hotel. *Third Class.* Situated on the beach, it resembles a typical motel. All 53 rooms face the water—as do the guests, since their rooms are so small and dark. Single rooms rent at LE 4, doubles at LE 5.50.

Hanoville Hotel. *Second Class.* A little farther west and a little step up from the Agami, but twice as large. Costs about double the Agami.

EL ALAMEIN: If you like to be first and love beaches, there are two sets of beaches farther west where few Americans or Europeans go. They will one day. These beaches are as fine as any on the Mediterranean. Despite plans to develop them— already each has decent hotels—the word has not yet reached international ears.

At Sidi Abdel Rahman beach, the water is turquoise, emerald, then cobalt as it leaves the milky sand that stretches for miles. El Alamein is the nearest town. Back in the desert the great World War II battle was fought in which Rommel lost his first engagement and the Allies first gained heart. Tanks and other relics are preserved in the town museum. Alamein today is lively, awakened by pipeline construction and new port facilities. By the end of this decade oil from Egypt's Red Sea fields will be shipped from here. Enjoy the beaches while you still can. (For about LE 5 a taxi will bring you the 60 miles from Alexandria.)

El Alamein Hotel. *First Class.* All 35 rooms face the sea, with balconies and French doors. The veranda is pleasant for drinks. Open from May through October. Compulsory half-board. Rooms run from LE 11.50 for singles to LE 13 for doubles. Egyptian Hotels Company.

MARSA MATROU: This is the last real town in Egypt before the Libyan border, 180 miles from Alexandria. It too has plans for major tourist development—the reason is the beaches east and west of town. Eastern beaches provide better water for swimming and have larger areas of sand. The beaches west of town offer spectacles—precipitous rocks that nestle quiet beaches and form breakers offshore for wave displays. One huge, hollow rock offshore is called Cleopatra's Bath. Swimming is dangerous in this area with rocks and breakers, but the view is well worth the look. A ferry leaves the town port every few hours for Cleopatra's Bath and beaches. Other fine beaches lie even farther west, but no regular transportation reaches them as yet.

Marsa Matrou is 180 miles from Alexandria. It can be visited by train, hired car, or even plane. Hotels here are very basic but serve for a beach existence. All are on the town corniche, by the beach.

Arous el Bahr. *Third Class.* The newest hotel, but small rooms. For our taste the hotel disco is not a plus. Open all year, not air-conditioned. Half-board is compulsory. Including breakfast and lunch or dinner, the cost for one person is LE 12.50, LE 21 for two.

Beau Site Hotel. *Fourth Class.* Only 33 rooms and spartan; the hotel also has a disco which is the most popular with town people but would be the least popular with us if we were staying here. Singles cost LE 5.50; doubles cost LE 7.

Lido Hotel. *Third Class.* About twice as large as the Beau Site and nearby, but older. Prices reflect its age. Singles can be had for LE 2 and double rooms run from LE 3 to LE 5.50.

AMENITIES

HOTELS

Hotels east and west of central Alexandria were discussed in the previous section. Here we will treat the best hotels in the city itself, places to stay while touring the sights. If you fail to find a room in the hotels listed here, the Egyptian Tourist Office on Saad Zaghlul Square will try to find you space in 25-odd other hotels that are third class or lower.

Cecil Hotel. *First Class.* (Saad Zaghlul Square.) The hotel exactly meets our expectations of Alexandria, in that way it is perfect. Do not come for newness or spotlessness, come for character. The elevator, the wood floors, the spacious rooms and furnishings that Clea (of Durrell's world) might have used, suit exactly. Front rooms look on the sea, back rooms are larger. The food is reasonably good for a hotel. Open all year, not air-conditioned. Compulsory half-board. Singles cost LE 10; doubles go for LE 11. Egyptian Hotels Company.

Hotel Beau Rivage. *First Class.* (434 Shari el Gueish, the Nile Corniche.) A very popular hotel that lures guests three and a half miles west of the center of town for its quiet and gardens. Bungalows on the back and rooms in the main building hold 50 parties. We recommend front rooms for their views. The food is quite good. Open all year, without air-conditioning. Full-board, for an extra LE 7.50 per person, required in summer; half-board, for LE 4.50 per person, required in the other seasons. Singles cost LE 12, LE 2 less without bath; doubles cost LE 14, without bath LE 13.

San Stefano Hotel. *First Class.* (Shari el Gueish, one block closer to center city than the Hotel Beau Rivage.) A larger hotel, more comfortable than its neighbor, this one we think fills up less quickly because it lacks the personality. We would call the food adequate. Open all year, not air-conditioned. Compulsory half-board. Singles cost LE 11, and doubles LE 12, but after the summer season LE 1 less each. Egyptian Hotels Company.

Windsor Palace Hotel. *First Class.* (17 al Shohada Street, one block back from the Cecil.) The location is central, the front rooms with sea views are large and recommended. We loved the old cage elevators and the grand staircase, but not the back, viewless rooms. Food we found standard. Open all year, without air-conditioning. Half-board required in summer for LE 4 per person extra. With views, singles cost LE 10.50, doubles LE 13.

Metropole Hotel. *Second Class.* (52 Saad Zaghlul Street, one block west of the Windsor Hotel.) Better than its present rating, refurbished, and centrally located, this is a reasonable choice. Open all year, not air-conditioned. Half-board required in summer. Single rooms cost LE 9.50 and doubles LE 14.

Hotel San Giovanni. *Second Class.* (205 Shari el Gueish, two miles east of Saad Zaghlul.) This hotel stands out in its class; too bad it has only 35 rooms. Its kitchen, which we think produces the best hotel food in town, makes a stay more special. Open all year, no air-conditioning. Half-board required in season. Double rooms with sea views rent for 10.50, LE 9 as singles.

LEAVING ALEXANDRIA

Trains leave for Cairo at 7:50 a.m., 9:20 a.m., 10:30 a.m., 11:40 a.m., 2:15 p.m., 3:30 p.m., 5:10 p.m., 6:25 p.m., and 7:25 p.m. A first-class ticket costs LE 2.56, second class is LE 1.50. It takes about two and a half hours to reach Cairo.

14.

Off Beaten Tracks

Here are three places where most tourists do not go. The first is away from normal routes, though it is a resort filled with tourists—unusual and international tourists, because most of the world has not yet heard about Hurghadah and its extraordinary scuba diving. The second is in the Delta, lying between Cairo and Alexandria and easy to reach. Although Delta ruins are not splendid, they are rich in historical associations—Tanis, for example, the probable site of the city which Jews built while enslaved and from which they began their Exodus. The third trip, for the adventurous, is Kharga Oasis—across 140 miles of desert where the absence of other tourists can be guaranteed.

HURGHADAH

Experts rate the Red Sea among the very best places in the world for scuba diving. The waters of this misleadingly named sea are electric blue and crystal clear, teeming with brilliantly colored fish that play among intricate coral formations. Empty white-sand beaches stretch in a thin line for 100 miles. So far only Hurghadah has been developed in this area. Hurghadah, the town, consists of dusty small houses that just fit between mountains and the sea. A marine museum and aquarium sit on the shore, displaying the incredible variety of local fish and the neighboring sea lions. Three miles south around a protected bay are modern hotels. At the north end is the Hurghadah Sheraton. Around to the south of the bay is the complex of cabins operated by Club Mediterranee.

For those who tire of the swimming, excursions can be arranged to Luxor, 150 miles away, and to Roman towns beside ancient porphyry quarries at Gebel Dukham and Gebel Farita, 30 and 60 miles southwest.

Hurghadah Sheraton. *Deluxe.* Modern, all air-conditioned, most of the 250 rooms have terraces with sea views. Half-board is compulsory at LE 6 per person. Single rooms start at LE 18, doubles at LE 21.

Magawish Hurghadah. Rooms are in air-conditioned chalets with two beds, bath, and sitting area. Like all Club Med camps, this one offers innumerable activities in the basic rate. Per person the cost is about LE 25, including three meals and the activities. Operated by Club Mediterranee and Misr Travel.

From Cairo there are five flights each week, leaving daily at 7 a.m. Return flights leave Hurghadah at 8:20 a.m. on Monday, Wednesday, Thursday, and Sunday, arriving in Cairo at 9:10 a.m. On other days the plane leaves at 10:25 a.m. You can also reach Hurghadah from Luxor, either by hiring a car and driver for the four-hour drive or by taking the town bus that runs between these cities. The bus schedule is variable, but you can check with the concierge of any Luxor hotel.

THE DELTA

You can spend a quiet day alone at ruins that stretch to the horizon in the Delta north of Cairo, returning in the evening.

All it takes is hiring a car and driver. The round trip covers 210 miles over fairly good roads through endless flat land-scapes. Two ancient sites are worth exploring—**Bubastis,** home of the cat goddess, and **Tanis,** the probable ancient Raameses.

The Delta was the most popular part of Egypt, an area of countless ancient towns. The land is low, only a few feet above sea level, and formerly was marshy. Such moisture erodes ancient buildings, even hard granite, and makes excavation all but impossible. What little survives today is mainly in chaotic jumbles where sharp eyes and good imaginations can find and reconstruct ancient temples and towns.

From Cairo, take the road through Heliopolis that leads to the airport. Two miles before the airport, turn left onto the road to Ismailia through the Delta. In 40 miles, at Belbeis, turn left onto the road to Zagazig. Just at the outskirts of Zagazig a major road connecting Alexandria to Port Said crosses; as soon as you turn right onto this road in the direction of Port Said, you are driving through Tell Basta, the former Bubastis.

Egyptians were the first people to domesticate the cat, and this place was sacred to the cat goddess, Bastet. It was also the home of the Lybian pharaohs of Dynasty XXII. The area covered with a jumble of blocks to the right of the road is the site of Bastet's temple, built by the Lybian pharaohs. Two hundred yards farther down the road and left is the ancient cat cemetery. Here tens of thousand of mummified cats were buried, many with lovely bronze cat statues. On the right are burned remains of a large Middle Kingdom structure of unkown purpose as well as later tombs.

Return to the road from Cairo and drive through Zagazig, taking the road to Hehya. Continue through Hehya and Abu Kebir to Fakus, a total of 40 miles. On reaching Fakus, pass by on the left, then left again to Kantir and Huseiniya. Soon after comes Giziret Saud, beyond which the large *tell* (hill) of Tanis may be seen. Take the right side of the fork to Tanis (also called San el Hagar).

The ruins are enormous, running for a mile or more in each

direction. Several excavations have been done and a new one is in progress, for the site intrigues students of ancient history. This may be the location of Avaris, capital of the Hyksos. It is also the likely candidate for the city called Raameses in the Bible, Ramesses by the Egyptians, constructed originally by Rameses the Great. Through the monumental gateway is a colossus of Rameses, then a complex of ruined temples. Just right through the gateway is a late royal necropolis. The best-preserved tomb is that of the pharaoh Psusennes which was discovered intact in 1952. All around lie carvings and statues in utter tranquillity.

KHARGA OASIS

Defended by the desert, Kharga is unspoiled. It is a genuine oasis, thanks to underground water, green in the midst of gray desert. Full of farms and palms and scattered villages, its population recently was increased by resettled Nubians displaced by Lake Nasser. Here few people speak English. Kharga sees perhaps ten tourists a month. The best accomodations are crude. This is raw Egypt.

The only place to stay is in the main village, also named Kharga. Here is a small **Rest House** run by the government and the third-class **Ibis Hotel** (closed as of this writing, although it may reopen).

Two miles north is the **Temple of Hibis,** commissioned by the Persian Darius I, who lost to the Greeks at Marathon. The ruins are quite lovely, embellished by later Roman emperors. North of the temple lie remains of a Roman town and a very early, pre-Coptic, Christian cemetery. Adobe tombs still contain bright paintings. An old Muslim town to the south consists of houses dug beneath the ground to avoid the hot sun. Farther south are two small Roman temples, then a string of little Ptolemaic temples.

Call ahead to make certain you have a room. Connections can be made at Cairo for the planes that leave at 6 a.m. on Wednesdays and Saturdays, or at Aswan on Thursday or Sunday at 11:05 a.m. You can instead drive from Assiut, which is 200 miles south of Cairo, 125 miles north of Luxor, across 140 miles of desert. Make certain your car is in good condition and make sure you take extra water in case of breakdown. Though the road is good and the distance can be covered in less than four hours, other cars are infrequent.

Appendix

HIEROGLYPHS

Ancient Egyptian is the second oldest written language, second by about one century to Sumerian—but the winner in conservatism. Over the centuries Egyptians developed other, faster ways to write, yet continued to use hieroglyphs in tombs and temples long after the time that languages evolve beyond the stage of pictures. The characters of their original writing had magical and religious associations, hence the name *hieroglyphs*, "sacred carving."

Hieroglyphs was a language that employed pictures, not a picture language. Each picture actually was a character with a fixed value as a sound, which combined with others to compose the sound of a spoken word, as we do with our alphabet. ⟨hieroglyph⟩ , for example, had nothing to do with the hand, stool, or loaf of bread which were pictured; the three characters conveyed sounds similar to our *d*, *p*, and *t*, respectively, forming the sounds of the word for "boat," *depet*. Vowels were frequently omitted, as if we were to write *cp* for "cup." The resulting ambiguities (*cop, cap, cope*, etc.) were eliminated by appending a picture to indicate the word's category. ⟨hieroglyphs⟩ , which could mean *prosperous*, *storehouse*, or the verb *proceed*, meant only the latter when followed by feet: ⟨hieroglyphs⟩ . The most common characters represented a single sound, but others represented two sounds: ⟨hieroglyph⟩ = *mt;* still others represented three: ⟨hieroglyph⟩ = *nfr*. Hieroglyphs could be written in either direction. They are read from top to bottom and towards the faces of the characters. Read left to right, ⟨hieroglyphs⟩ says "Magic is everyplace;" ⟨hieroglyphs⟩ says the same thing, read right to left. The picture potential of their language was not ignored by the Egyptians. A single stroke below or beside a character could make it function as a depiction. Normally, represented the sound *r*, but  meant a mouth. Two such strokes or three, however, made a word dual or plural. Hieroglyphs came complete with a grammar, like any other language. The verb went at the beginning of a sentence, though certain particles preceded even verbs; adjectives followed their nouns, and so on.

A pharaoh's name was written in a unique way, inside a cartouche—an oval formed around the name by rope tied at the end, to symbol universal dominion. The pharaoh Khufu, who erected the Great Pyramid, would be written , Ptolemy 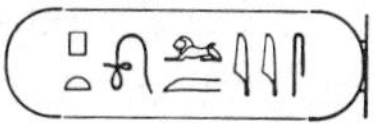, and, while Cleopatra was pharaoh, her name was written . From the time of the Middle Kingdom on, every pharaoh had five names. Two of these names, called the Great Names, were written inside cartouches. Either of these cartouches was apt to designate a given king. The great pharaoh Thothmoses III, for example, commonly was designated by the cartouche 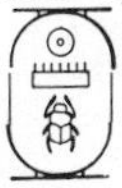, which was his prenomen, Menkheperra, instead of his nomen, Thothmoses. All of which makes learning the names of Egypt's 600 pharaohs a difficult enterprise.

Hieroglyphs hold few mysteries for scholars today. Only rarely used words, some place names, and some words for plants, fish, and animals are unclear. However, we must confess that the beautiful hieroglyphic characters usually are more interesting to look at than to read. Inscriptions almost always repeat set phrases. Typical are: "The pharaoh so-and-so, may he live eternally for a hundred thousand years, given life like Ra forever," or, "The son of the courtier———, born of the lady———, so-and-so, made this and is justified [a euphemism for dead]."

ARABIC PHRASES

Arabic seldom is necessary since every Egyptian pupil learns English. Egyptians are eager to use what they have learned. They run to get help when their own competence is inadequate to the task. A few phrases are, frankly, unlikely to solve anyone's problem in an extreme situation where Arabic would be necessary. But, on occasion, a few words in Arabic might be fun—for the surprised and warm response returned by the hearer.

Good morning. . . . . Sah-bah ill care

Good evening . . . . Masah bill care

Hello. . . . . Sah-ee-dah

Goodbye (the one leaving). . . . . Sah-ee-dah

Goodbye (the one remaining,
   or who speaks second). . . . . Ma-sah-lah-ma

Yes. . . . . Eye-wah

No . . . . Leh

Please (by a male) . . . . Min-fad-lack
   (by a female) . . . . Min-fad-lick

Thank you. . . . . Show-krahn

You are welcome . . . . Ahf-wan

God willing. . . . . In-sha-lah

What is your name?. . . . . Is-mock eh?

My name is. . . . . Is-me. . . .

Do you speak English? . . . . Bit-call-him in-glaze-ee

I do not speak Arabic. Ah-na ma bak-call
                                               eemch ah-rah-bee

I speak English . . . . ah-na bit-call-him
                                                in-glaze-ee

Go away. . . . . Em-she

Hurry . . . . Yah-lah

Stop . . . . Wah-off

Is it possible? .... Moom-kin?

Impossible .... Mish-moom-kin

Where is. .... Fain. . .
    the restaurant .... Met-ahm
    the museum............................. Met-cough
    the mosque................................. Guh-ma

I am hungry (if male)..................... Ah-na goo-dan
           (if female) .... Ah-na goo-ah-na

I want....................................... Ahh-yiz

The bill............................ Fah-too-ray/heh-saab

A toast:......................... Hah-nee-an yah-see-deh

How much? .... Ah day?

Bad .... Bat-tal

Not bad.................................. Mish bat-tal

Very good .... Kwice cah-tier

Good .... Kwice

Not good.................................. Mish kwice

Cheap.. Re-keys

Expensive .... Gah-leh

Old.. Ah-deem

New... Geh-deem

One .... Wa-kid

Two .... It-main

Three .... Tah-lah-teh

Ten... Ahsh-are

One hundred.................................. Me-ya

Egyptian Pound .... Geh-nay

Piaster .... Ersh

DATES

Predynastic Period (c. 4000–3100 B.C.)
Art and towns in Egypt but only the rudiments of writing and no pharoah.

Early Dynastic Period (c. 3100–2686 B.C.)
Dynasty I (c. 3100–2890)   Narmer-Menes c. 3100–?
Dynasty II (c. 2890–2686)   —

[Approximate date of the biblical flood: 2700 B.C.]

Old Kingdom (c. 2686–2181 B.C.)
Dynasty III (c. 2686–2613 B.C.)

—

	Zoser	c. 2667–2648 B.C.

Dynasty IV (c. 2613–2498 B.C.)

	Sneferu	c. 2613–2589 B.C.
	Khufu	c. 2589–2566 B.C.

—

Khaefra   c. 2558–2533 B.C.

—

Menkaura   c. 2532–2504 B.C.

[Rise of Minoan civilization: c. 2500 B.C.]

Dynasty V (c. 2498–2345 B.C.)

—

Unis   c. 2375–2345 B.C.

Dynasty VI (c. 2345–2181 B.C.)

—

Pepi II   c. 2278–2188 B.C.

—

First Intermediate Period (2181–2040 B.C.)
Dynasties VII–X

Middle Kingdom (c. 2040–1786 B.C.)
Dynasty XI (c. 2133–1991 B.C.)

—

Montuhotep II 2060–2010 B.C.

—

Dynasty XII (1991–1786 B.C.)

Amunemhat I	1991–1962 B.C.
—	
Senusert III	1878–1843 B.C.
Amunemhat III	1842–1797 B.C.
—	

Second Intermediate Period (1786–1570 B.C.)
   Dynasties XIII–XIV (1786–?)
   Dynasties XV–XVI "Hyksos" (1684–1567 B.C.)
   Dynasty XVII (1650–1567 B.C.)

—	
Kamose	?

New Kingdom (1570–1086 B.C.)

[*Chinese civilization begins with the Shang Dynasty: c. 1500* B.C.]

Dynasty XVIII (1567–1326 B.C.)

Ahmose	1570–1546 B.C.
Amunhotep I	1546–1526 B.C.
Thothmoses I	1526–1512 B.C.
Thotmoses II	1512–1504 B.C.
Hatshepsut	1505–1482 B.C.
Thothmoses III	1504–1450 B.C.
Amunhotep II	1450–1425 B.C.
Thothmoses IV	1425–1417 B.C.
Amunhotep III	1417–1379 B.C.
Amunhotep IV (Akhenaten)	1389–1372 B.C.
Smenkara	?
Tutankhamun	1372–1360 B.C.
Ay	1360–1356 B.C.
Horemheb	1356–1326 B.C.

Dynasty XIX (1325–1200 B.C.)

Rameses I	1325–1322 B.C.
Seti I	1322–1304 B.C.
Rameses II (the Great)	1304–1237 B.C.
Merenptah	1236–1223 B.C.
—	

[*Trojan War: c. 1200* B.C.]
[*Olmecs, first American civilization: c. 1200* B.C.]

Dynasty XX (1200–1086 B.C.)

—

Rameses III   1198–1166 B.C.

—

Late Period (1085–332 B.C.)
   Dynasty XXI (1085–945 B.C.)
   Dynasty XXII "Libyan" (c. 945–730 B.C.)
   Dynasties XXIII–XXIV (c. 730? 715 B.C.)
   Dynasty XXV "Nubian" (716–666 B.C.)
   Dynasty XXVI "Saitic" (665–525 B.C.)
   Dynasty XXVII "Persian" (525–404 B.C.)

[*Parthenon begun: 447* B.C.]

   Dynasties XXVIII–XXX (404–343 B.C.)
   Dynasty XXXI "Persian II" (343–332 B.C.)

Alexander the Great (332–323 B.C.)

Ptolemies (304–30 B.C.)

Roman Period (30 B.C.–4th century A.D.)

Coptic Period (4th century A.D.–640 A.D.)

Arab Conquest (641 A.D.)

Principal Gods and Goddesses of Ancient Egypt

OSIRIS
(Lord of the Netherworld)

ISIS
(Wife)

HORUS
(Son-Pharaoh)

Seth
(Catastrophe)

Amun
(Father)

Mut
(Mother)

Ptah
(Creation)

Thoth
(Science)

Maat
(Order)

Hat-hor
(Sky-Motherhood)

Anubis
(Mummification)

Min
(Fertility)

Sekhmet
(Lion)

Sobek
(Crocodile)

Apis
(Bull)

Nut
(Sky)

Hapi
(Nile)

Touris
(Fertility)

Bes
(Motherhood)

—FROM
E.A. WALLIS BUDGE
Amulets and Talismans

Index